The USE *and* ABUSE *of* MEMORY

The
USE *and* ABUSE
of MEMORY

Interpreting World War II in Contemporary European Politics

Christian Karner and Bram Mertens, editors

Transaction Publishers
New Brunswick (U.S.A.) and London (U.K.)

This book is printed on acid-free paper that meets the American National Standard for Permanence of Paper for Printed Library Materials.

Library of Congress Catalog Number: 2013005080
ISBN: 978-1-4128-5194-7
Printed in the United States of America

Library of Congress Cataloging-in-Publication Data

The Use and Abuse of Memory: Interpreting World War II in Contemporary European Politics / Christian Karner and Bram Mertens, editors.
       pages cm
  1. World War, 1939–1945—Historiography—Political aspects—Europe. 2. World War, 1939–1945--Influence. 3. Europe--Politics and government—1945- 4. Collective memory—Europe. I. Karner, Christian, author, editor of compilation. II. Mertens, Bram, author, editor of compilation.
  D743.42.N37 2013
  940.55—dc23

                                                        2013005080

Contents

Introduction: Memories and Analogies of World War II

Christian Karner and Bram Mertens

This is a book about the presence of the past in the present. More accurately, it is a book about the enduring and arguably renewed prominence of narratives about and allusions to the Second World War across Europe. To a degree, this is well-trodden academic territory (e.g., see Huyssen 2003): there is a large, well-known, and continually growing body of literature on European memories of World War II (e.g., Müller 2002; Lebow et al. 2006; Biess and Moeller 2010; Pakier and Stråth 2010). Similarly, the more fundamental point about the relevance of the past to the present or, conversely, of present circumstances to socially circulating and politically consequential narratives of the past is a key component of literature on the so-called "memory boom" of recent decades. Regula Ludi, for example, echoes the well-established insight that "representations of the past . . . depend on a frame of reference informed by present needs, concerns and values" (2006: 213). Similarly, Hannes Heer and Ruth Wodak refer to "history as a retrospectively composed and meaning-endowed narrative" (2008: 1).

In terms of subject matter and underpinning ontological assumptions, then, this book continues some influential and well-established trajectories of recent academic enquiry. What we hope to add to the existing literature can be summarized as follows. Firstly, this is a distinctly interdisciplinary project, involving historians, sociologists, anthropologists, linguists, political scientists, and contributions to various area studies; we aim to demonstrate that an understanding of the numerous and diverse invocations of World War II witnessed since the middle of the twentieth century and, perhaps with even greater frequency, in the early twenty-first century across and beyond Europe not only benefits from, but also requires a wide-ranging combination of theoretical paradigms, disciplinary frameworks, and methodological approaches. Secondly, this project is unusual in its geographical breadth, in combining analyses of national and transnational contexts that stretch across Western, Central, and Eastern Europe, and include Scandinavia as much as the Mediterranean. Thirdly, taken as a whole, the analyses presented in what follows cast their eyes particularly widely in terms of *how*, *where*, and *to what effect* the Second World War has been remembered: this includes discussions of large-scale ideological efforts at nation-building—or nation-reasserting—by political elites, as well as patterns of everyday sense-making by so-called ordinary social actors; it includes discussions of how a particularly painful and violent part of the past is used and abused across a wide range of social realms, from the media to educational institutions, from film and literature to cross-border controversies, from exhibitions to academia, and from enormously consequential political decisions to the seemingly banal and biographical. We discover across the following chapters that individual and collective memories and references to the history of the Second World War that provide an interpretative frame for present circumstances recur across diverse signifying practices and are articulated from a wide range of institutional positions. Fourthly, and related to the previous point, the following analyses also demonstrate that World War II continues to be a prominent, near ubiquitous point of reference not only across Europe but also across the political spectrum: while the Left and Right of course differ enormously in their respective motivations for invoking World War II, and in the political effects achieved thereby, they appear to share—their defining ideological differences and mutual opposition notwithstanding—a basic consciousness of the enduring legacies, relevance, and trauma of this most murderous and destructive of historical ruptures. Each of these four dimensions warrants detailed and critical discussion.

The continuing relevance and resonance of the Second World War as a monumental turning point in world history is of course not surprising. Its scale, global reach, intensity, brutality, cost to human life and humanity are as well-known as they are unparalleled. More than six and a half decades after the world discovered the previously unimaginable horrors of the Nazi extermination camps, and after the dropping of the nuclear bombs on Hiroshima and Nagasaki, the memories are eminently with us—also with those of us who were not there but who have inherited and assimilated certain memories and narratives of the bloodiest of chapters in human history. In academic and human terms, preserving awareness of this past should be an ethical imperative and is of course far preferable to the alternative of amnesia, an alternative (most) European societies practiced in the immediate postwar era (Judt 2002). Yet, and as already implied, the ideological content and form, the structural contexts and effects, and the ethics of any and all of these countless memories and narratives demand attention, reflection, and debate. Moreover, while the passing of generations is bound to affect the content and transmission of memories and narratives of the Second World War, it does not inevitably deplete their personal salience. Many, most likely all contributors to and readers of this volume, will be children, grandchildren, or great-grandchildren of people who—depending on their social positions, ethnicity, nationality, and biographical circumstances— variously endured, experienced, suffered in, survived, contributed to, died, or were murdered in World War II. This, in itself, calls for a historical, intergenerational form of what C. Wright Mills (1959) famously defined as the "sociological imagination": the ability to see the historical beyond and in the biographical, the structural or public in the only seemingly private. As Marla Morris argues (2002: 1) with regard to the Holocaust, "the past is present in the here and now and continues to get re-played, re-lived and re-worked. For each passing generation, difficult memories . . . remain . . . [and] leave their mark on Jews, Germans and others."

To set the scene for the subsequent chapters, this introduction begins with a brief discussion of a handful of randomly selected snapshots of some of the innumerable recent instances of allusions to World War II. The intention here is not to develop properly contextualized analyses but merely to highlight that the Second World War is indeed referenced and used for multiple purposes, by very differently positioned social actors arguing, interpreting, and politicizing with varying degrees of consciousness and reflexivity. We continue this by highlighting a number of themes and questions that underpin and meander through important parts of the subsequent contributions to this book. These are questions about nation-states and Europe as spaces of collective and contested memories and narratives of the past; questions about the (mis)uses of historical analogies; epistemological questions about the relationship between memories and historiography; and issues

3

raised by the literature on the Holocaust, its historical singularity, yet potential recurrence.

Unlimited Relevance?

Building on Andreas Huyssen's (2003: 15) observation that "the geographic spread of the culture of memory is as wide as memory's political uses are varied," we here focus more specifically on references to the history of the Second World War that are indeed ubiquitous across and beyond Europe in the early twenty-first century, wherever we draw its geographical and cultural-political borders. This is demonstrated by an even half-alert reading of everyday conversations, political debates, and media coverage in any European nation state, and it was further corroborated by the sheer number of proposals the call for papers underpinning this book generated. Any selection of relevant examples is thus bound to be arbitrary and not representative of the full range of allusions, analogies, and other comparisons in circulation. What follows here is but a random and short list of some such invocations, the purpose of which is to draw attention to their ideological diversity, the apparent malleability of a particular point of historical reference, and to thereby raise a basic question: What do such heterogeneous allusions suggest about this particular past and, as importantly, about the present?

At the most recent European elections, the UK Independence Party's campaign centered on the iconic image of Winston Churchill, through whom UKIP—which eventually emerged as the second strongest British party contesting these elections—sought to articulate its staunch anti-EU politics. Not surprisingly, such discursive and visual strategies were also criticized—by a Conservative Party politician on the BBC's *Question Time* for example (21 May 2009)—for being inaccurate, thoroughly de-contextualized, and historically distorting. In the British context, but clearly not only there, World War II appears to be particularly conducive for the articulation of EU-skepticism. In March 2010, for example, the *Daily Express* described Europol as a "New EU Gestapo spy[ing] on Britons" (Reynolds 2010). In historiographical terms, such linking of utterly incomparable institutions and contexts is at best ridiculous and, at worst, highly irresponsible. However, what is at stake in such claims is clearly not historical accuracy but the articulation of a political position, with history being reduced to rhetoric. In this particular case, the paper's political position was thrown into even sharper relief in its subsequent campaign to "get Britain out of Europe," based on its proclamation that "we want our country back" (*Daily Express* 25 November 2010: 1). In Georgia, meanwhile, near what some consider the European continent's most easterly boundaries, a popular musician and leading figure in the opposition movement has drawn deeply disconcerting comparisons between his country's Second World War history and its present state (*Deutsche Welle* TV 4 June 2009). And in Belgium, at the heart of Europe, the chairman of the FDF, Olivier Maingain, compared the policies of the Flemish regional government to "practices worthy of the German occupation" (*La Libre Belgique* 31 March 2010), whereas Filip Dewinter of Vlaams Belang accused the francophone parties of seeking *Lebensraum* in Flanders (VRT TV 3 June 2010). The staggering, sometimes deeply disconcerting ideological malleability of alleged analogies of the Second World War—even articulated for mutually exclusive political purposes—has also been observed in a Scandinavian context:

> Swedish politicians not only have used Hitler and the Holocaust to combat the EMU and [to] support the undersigning of the EU constitution, but have also placed NATO's bombings of Belgrade in 1996 [*sic*] on equal footing with the Holocaust. . . . Equating the Israeli treatment of the Palestinians to the Holocaust is a particularly troublesome political use of history in the early twenty-first century. (Karlsson 2010: 53)

Not only sections of the media, political parties in very different national contexts, and politicians of different persuasion can be observed linking their agendas to symbols, narratives, and concepts or institutions closely associated with World War II. During his UK visit in 2010, Pope Benedict compared "aggressive atheism" to Nazism (Doughty 2010). An ideologically very different critique, aimed at the power yielded by banks and financial markets, was recently formulated by Jean Ziegler, Swiss left-wing sociologist and staunch critic of economic globalization. In an interview with Austrian comedian, actor, and author Alfred Dorfer, Ziegler suggested that "stock exchange scoundrels" (*Börsenhalunken*) ought to face a "Nürnberg-style human rights court" (ORF 2 25 July 2011). Irrespective of one's (dis)agreement with Ziegler's politics, basic questions relevant to this book arise: Was this another thoroughly decontextualized comparison that distorts both contexts—Nazism and the hunger inflicted on those most chronically excluded from today's global economy—being linked to one another? Or was it a justifiable rhetorical tactic to draw attention to how contemporary suffering and the deaths of millions are man-made and hence preventable? Furthermore, are such allusions always made consciously, or can they also reflect a sense-making process, in which individuals sometimes draw less reflexively on widely known symbols or historical episodes as points of reference and comparison?

However (un)consciously formulated, such (everyday) interpretations both make sense of a given situation and formulate a preferred response to it (see Karner 2010; 2011). As such, they are of course not peculiar to debates among politicians and academics, but they suffuse social life much more widely. One example of a bottom-up and politically positioned interpretation of current affairs, which also drew on the history of Nazism as a point of reference, was recently articulated by a listener calling in to a discussion on BBC Radio 4 (2 July 2011). In a critical response to calls by a Conservative politician for British workers to be "given a [fairer] chance," the listener in question argued that current "economic problems aren't migrants' fault, just like the economic problems in Germany in the 1930s weren't the Jews' fault."

This random selection of some recent allusions to World War II begins to capture their use to, and by, people positioned very differently on existing hierarchies of power and status, across the ideological spectrum and across nation states. While the real prevalence of such invocations will only emerge in subsequent chapters, this preliminary discussion already points to two key insights. First, the Second World War is now firmly embedded in many Europeans' historical (semi-)consciousness and life-worlds, to the extent that it can be readily employed as an interpretative anchor (see also Jaspal and Yampolski 2011) and point of reference that others will recognize. Second, the allusions above reflect not only the continuing presence of the Second World War in the minds and rhetoric of Europeans (and others), they also say at least as much about those present circumstances being discursively linked to the period of the 1930s and 1940s. As such, however problematic allusions to the Second World War may be, they also provide a glimpse into what those enunciating them perceive to be key problems or defining issues in the here and now: from European integration to power struggles within nation states, from contemporary transnational controversies to secularism or the inequalities and injustices of our now inescapably global economy. As this book demonstrates, the extent of the asserted comparative relevance of World War II is staggering, as is the range of contemporary issues it is linked to, and the variety of political purposes pursued thereby. Before we can turn to a selection of more detailed analyses, however, a number of preliminary conceptual questions remain to be addressed.

Mythscape(s)

In a seminal article on the role of (narratives of) the past in the "dynamics of national identity formation," Duncan Bell argues for the notion of a national "mythscape" as opposed to the more widely employed concept of "collective memory." A mythscape is defined as "the temporally and spatially extended discursive realm wherein the struggle for control of people's memories and the formation of nationalist myths is debated, contested and subverted incessantly" (Bell 2003: 66). This formulation contains two important and inter-related insights. First, not only national identities but also their constitutive myths require ongoing ideological work and reproduction. Second, national mythscapes are internally contested domains, wherein "governing" and "subaltern" myths (Bell 2003: 74), or dominant and "countermemories" (Kansteiner 2006: 134), clash. There is no singular, all-encompassing narrative of the national past; instead nations are "contested terrain[s] on which groups with competing memories struggle to generalize their ideal conception of society" (Levy and Dierkes 2002: 244).

Several of the contributions to this book demonstrate the applicability and usefulness of the concept of the mythscape in a variety of national contexts. This having been said, our concerns are of course more narrowly delineated and focused firmly on the role—in some contexts the obvious centrality—of World War II within various national mythscapes. As such, we build on Thomas Wolfe's observations (2006: 279) that the Second World War has "transformed all politics into politics of memory" and that its "catastrophe . . . was so enormous that no national narrative can avoid it." However, our analyses of the place of World War II across various European national mythscapes go further. For example, several contributions ask searching questions about the precise discursive workings and various manifestations of both governing and subaltern narratives of this particular historical era. Theoretically, two concepts associated with different forms of discourse analysis are relevant in this respect. For any one mythscape, we suggest, it pays analytical dividends to pay close attention to what Michael Billig terms the "deixis" (1995: 11) at work in relevant discourses: Forms of "rhetorical pointing"—as manifest in the use of the personal pronouns *we* and *they*, *us* and *them*, as well as in other linguistic means of reproducing boundaries of belonging and exclusion—thus reflect who remembers and how, which "in-groups" and "out-groups" are being (re)produced thereby. Similarly, questions arise as to the "structure of arguments," or *topoi* at work in such discourses. A topos is defined as "parts of argumentation that belong to . . . either explicit or inferable premises . . . that connect the argument . . . with the claim" (Reisigl and Wodak 2001: 74–75). Applied to our concerns, this invites examinations of the form of different memory discourses, the tropes and interpretative lenses—such as topoi of danger, threat, peace, solidarity, rights, or "East and West" (Krzyżanowski 2009)—employed therein. In this respect, some of the following analyses also connect with Fogu and Kansteiner's notion of the "poetics of history": Culturally shared yet contested historical narratives that utilize their own "poetic arsenal [in] relation to the present . . . a rhetorical enframing of the memory of recent events by tropes derived from an already institutionalized historical culture," such as—for instance—the Swiss example of "national traditions iconized in a historic site" (2006: 302–303).

Finally, the notion of the mythscape also enables us to raise important questions about the potential for European memory cultures. The consensus in recent literature is that these continue to be "nationally segmented" (Pakier and Stråth 2010: 12), that "Europeanization" has been accompanied by a "nationalization of history" (Karlsson 2010: 39), and that the "politics of memory take place primarily within a national frame of reference" (Fogu and Kansteiner 2006: 293). Not only can "the overwhelming majority of ordinary Europeans . . . hardly be supposed to be framing their recollections in a European fashion," argues Konrad Jarausch (2010: 313; 317), but the EU "must refrain from mandating a 'Brussels version' [of history] from above, because imposed memories tend not to produce viable roots." Several contributions to the present volume (see, for example, the respective chapters by Burridge, Karner, Lialiouti and Bithymitris, Zhurzhenko) provide further empirical evidence, from a variety of national contexts, that local or national memories do indeed tend to internally divide any potentially emerging European framework of remembrance. Indeed, the concept of mythscapes, whether on national or potentially on European levels, would lead us to expect nothing less, for they are by definition internally heterogeneous and contested. At the same time, other contributions (e.g., chapters by Grunwald, Schult, and Popescu) demonstrate that some significant memory debates in which World War II plays a prominent role occur across national boundaries, in transnational spaces of disagreement and struggle. Moreover, acknowledgement of the continuing hegemony of nation-focused frameworks of memory should not make us overlook important recent literature (Cram 2009), according to which national identities can and do coexist with an emerging "banal Europeanism." And although national frameworks clearly continue to be dominant, this must not lead us to leave earlier histories of nation-building and the role of inevitably selective historical accounts in those processes unexamined and problematically naturalized. By contrast, the notion of mythscapes, whether national or European, enables us to keep our eyes firmly set on the ideological processes and struggles surrounding all efforts at building and reproducing identities and political legitimacy.

On Analogies

In a discussion of the various "uses of history" in the context of contemporary "Europeanization," Klas-Göran Karlsson argues that "crises . . . are hotbeds of . . . time-transcending historical thinking," seeing history being utilized by "groups . . . satisfy[ing] certain needs or look[ing] after certain interests" (2010: 45). In terms of his typology of such (mis)uses, Karlsson's outlines of "existential" and "ideological"/"political" uses respectively (2010: 47–52) are particularly relevant to the following discussions. He detects existential uses in postindustrial preoccupations with issues of "belonging, self-expression and the quality of life." These arguably capture some of the everyday historical comparisons analyzed in this book, through which ordinary social actors make sense of the social circumstances they confront at the beginning of the twenty-first century. Seemingly quotidian and generally unnoticed as their analogies may be, they are of course nonetheless political in the discourse analytical sense, which defines all written and spoken language as forms of social practice that emerge out of existing structures of power, which they in turn help reproduce or subvert (e.g., Weiss and Wodak 2003). The historically framed opinions and everyday interpretations of ordinary citizens thus need to be seen as ideological and politically charged. Yet, there are other, structurally more immediately consequential uses of history—instrumentalizations of the past by politicians and intellectuals seeking to "convince, influence, rationalize, mobilize and authorize" (Karlsson 2010: 50). Belying historiographical imperatives to provide contextualization and evidence, such top-down invocations of the past tend to strive for a simple "transfer effect between 'then' and 'now,'" in the service of alleged "lessons from the past to be learned and taught by posterity" (Karlsson 2010: 52). In other words, what distinguishes existential from such more prominent political (mis)uses of history is not the presence or absence of ideology, but the institutional positions—those of ordinary citizens and members of decision-making elites respectively—from which they are articulated.

Also highly relevant in this context are Jan-Werner Müller's comments on the "[mis]use of memory" through historical analogies (see also Whitling 2010: 91). Müller points out that even though such analogical projections from the past to the present or an anticipated future are often misleading, many policy-makers, journalists, and historians "cannot resist making them." The reasons for the frequently "poor results" of such analogical reasoning are twofold: they "reduce complexity and short-circuit critical reflection" and they are self-interested, aiming to "create 'instant legitimacy'" (Müller 2002: 27). Elsewhere, Müller reminds us of one particularly controversial and "irresponsible reference to the past"—Silvio Berlusconi's likening of a German MEP to a "concentration camp guard" in 2003—and observes that the Holocaust has become a particularly widely (mis)used "anchor" to analogical reasoning:

> Memories of the Holocaust have served to legitimate both multicultural integration and humanitarian intervention. . . . Frequently drawing on the history . . . of the Holocaust is bound to open a Pandora's box of problems unavoidably associated with historical analogies. James Bryce's judgment . . . that "the chief practical use of history is to deliver us from plausible historical analogies" will not deter politicians, intellectuals and citizens from rummaging through the past. . . . [The] ethical question about the use of analogies . . . has been debated most extensively in connection with extracting "lessons" . . . from the Holocaust. Drawing such lessons, as laudable as it might be in the abstract, can be part of a strategy of consolation . . . rather than a more painful strategy of confronting the past. (Müller 2010: 32–34)

While there is more to be said about purported lessons from, or comparisons with, the Holocaust (see below), for now we also ought to take note of Karlsson's abovementioned emphasis on *crises* as ideal typical structural conditions of possibility for the kind of analogical thinking and arguing examined in this book. This partly echoes Stråth and Wodak's (2009: 26–32) focus on crises and "value mobilization" in the context of "political instrumentalizations of history" (and the role of the media in them). As has already been stressed, the invocations of World War II examined by our contributors reveal at least as much about the present as they do about contextually available and more or less widely circulating narratives of the past. By virtue of the links established between a deeply traumatic past and the present, we are offered a window onto aspects of contemporary life and politics variously experienced as most anxiety-inducing, most unjust, most dangerous, or most inhumane. However, all of this raises difficult epistemological and ethical questions, which form part of the wider context to our analyses and to which we turn next.

Memory: Epistemology and Ethics

Questions about the relationship and relevance of memory to historiography form part of the conceptual backdrop to this book. These questions are widely debated and contested. Not surprisingly, our contributions also reflect different, sometimes competing positions rather than a theoretical consensus. The crux of the issue is captured by Fogu and Kansteiner: Collective memory, they observe, is a "slippery phenomenon"—"not history . . . in the academic sense but . . . sometimes made from similar material." Moreover, memory studies and "the postmodern challenge" have triggered various responses, leading some historians to query any "radical" distinction between history and memory, given that "conscious and unconscious selection, interpretation and distortion" can feature in both; others, meanwhile, insist on the "epistemological integrity" of good historical scholarship, its "demand for proof," and resistance to "deformation" and "malleability" by "present needs" that are seen to define memory (Fogu and Kansteiner 2006: 285; 299).

A similar account of such paradigmatic differences emerges from Dominick LaCapra's *History and Memory after Auschwitz.* A first, often neo-positivist position thus "define[s] itself against" memory, as a "demythologizing form of secular enlightenment" skeptical of the "tricks" and purported unreliability of memory; a second position, by contrast, sees memory as "authentic, existentially rich," as history's "essence" or "matrix and muse." Yet, there is arguably some theoretical middle ground, where memory is seen as neither identical with, nor opposite to, history; where their relationship is acknowledged to "vary over time," with memory being treated as both "a crucial source for history" and as having "complicated relations to documentary sources"; and despite its recognized weaknesses—"falsifications, repressions, displacements, and denials"—"memory may nonetheless be informative" (LaCapra 1998: 16–19).

At their most basic, then, these debates center on the status of historiographical truth and on the relevance of individual and collective memories for obtaining it. The complexity of these discussions and their resonance in Europe's politics of World War II remembrance emerges from the following account:

> The politics of memory in postwar Europe has an obvious starting point (1945), some critical turning points . . . but *no endpoint*. While there are undeniably *distorted constructions* of World War II . . . that still need to be confronted, discredited, and replaced, there is *no objective truth* or reading of the past to take their place. Nor do the same aspects of the past have enduring relevance; they change as a function of contemporary problems and needs. (Lebow 2006: 36, *italics added*)

The epistemological implications of this warrant careful thought by anyone concerned with the(se) politics of memory. How does this relate, for instance, to Timothy Garton Ash's (2002: 281–282) "allergy to some of the . . . ludicrous frivolities of postmodern historiography" and his insistence that with proper scholarly care (i.e., thorough contextualization, skilled balancing of "intellectual distance" and "imaginative sympathy" with all historical actors involved) "a truth . . . not a single absolute Truth with a capital T, but still a real and important one" can be extracted from the most corrupted of files and the most problematic memories? Obviously, special responsibility falls on our collective academic shoulders in finding and circulating such truths, with a lower case *t*, which are capable of "confronting, discrediting and replacing" those distorted and deeply troubling constructions of World War II also in wider circulation. And clearly, epistemological reflexivity and humility are not inevitably tantamount to the kind of postmodern hyper-relativism that can be conducive to such distortions.

With regard to the relationship between memory and historiography, it seems to be stating the obvious that triangulation of sources and detailed, wide-ranging contextualization can and usually does differentiate the latter from the former. And while some recent scholarship corroborates that biographical memories are framed by the present and can also be a form of co-constructing identities involving researcher and research participant (Harding 2006), this of course does not detract from the existential centrality of memory, nor from its importance as a form of historical and social scientific data. Indeed, regarding memories as data that requires interpretation and analysis offers one possible conceptualization of the relationship between memory and historiography. As such, we may turn to the sociologist Anthony Giddens (1984) and his notion of the "double-hermeneutic." This captures the fact that all social actors already interpret their lives and life worlds, which is what qualitative (interview- and other) data tends to capture; the analyst's task—on a secondary hermeneutic level—then consists of contextualizing and interpreting an already pre-interpreted reality. Translated into our terms, memories as recalled by social actors or transmitted in public operate on an immediate, primary level of sense-making; (social/) historical analysis, on the other hand, contextualizes and makes sense of that which has already been made meaningful by those remembering or talking about the past. Yet, how such secondary interpretations unfold, which paradigmatic assumptions and theoretical frameworks they may employ or contest, are key decisions that will shape any given analysis. Put differently, the double-hermeneutic arguably both captures the research process and reminds us of our inevitable positionality. We all—social actors and analysts alike—remember, talk, write, and interpret from particular institutional, ideological, epistemological, and ethical positions.

Finally, returning to Lebow's above quotation and in spite of the fickleness of public attention and collective memories, there is a very strong, we would argue irrefutable ethical case for certain "aspects of the past"—particularly the Holocaust—to be given enduring relevance (see Morris 2002). Important moral questions also arise in the face of political attempts, from within different ideological camps, to co-opt and use the past for present purposes (see, for example, Rees 2010) and, more generally, given the mutual embedded-ness of memory and power: in the words of Jan-Werner Müller (2002: 12), "how should we treat a difficult past?" Nowhere are such questions more salient than with regard to studies and remembrance of the Holocaust.

The Holocaust: Singularity and (Potential) Recurrence

World War II comparisons of the kinds analyzed in this book are not restricted to everyday talk, political rhetoric, or various allusions in the media or other parts of the public sphere. Academics are far from immune to analogical thinking. This is illustrated by Irving Horowitz's important critique of the "ideological uses of social science," which

include decontextualized, leveling comparisons or analytically unhelp-
ful and ethically problematic definitional conflations. Horowitz offers
much-needed deconstructions of some staggering, deeply troubling
"rhetorical outbursts" linking Nazism to Zionism (1994: 29–30) or of
scholarly definitions of Apartheid as a form of genocide. Its abhorrent
racism notwithstanding, Horowitz points out that "it does not serve
the victims nor anyone else to present South Africa[n apartheid] as a
case of genocide—which implies the . . . destruction of a people" (1994:
165). Such conflations are not only historically inaccurate but, one
fears, inadvertently or otherwise attempting to "relativize the Jewish
case as one of many, consequently disregarding the specificity . . .
[of] the Nazi Holocaust" (Horowitz 1994: 165).

Perhaps the most well-known manifestations of such ideologically
motivated leveling comparisons occurred in the German Historians'
Dispute (*Historikerstreit*) of 1986. More particularly, Ernst Nolte's
much-debated position was based on the construction of Nazism, and
therefore also the Holocaust, as allegedly comparable or continuous
with other totalitarianisms. It was, as shown by LaCapra (1998: 49–50),
informed by very particular "interpretive procedures"—"the comparison of Nazi crimes with other forms of modern genocidal phenomena
(particularly Stalin's Gulags)," which effected a "relativizing" or "air-
brushing" of Auschwitz and sought to articulate a "positive narration"
of national identity unburdened from the moral imperative to mourn
the victims of the Shoah. As we also know, the *Historikerstreit* was a
key moment in the German history of World War II remembrance and
ultimately resulted in a "fragile consensus" concerning the singularity
of the Holocaust and its "profound ramifications for German identity
and politics" (Beattie 2006: 153).

It has also been shown that academic and other comparisons, as
well as attempts to make sense of present circumstances by analogy
to selective representations of the past, feature not only in public controversies but also in seemingly more quotidian statements, positions,
and debates. Samuel Moyn's recent analysis (2010) of a shift in postwar
interpretative frames is highly relevant here. An earlier "concentration camp paradigm," Moyn shows (2010: 49–57), was thus gradually
replaced by the "extermination camp paradigm." While both serve(d)
as rhetorical and interpretive synecdoches, in which a particular,
selected part stands in for the whole, their focus and political effects in
terms of the historical analogies they enable differ(ed) sharply. While
the concentration camp synecdoche subsumed the Shoah under wider

"Nazi criminality" and even other "camp systems" of oppression, internment, and exploitation, the extermination camp synecdoche moved
the focus firmly onto the systematic murder of Jews as Jews. In light
of a recent revival of the concentration camp paradigm, notably by the
Italian philosopher Giorgio Agamben, Moyn concludes by spelling out
the moral and political implications of all forms of synecdoche: their
inevitable selectivity encourages not only a ranking of horrors but also,
through the analogies they allow, "different sorts of attention in the
present" (Moyn 2010: 61–62). Clearly, these issues resonate in parts
of this book, where they are developed further.

At the same time, there are other, more benign, and much-needed
attempts to detect traces of the past in the present and to interpret
them as warnings. Much of what in the German-speaking world now
falls under a *Wehret den Anfängen* ("beware and fight the beginnings")
response to contemporary ills reflects a historical consciousness
focused on totalitarianism and the possibility of a recurrence. More
generally, the ability to detect similarities across time and to com-
municate them to the public is part of a disciplinary *raison d'être* and
intellectual self-understanding for many in the social sciences and
humanities. Part of the challenge, then, appears to be this: When to
insist—for epistemological and ethical reasons—on historical particularities that defy easy, decontextualized analogies; and how, conversely,
to detect real structural or ideological similarities. This challenge also
underpins much scholarship on the Holocaust. Important recurring
themes include the argument that the Shoah ultimately defies representation, easy pedagogical lessons, and comprehension (e.g., Eppert
2002; Morris 2002). In a similar vein, there are passionate calls against
any political instrumentalization of the Holocaust, including instances
where it is used as "template for past, present or future genocides,"
thereby reducing its victims to "rhetorical devices used to condemn
contemporary atrocities" (Weaver 2002: 159). Conversely, on the other
end of what one may regard as an interpretative spectrum, we encounter
analyses keen to point at purported continuities between Nazism and
various contemporary phenomena: James Watson's discussion (2002)
of the alleged, partial continuities (on the levels of biopolitical thinking
and governmentality) between Nazi "racial hygiene" and the contemporary production and exclusion of a "superfluous global 'underclass'"
is a case in point.

Meanwhile, some of the most influential contributions to research on
the Holocaust seemingly occupy a more nuanced middle ground (their

diverging analyses and mutual disagreements notwithstanding)—in reflecting the singularity of the Holocaust *and* in revealing conditions of possibility that can recur. Yehuda Bauer premises his approach on firm epistemological and political opposition to any view of the Holocaust as "something mysterious" or inexplicable. The analysis he proposes stresses the central roles played by a racist ideology, a "pseudo-intellectual elite with a genocidal program," and widespread, though perhaps latent anti-Semitic attitudes capable of being formed into a consensus in the context of social crises (Bauer 2001: 38; 45; 104–105). Although their respective explanatory models differ, Raul Hilberg and Zygmunt Bauman famously offer analyses that also point toward an underlying structure that makes a recurrence of the Holocaust—and therefore also comparisons—possible. While Hilberg (1996) uncovers a bureaucratic "destruction process," Bauman (2003) emphasizes the coming together of three distinctly modern phenomena—"deep social dislocation," bureaucratic organization, and a totalizing blueprint for a radically different social order. Such explanatory models not only acknowledge that further Holocausts remain distinct possibilities, but they arguably also point at the societal realms and the kinds of discursive shifts to be looked at for meaningful comparisons and justified or necessary warnings. The singularity-and/or-comparability issue is approached in yet another way by Dominick LaCapra:

> [T]he Holocaust was "unique" in a specific, nonnumerical and noninvidious sense. In it an extreme threshold or outer limit of transgression was crossed, and whenever that threshold . . . is crossed, something "unique" happens and the standard opposition between uniqueness and comparability is unsettled, thereby depriving comparatives (especially in terms of magnitude) of a . . . foundation. (1998: 6–7)

Calling for an "ethical turn" in critical theory, LaCapra therefore does not make an argument about numbers or social structures, but about the profound implications of every genocide for all of humanity.

These, then, are the contours of some of the wider debates within which this edited collection is embedded. Our aim is to capture, contextualize, and make sense of some of the countless allusions to the Second World War made across Europe—in its widest geographical and cultural definition—in the early twenty-first century, as well as their (dis)continuities with earlier decades. We will discover, not surprisingly, that the historical and symbolic referents provided by the Second

World War today still include the full range of "individual and collective experiences" that defined it: "population displacements, mass starvation, internment, forced migrations, aerial bombardments . . . ethnic cleansing and genocide . . . [being] victims, accomplices, bystanders and perpetrators" (Biess 2010: 2). The following contributions focus on some of the innumerable instances—some of them highly controversial and much discussed, others part of mundane everyday discourse—of memories of invasion, occupation, oppression, genocide, and other facets of World War II being used and abused as points of reference and interpretation for present circumstances. Empirically and theoretically wide-ranging, our analyses detect contemporary references to, and instrumentalizations of, memories of World War II for various rhetorical purposes in the contexts of national or transnational power struggles and across diverse forms of data: from political rhetoric to everyday language; from relevant media discourse to representations of (or mere allusions to) the Second World War in art; from school textbooks to readers' letters to newspaper editors; from public rituals of commemoration to life histories or intergenerational variations in how World War II is talked about. Jointly, the following analyses illustrate how such diverse politics of memory are used to interpret, predict, and respond to some of the social, political, and economic challenges widely perceived to define the here and now.

Moreover, various conceptual questions surface in different parts of this book, including the following: How are memories of the Holocaust invoked, or sometimes silenced, in contemporary discussions surrounding European identity and integration? More broadly, how, where, and for what purposes are memories and narratives of World War II selected and articulated today? How and where are such narratives contested? What is the relative relevance of, for instance, national and European politics, economic globalization, and the current debt crises to any such invocations of—and interpretative struggles over—the past? Can competing historical narratives be meaningfully described—in Gramscian terminology—as "hegemonic" and "counter-hegemonic" respectively, and, if so, in relation to which scale of contemporary politics (i.e., local, regional, national, European, global)? What forms of politics are facilitated by analogical thinking? Which wider theoretical debates (e.g., regarding social memory, civil society, or discourse-analytical approaches to studying language in social context) advance our understanding of past or contemporary discursive contests over World War II? How do ideological struggles over memory connect with contemporary debates about migration, multiculturalism, integration, and identity politics? What are our intellectual and ethical responsibilities in responding to historical inaccuracies, distortions, omissions, or abuses?

While these questions cut across the different chapters of this book, our contributors take readers on a journey meandering across Europe, from West to East, and from North to South and back again. In terms of geographical scale, we begin with a broad, pan-European view, followed by a series of more narrowly, predominantly nationally delineated chapters, before concluding with another discussion of distinctly transnational dimensions, and an epilogue offering further reflections. More concretely, Henning Grunwald begins with a discussion of genocide memorialization and Europeanization, which covers wide historical grounds since the Second World War and considerable geographical distances, thus offering important conceptual and empirical contextualization to the case studies that follow. These subsequent analyses focus, respectively, on a series of parliamentary debates in the United Kingdom (Burridge); on a recent Swedish controversy with wider European resonance (Schult); on German narratives of wartime suffering (Wilds); on the Flemish counter-memory of the Second World War in the context of Belgium's postwar history and ethnolinguistic division (Mertens); on historical analogies drawn and invocations made by former French president Nicolas Sarkozy (Smith); on the interplay of memories of World War II, political legitimacy, crises, and transformations in postwar and contemporary Italy (Thomassen and Forlenza); on the rhetorical framing and political instrumentalization of Greek anti-German sentiments in a deep and deepening debt and austerity crisis (Lialiouti and Bithymitris); on conflicting narratives of the Second World War encountered in school textbooks in the post-Yugoslav states of Croatia, Bosnia and Herzegovina, Serbia, and Montenegro (Mihajlović Trbovc and Pavasović Trošt); on Austria's national mythscape (Karner); on the discursive framing of memories of World War II across Polish generations (Duszak); on the complex and enduring significance of the Molotov-Ribbentrop Pact to Ukrainian collective memory (Zhurzhenko); and on the reception of a particular example of installation art in Germany, Holland, and Lithuania (Popescu).

However, this book can also be read—and its chapters be grouped—thematically. In addition to the easily discernible national foci, there are transnational, distinctly European dimensions (see, in particular, chapters by Grunwald, Karner, Schult) and both regional and comparative discussions (e.g., Mertens, Mihajlović Trbovc and Pavasović Trošt, Popescu). In terms of approaches and the materials or domains selected for analysis, different chapters variously focus on art (Popescu, Schult); on memory narratives and counter-narratives formulated by historians (see Smith, Wilds), in the realm of the everyday (see Duszak, Karner), by politicians (e.g., Burridge, Lialiouti and Bithymitris, Mertens; Smith, Zhurzhenko), or indeed across these various layers of social reality (Grunwald, Karner, Lialiouti and Bithymitris, Thomassen and Forlenza, Wilds). While some chapters illuminate the interface between the state and people's ordinary life-worlds (Mertens, Mihajlović Trbovc and Pavasović Trošt, Popescu), others contain elements of theoretical and conceptual development relevant to memory studies more widely (e.g., Duszak, Grunwald, Karner, Wilds, Zhurzhenko). Arguably most significant, however, is the earlier mentioned and recurring focus on the salience and wider resonance of particular memories in the context of previous and contemporary crises—many of them profoundly structural, others primarily perceived crises (e.g., Burridge, Grunwald, Karner, Lialiouti and Bithymitris, Mertens, Smith, Thomassen and Forlenza, Wilds).

"The further we get from the Second World War," Dan Stone observes (2010: 467), "the more fierce the battle over its meaning grows." We confidently hope that the analyses presented here advance our collective understanding of, and ability to respond to, some of the many "new contests in Europe's ongoing memory wars" (Stone 2010: 468).

References

Bauer, Yehuda. 2001. *Rethinking the Holocaust*. New Haven: Yale University Press.

Bauman, Zygmunt. [1989] 2003. *Modernity and the Holocaust*. Cambridge: Polity.

Beattie, Andrew. 2006. "The victims of totalitarianism and the centrality of Nazi Genocide." In *Germans as Victims*, ed. Bill Niven. Basingstoke: Palgrave Macmillan.

Bell, Duncan. 2003. "Mythscapes: memory, mythology, and national identity." *British Journal of Sociology* 54 (1): 63–81.

Biess, Frank. 2010. "Histories of the aftermath." In *Histories of the Aftermath*, eds. Frank Biess and Robert Moeller. New York/Oxford: Berghahn.

Biess, Frank and Robert Moeller, eds. 2010. *Histories of the Aftermath: The Legacies of the Second World War in Europe*. New York/Oxford: Berghahn.

Billig, Michael. 1995. *Banal Nationalism*. London: Sage.

Cram, Laura. 2009. "Introduction: banal Europeanism." *Nations and Nationalism* 15 (1): 101–108.

Doughty, Steve. 2010. "Aggressive atheism and Nazi echoes." *Daily Mail* 17 September: 6.

Eppert, Claudia. 2002. "Throwing testimony against the wall." In *Difficult Memories: Talk in a (Post) Holocaust Era*, eds. Marla Morris and John Weaver. New York: Peter Lang.

Fogu, Claudio and Wulf Kansteiner. 2006. "The politics of memory and the poetics of History." In *The Politics of Memory in Postwar Europe*, eds. Richard Lebow, Wulf Kansteiner, and Claudio Fogu. Durham and London: Duke University Press.

Garton Ash, Timothy. 2002. "Trials, purges and history lessons." In *Memory & Power in Post-War Europe*, ed. Jan-Werner Müller. Cambridge: Cambridge University Press.

Giddens, Anthony. 1984. *The Constitution of Society*. Cambridge: Polity Press.

Harding, Jennifer. 2006. "Questioning the subject in biographical interviewing." *Sociological Research Online* 11 (3), http://www.socresonline.org.uk/11/3/harding.html.

Heer, Hannes and Ruth Wodak. 2008. "Introduction." In *The Discursive Construction of History*, eds. Hannes Heer, Walter Manoschek, Alexander Pollak, and Ruth Wodak. Basingstoke: Palgrave Macmillan.

Hilberg, Raul. 1996. *The Politics of Memory*. Chicago: Dee.

Horowitz, Irving. 1994. *The Decomposition of Sociology*. New York/Oxford: Oxford University Press.

Huyssen, Andreas. 2003. *Present Pasts: Urban Palimpsests and the Politics of Memory*. Stanford: Stanford University Press.

Jarausch, Konrad. 2010. "Nightmares or daydreams?" In *A European Memory?* Eds. Małgorzata Pakier and Bo Stråth. New York/Oxford: Berghahn.

Jaspal, Rusi and Maya Yampolsky. 2011. "Social representations of the Holocaust and Jewish Israeli identity construction." *Social Identities* 17 (2): 201–224.

Judt, Tony. 2002. "The past is another country." In *Memory & Power in Post-War Europe*, ed. Jan-Werner Müller. Cambridge: Cambridge University Press.

Kansteiner, Wulf. 2006. "Losing the war, winning the memory battle." In *The Politics of Memory in Postwar Europe*, eds. Richard Lebow, Wulf Kansteiner, and Claudio Fogu. Durham and London: Duke University Press.

Karlsson, Klas-Göran. 2010. "The uses of history and the third wave of Europeanisation." In *A European Memory?* Eds. Małgorzata Pakier and Bo Stråth. New York/Oxford: Berghahn.

Karner, Christian. 2010. "The uses of the past and European integration: Austria between Lisbon, Ireland and EURO 08." *Identities: Global Studies in Culture and Power* 17 (4): 387–410.

Karner, Christian. 2011. *Negotiating National Identities: Between Globalization, the Past and the "Other."* Farnham: Ashgate.

Krzyżanowski, Michał. 2009. "The discursive construction of Europe and values in the coverage of the Polish 1981 'state of war' in the European press." In *The European Public Sphere and the Media*, eds. Anna Triandafyllidou, Ruth Wodak, and Michał Krzyżanowski. Basingstoke: Palgrave Macmillan.

LaCapra, Dominick. 1998. *History and Memory after Auschwitz*. Ithaca: Cornell University Press.

Lebow, Richard. 2006. "The memory of politics in postwar Europe." In *The Politics of Memory in Postwar Europe*, eds. Richard Lebow, Wulf Kansteiner, and Claudio Fogu. Durham and London: Duke University Press.

Lebow, Richard, Wulf Kansteiner and Claudio Fogu, eds. 2006. *The Politics of Memory in Postwar Europe*. Durham and London: Duke University Press.

Levy, Daniel and Julian Dierkes. 2002. "Institutionalising the past." In *Memory & Power in Post-War Europe*, ed. Jan-Werner Müller. Cambridge: Cambridge University Press.

Ludi, Regula. 2006. "What is so special about Switzerland?" In *The Politics of Memory in Postwar Europe*, eds. Richard Lebow, Wulf Kansteiner, and Claudio Fogu. Durham and London: Duke University Press.

Mills, C. Wright. 1959. *The Sociological Imagination*. Oxford: Oxford University Press.

Morris, Marla. 2002. "A difficult road: talk in (Post) Holocaust voices." In *Difficult Memories: Talk in a (Post) Holocaust Era*, eds. Marla Morris and John Weaver. New York: Peter Lang.

Moyn, Samuel. 2010. "In the Aftermath of Camps." In *Histories of the Aftermath*, eds. Frank Biess and Robert Moeller. New York/Oxford: Berghahn.

Müller, Jan-Werner. 2002. "Introduction." In *Memory & Power in Post-War Europe*, ed. Jan-Werner Müller. Cambridge: Cambridge University Press.

Müller, Jan-Werner. 2010. "On European memory." In *A European Memory?* Eds. Małgorzata Pakier and Bo Stråth. New York/Oxford: Berghahn.

Pakier, Małgorzata and Bo Stråth. 2010. "A European Memory?" In *A European Memory?* Eds. Małgorzata Pakier and Bo Stråth. New York/Oxford: Berghahn.

Rees, Arfon. 2010. "Managing the history of the past in the former Communist states." In *A European Memory?* Eds. Małgorzata Pakier and Bo Stråth. New York/Oxford: Berghahn.

Reisigl, Martin and Ruth Wodak. 2001. *Discourse and Discrimination*. London/ New York: Routledge.

Reynolds, Mary. 2010. "New EU Gestapo spies on Britons." *Daily Express* 26 March, http://www.express.co.uk/posts/view/165256/New-EU-gestapo-spies-on-Britons. Accesssed 29 March 2010.

Stone, Dan. 2010. "Beyond the 'Auschwitz syndrome': Holocaust historiography after the Cold War." *Patterns of Prejudice* 44 (5): 454–468.

Stråth, Bo and Ruth Wodak. 2009. "Europe-discourse-politics-media-history: constructing 'crises'?" In *The European Public Sphere and the Media*, eds. Anna Triandafyllidou, Ruth Wodak and Michał Krzyżanowski. Basingstoke: Palgrave Macmillan.

Watson, James. 2002. "Philosophy and reified consciousness in the age of genocide." In *Difficult Memories: Talk in a (Post) Holocaust Era*, eds. Marla Morris and John Weaver. New York: Peter Lang.

Weaver, John. 2002. "Silence of method." In *Difficult Memories: Talk in a (Post) Holocaust Era*, eds. Marla Morris and John Weaver. New York: Peter Lang.

Weiss, Gilbert and Ruth Wodak, eds. 2003. *Critical Discourse Analysis*. Basingstoke: Palgrave Macmillan.

Whitling, Fredrick. 2010. "*Dominatio Memoriae* and the power of remembrance." In *A European Memory?* Eds. Małgorzata Pakier and Bo Stråth. New York/ Oxford: Berghahn.

Wolfe, Thomas. 2006. "Past as present, myth, or history?" In *The Politics of Memory in Postwar Europe*, eds. Richard Lebow, Wulf Kansteiner, and Claudio Fogu. Durham and London: Duke University Press.

1

Genocide Memorialization and the Europeanization of Europe

Henning Grunwald

In his book *Europe Does Not Need the Euro*, the German populist Thilo Sarrazin argues that Chancellor Angela Merkel is clinging to the Euro in misguided atonement for German sins in World War II. History, or rather a misreading of history, holds her hostage. In a precise reversal of this accusation, the British *New Statesman* charges her with forgetting these (and other) lessons of the past. More pernicious than Iran's quest for nuclear capabilities, Merkel is the greatest threat to Europe (and the world) since Hitler (Sarrazin 2012, anonymous leader, *New Statesman* 141, 25 June: 7).

Others are even more explicit. In the *Daily Mail*, Simon Heffer writes that the Euro bailout amounts to an "economic colonisation of Europe by stealth by the Germans." "Once," Heffer continues, it would have "taken an invading military force to topple the leadership of a European nation. Today, it can be done through sheer economic pressure." We are witnessing, in other words, the "rise of the Fourth Reich," in which Germany is "using the financial crisis to conquer Europe . . . a loss of sovereignty not seen . . . since many were under the jackboot of the Third Reich." Such arguments are by no means to be found only in the popular and conservative British press. The *Guardian's* Simon Jenkins warns of "German supremacy," which would bring us "back to the ghoulish first half of the 20th century." It's a good thing, he muses, that contemporary "Germany has no panzer divisions" (Evans 2011: 23).

Against the backdrop of the Euro crisis, this volume and the Nottingham conference where it was conceived appear timely and topical. Nonetheless, the editors wisely resisted the temptation of making the crisis-spawned surge of rhetoric saturated in suspect claims about Europe's past an explicit focal point of our deliberations. Whether (and how) one can extrapolate from Europe's past to its future is a far more fascinating and complex question than the knee-jerk fashion in which many such arguments are deployed would suggest.

In what follows, I will attempt to survey European memory regimes since 1945, in broad brushstrokes and necessarily without any claims to comprehensiveness. Still, I hope that the many and obvious omissions and shortcomings are at least partially offset by the attempt, in contrast to the great majority of contributions, to eschew a national focus when considering European memory politics. What I hope to achieve are two things. Firstly, to remind readers of the historicity of founding myths and identity ascriptions, including European ones. Such ascriptions pretend as though they had always already existed when in fact they can wax and wane—and sometimes be produced—with astonishing speed, under very specific conditions.

Take for example the rhetorical equation of Germany with Nazi-era aggression and state crime. The last wave of such rhetoric swept over Britain in the early 1990s. It was in fact an expression of anxiety—about reunification. Among historians, the meeting Margaret Thatcher convened at Chequers is legendary. It discussed, in the words of a participant, the "abiding part[s] of the German character: in alphabetical order, angst, aggressiveness, assertiveness, bullying, egotism, inferiority complex, sentimentality." But you did not have to be conservative to fear a German backsliding into jackboots. The *Economist*, for instance, thought it likely that a reunified Germany would seek its own nuclear deterrent. The *Daily Mirror*, infamously, had footballer Stuart Pearce scream "Achtung! Surrender. For you, Fritz, ze Euro 96 championship is over" on its front page as it "declare[d] football war on Germany . . . England's old enemy . . . defeated in two world wars and one World Cup." As Richard Evans reminds us, before this wave of national anxiety, the primary British association with Germany was economic efficiency, dependability, et cetera, positive attributes much like the ones prevalent about Germany in Greece before the current crisis (Evans 2011: 24).

Secondly, I want to take a look at the European and Europeanizing dimensions of the violent and genocidal past of the "dark continent" (as Mark Mazower has labeled twentieth- century Europe) and of the representations of this past. Most papers assembled here focus on national discourses and practices of memory, and the national contro- versies they provoke or catalyze. There can be little doubt, however, that memories and memorialization, both popular and institutionalized, inform and underpin European identities and discourses. Fragile and contingent as European-ness, however defined, is revealed to be in the twin absence of a European public sphere and (powerful) democratic representation on the European level, there is more to the evocation of the war-torn, genocidal past than mere reassertion of national particularism. The *en masse* enslavement of forced laborers in World War II, the forced resettlement of millions of ethnically defined undesirables in the course and wake of conflict, and the destruction of the European Jews were crimes transnational in their conception, perpetration, and certainly in their consequences. To what degree is this true also of their memorialization? Is Europe really on the verge of becoming a "community of memory," as Aleida Assmann argues? Or do the last few years since the onset of the sovereign debt crisis not highlight the divisive potential of remembering Europe's violent twentieth century? How much does Europe owe (in both senses of the word) to the "negative founding myth" that Dan Diner sees in the Holocaust (Assmann 2007, Diner 2003)?

My argument is that, despite attempts at political manipulation, the memory and memorialization of genocide had a Europeanizing dimension. This is true, I argue against Tony Judt and Jeffrey Herf, even with the "freezing of memory" (or the "memory hole") during the Cold War (Judt 2002: 157, Assmann 2007: 15). The alignment with ideological exigencies was neither complete nor unambiguous, nor is it likely ever to be.

Take the vociferous reactions to Ronald Reagan's travel plans in 1985. During his visit to Bitburg military cemetery Reagan made remarks that seemed to equate the German soldiers buried there with the Jews killed in the SS camps (both termed "victims"). The speech provoked an outcry, and as a consequence a visit to Bergen-Belsen concentration camp was hastily tacked on to the itinerary. There, however, protesters not only demonstrated against Reagan's visit, but also against the perceived marginalization of Holocaust memory in West German political culture. In deliberately leaving camp memorials out of the initial plans for Reagan's visit, no doubt the last thing Chancellor Kohl's aides envisaged were German policemen manhandling Hasidic protesters to clear the way for the presidential motorcade into Bergen-Belsen. Meanwhile, Youri Vorontsov, Soviet ambassador to France, laid a wreath in Oradour-sur-Glane, site of an infamous SS massacre in 1944, to honor the "eternal memory of French patriots and Soviet patriots." This move, poignantly affirming the European and historical friendship binding

France and the Soviet Union, attracted not only the applause of the French CP, but also the much more unlikely acclamation of Margaret Thatcher (Rousso 1986: 55–6).

The Bitburg affair signals one of the ways in which the manipulation or political cropping of wartime memories was limited and could even prove counter-productive. Contrary to Kohl's intentions, more, not less attention was paid to the Nazi persecution of the Jews, and the ahistorical and insensitive Americanization of Holocaust memory contrasted unfavorably with the European affirmation of anti-Fascist solidarity.

The relationship between (collective) memory of genocide and a strengthening European identity is complex. Not only is Holocaust memory tied to factors transcending Europe, but even insofar as it is a European phenomenon presents itself as fraught with contradictions. Indeed, while memory can serve as a unifying force, it can also prove divisive, not only erecting barriers between communities but also creating fractures within them. As Konrad Jarausch puts it, "efforts to cope with German catastrophes" has resulted in "an insecure memory culture, full of taboos and given to controversy," and the "emphasis on particular suffering has prevented the realization of the interconnectedness of the historical sources of pain which might encourage greater compassion." The "intensely partisan politics of memory" have failed to give rise to a "coherent and generally accepted reading of the German past" (Jarausch 2001: 189–91). Hence, the notion of France as a country of resisters relegated stories about French complicity in the deportation of Jews to the margins of newspapers and national identity. It is emblematic for this that French guilt in the *Rafle*, the roundup of some 13,000 Parisian Jews almost exactly seventy years ago, in July 1942, and French complicity in Nazi crimes more generally, was only acknowledged in 1995, by Jaques Chirac. Just as Polish self-categorization as the primary sufferers of Nazi occupation was cast in national and then political terms, thus leaving little room for the commemoration of Jewish victims as such, so the Austrian self-stylization as the Nazis' first victims obstructed acknowledgment of Austrian responsibility in the genocide and supported a general view that:

> All suffering of the Jews during this period was inflicted upon them by the Germans and not by the Austrians; Austria bears no guilt for all of these evil things, and where there is no guilt, there is no obligation for restitution. (Uhl 2005: 57)

Holocaust memory, in other words, is by no means the driver of a straightforward, unidirectional process of Europeanization.

This paper has three parts. The first discusses the concepts involved, namely collective memory, collective identity, and Europeanization. A second, more empirical section aims to survey memory regimes from 1945 to 2000, while the third comments on the implications for the future (if any) of Europeanization.

Collective Memory and Europeanization

Both the study of Holocaust memory and the study of Europeanization have expanded greatly in the last two decades. Are these two developments related? The existence of a memory boom (or wave, or even mania) in the humanities is no longer disputed, merely celebrated or bemoaned (Confino 2006: 170–1, Lenz 2007: 7, Kansteiner 2002: 182). Certainly, surging interest in Holocaust memorialization is an important factor in the disciplinary ascendancy of memory studies. Jan-Werner Müller argues that the Holocaust, by virtue of passing from "communicative memory" (i.e., living) into "cultural memory" drives a preoccupation with memory as "a final battle over the content of a future cultural memory is being waged by witnesses and as the intellectual legacies to be passed on and the dominant representations of the past are being contested" (Müller 2002: 13–17). Jeffrey Olick links to the Holocaust the increase in redress claims and the "politics of victimization and regret" as strategies for political conflict in multicultural societies, while Aleida Assmann underscores this point in less stark terms when she argues that the Holocaust provides a language and a template for the perception and articulation of other traumatic experiences (Assmann 2007: 14, Müller 2002: 16, note 65). Whether or not one agrees with Pierre Nora's assertion that "whoever says memory says Shoah," it is clear that one can plausibly argue for a link, a mutual reinforcement between Holocaust memorialization and memory studies (Raulff 1998).

But what about Europeanization? For that, we must first take a look at the terms *collective memory* and *collective identity*. Collective memory can be defined as "collectively shared representations of the past." Most users trace their understanding of the term to Maurice Halbwachs (a student of Durkheim), though many are uncomfortable with his emphasis on the social determination of memory (Kansteiner 2002: 181). In most contexts, collective memory implies a constructed and somehow official, elevated version of the past—*Gedächtnis, Andenken* rather than *Erinnerung*. Official memory is often infused with a *telos*, most pertinently that of the nation. In the words of Jeffrey Olick, "memory and the nation have a peculiar synergy. Even when other identities compete with or supplant the national in postmodernity, they draw on the expanded role for memory generated in the crucible of the nation-state" (Olick 1998: 379, Delanty 2005: 95–6). Despite their best intentions, even scholars interested in applications of the concept transcending the nation-state find it hard at times to escape the implications of this synergy (Müller 2002: 3, 27).

For us today, inquiring into the relevance of memory and memorialization of trauma and genocide for European identity, this is anything but a trivial point. How closely is the construction of Europe related to the—in retrospect highly deliberate—construction of national communities? The creation of a shared and to some extent mythical past, imbued with the values and meanings a nation's self-appointed intellectual midwives, from Treitschke to D'Annunzio, wished to espouse has been widely commented on (see Patel and von Hirschhausen 2010 for an overview). Collective memory is emphasized by those arguing for an emerging European identity as well as by those contesting it. Klaus Eder and Willfried Spohn, for example, set out to investigate "transnational interest networks, transnational institutions and transnational communications spheres as mechanisms of the evolution of a European civic identity and memory." Does it smack of Treitschkean teleology, Europeanized, to posit "the development of a European identity due to the reconstruction of national identities in an emerging Europe public sphere, where collective memories are contrasted, debated and reorganized" (Spohn 2005: 1–2)? Pieter Lagrou and Tony Judt, by contrast, emphasize the elaborate and conflict-laden construction of particular versions of the recent past, the contested nature of war memories, and the difficulties in reconciling them (Lagrou 2000; Judt 2002). Lutz Niethammer connects the very origins of the term *collective identity* in the writings of Carl Schmitt, Georg Lukács, and Carl Gustav Jung to a sense of crisis; it is worth asking, then, whether the current popularity of the term is not an index of the *lack* of a clear sense of purpose and direction for the European project (see Assmann 2007: 12).

Less contentious than the emergence of *a* European identity is probably the adaptation of national identities in light of increased European experiences. For evidence of increasing European experiences, we have but to think of the revolution in European travel wrought by budget airlines, deregulation, and the Schengen accord; of the European convertibility (at least in principle) of tertiary education credits and the resultant Europeanization of studies; of the links fostered by trade and business; or of the popularity of European competition in sports like soccer, handball, and golf. As much as, and quite probably more than increasing political cooperation and supra-national governance, this everyday Europe exerts pressure on the adaptation of national identities. Nonetheless, political science has used Europeanization primarily as a means of measuring the adaptation of national political institutions, legal frameworks, and governance to EU standards (usually prior to or following admission to the Community).

Europe is identified as a space of particularly dense and contested collective memory or memories (Osiel 1995: 476–7, Dewandre 1994: 97). This is often inextricably linked with Europe as the site of the Holocaust. As Dan Diner states, "Europe—the realm of the old continent [is] where the Holocaust was after all perpetrated, and where its remembrance certainly has a real impact on political discourse and political reality to come" (Diner 2003: 39). Aleida Assmann takes the point up:

> In Europe, the historical site of the German genocide of the Jews, Holocaust memory has a different quality and resonance. . . . In Europe this memory is anything but abstract and removed, but rather deeply engraved in local and national history. (Assmann 2007: 14)

Such statements reveal the palpable move away from considering national contexts in isolation and toward a more transnational perspective (Karlsson 2003: 7). Scholars disagree, however, on whether there is an adaptation of national identities to accommodate another layer of identity (Kohler-Koch's model), or whether we are beginning to witness a supplanting of separate and incompatible national memories with a European collective memory, or at least with a permanent substantial modification of national memories to allow for their partial merging into a "shared collective memory," as Assmann and Müller appear to suggest.

Holocaust Memorialization in Postwar Europe

Although the horror of the camps forbids romanticizing the internationalism of the forced community of victims they created, it is striking that affirming international solidarity within the camp community played a prominent role in shaping inmates' ideas about memorializing their plight and defiance. A little more than a week after the liberation of Buchenwald, for example, on 19 April 1945, in a carefully choreographed ceremony, a temporary memorial was dedicated by a committee of survivors. Though most of the inmates and most members of the organizing committee were German, it was a matter of course that the pledge of remembrance and anti-Fascist defiance was read out in a number of languages. The highlight of the ceremony was an oath to continue the struggle—"We will only cease our struggle when the last of the guilty ones has been sentenced in the court of all nations"—that cast an international community ("of all nations") as the counterweight to Nazi oppression (Knigge 1997: 94–5).

Both the makeshift nature of the memorial and its placement on the *Appellplatz* indicate that the actual memorial was to be the camp itself, the preservation of which most survivors assumed as a matter of course—both in Buchenwald and elsewhere. In fact, before the Americans transferred control of Weimar and its surroundings to the Soviets, the camp was used as a kind of memorial-cum-educational facility. In a somewhat macabre reenactment using the bodies of inmates overcome by their debilitation *after* the liberation, one thousand or so Weimar citizens were escorted through the camp grounds on General Patton's orders in order to demonstrate the extent of the horror. Former inmates volunteered for demonstrations of the atrocities committed against them using straw puppets dressed in prisoner's garb. The inmates' committee even proposed to commit the SS guards themselves to serve as a permanent, living memorial: dressed in the same clothes as their former charges, living in the same quarters, with the same rations, and spending their lives tending to the exact preservation of the camp sites, including pulling weeds out of the parade ground (Hoffmann 1997: 10–11, 97–8).

When the Socialist Unity Party (SED) took control of camp memorialization, the idea of maintaining the camps themselves as memorials was made impossible by their continued utilization as "special" labor and internment camps. Around a quarter of the twenty-eight thousand inmates of Soviet Special Camp 2 are estimated to have perished (Hoffmann 1997: 117–8). What remained, however, was the desire to record the international dimension of both the suffering and the community it forged. Hermann Henselmann, the director of the Academy of Fine Arts at Dessau, was commissioned to design a memorial. He envisaged linking the name of Buchenwald, like that of Goethe, indelibly to Weimar, "and I mean that in positive sense: Through the suffering of the terror, inmates from thirty-six nations are forged into the solidarity of the new Europe." Water, the "symbol of life," was to spout from thirty-six individual outlets and fuse into one stream, while soil from each country was to be ceremonially buried at the site, in central Weimar.[1]

As Volkhard Knigge observes, this projected memorial did "not simply announce the arrival of an entirely new world" but sought:

> to convey how this world came to be. From the night of fascism . . . springs new life . . . through the martyrdom, death and solidarity of the KZ inmates. The concentration camp is not only the germ cell of the new Germany, but of a new Europe. (Hoffmann 1997: 102)

In the course of the 1950s and 1960s, the logic of the Cold War division of Europe asserted itself ever more strongly upon the contours of camp memorial sites. In their (winning) 1952 conception for the Buchenwald memorial on the Ettersberg, Bertolt Brecht, Reinhold Lingner, and sculptor Fritz Cremer envisaged an ensemble that was both a stage (literally: it is a thirteen-thousand-spectator amphitheater) for commemorative performance and an embodiment of Cold War doctrine. A group of figures—inmates—twelve meters tall on a base measuring fifteen meters, stares belligerently west, with clubs and rifles raised. The motto "Here freedom began—when will it embrace everyman?" ("*Hier fing die Freiheit an—Wann wird frei sein jedermann?*") is chiseled into the base. "The stony inmates . . . all look westwards with an expression of worried concern on their faces. Their posture and gestures, however, express their determination to fight for the definitive destruction [*endgültige Vernichtung*] of fascism in a united Germany," the artists explain (Knigge 1997: 127–35).

As the inmates were reduced to the archetypal Communist resister, the largest group of victims, the Jews, dropped from sight. This was unsurprising, perhaps, in a year when the East German Jewish Communist Paul Merker was implicated in the cosmopolitan plot revealed by the defendants in the Slansky trial in Prague. Merker's advocacy for restitution payments from East Germany to Nazi victims was smeared as treason, designed to starve the GDR financially, thus making it more easily penetrable by international finance. Neither the absurdity of the charge nor the ancestry of the language in which it was couched requires commentary. Merker's personal tragedy aside, it is striking how successfully *East* German implication in the genocide was marginalized. In the open-ended question "what is significant in German history," 13 percent of respondents in the West, but only

1 percent of respondents in the East replied "the Holocaust" (compared to 23 percent and 36 percent, respectively, for "the Second World War") (Wolfgram 2006: 58–9).

The year 1952 saw both the signing of the Luxembourg accords between Germany and the State of Israel and the Conference of Jewish Material Claims against Germany (the Claims Conference for short). Though fraught with many problems—not least the fundamental one of whether *Wiedergutmachung* (restitution, atonement, "making good again") could be achieved at all, and if so, whether it could be done with material restitution—this was a revolutionary departure. The settlement recognized the rights of the Jewish people (rather than of nations), which international law had not previously known (Ludi 2006: 429). By the year 2000, more than 100 billion DM had been paid out, and even Jeffrey Herf calls this "a remarkable achievement." Less well-known are the accords Germany struck with eleven Western European States for compensation of their citizens, usually in the form of lump sum payments. These are interesting because, concluded between 1956 and 1964, they overlapped with a crucial period in the formation of the European Economic Community. Strikingly, the Western countries conducted the negotiations in a spirit of restraint vis-à-vis Germany, anxious not to sully public perceptions of the NATO ally, as Schrafstetter (2003) has shown.

The logic of the Cold War meanwhile imposed itself on the memorialization of the War and the Holocaust in other ways, too. From East of the Iron Curtain, only Yugoslavia sent a representative to the official West German dedication of the Bergen-Belsen memorial in November 1952. The message of remorse and shame (*"Diese Scham nimmt uns niemand ab"*) which President Heuss delivered there was typical of the élite remembrance that he, Kurt Schumacher and, more ambiguously, Adenauer encouraged but that did not translate into stringent judicial persecution of the perpetrators in West German society. Regula Ludi and Patrick Hutton (Ludi 2006, Hutton 2008: 588) have emphasized that these memory politics were designed explicitly to disconnect ordinary Germans from having to acknowledge their own culpability in NS crimes (Herf 2002: 190–2). As in other West European countries, the exigencies of bolstering national pride and patriotism as well as the continuing reliance on deeply compromised élites called for playing down the involvement of ordinary people in state crime.

In Poland, where the camp sites *were* preserved, the opening of the Auschwitz memorial in April 1967 made explicit what the Buchenwald memorial stopped just short of proclaiming. Camp survivor and Polish Prime Minister Cyrankiewicz enjoined the Federal Republic to give up policies with "National Socialist pedigree," to recognize Poland's western frontier, and to renounce its "lusting after atomic weapons." Soviet General Pietrenko, who had helped liberate the camp in 1945, called on the US to stop the war in Vietnam. At the same time as the victims were stylized and honored as resisters and martyrs, they were also marked as Polish patriots. Nothing encapsulates this more clearly than the ritual conferring of the highest order of the Polish People's Republic—the Grunwald Order—upon the victims/martyrs (a giant replica was prominently integrated into the memorial); but we might also cite the red triangle (marked with the letter P for Poland) that was used liberally in the memorial. "Catholic-Communist Martyrology left no space" for those not mandated by the official version of resistance and sacrifice by Poles and Communists: gypsies, homosexuals, prostitutes, and so forth. While Jews were given their own pavilion amongst the nations, it proved short-lived; within a few short months, the onset of the Yom Kippur War had occasioned its closing for "repairs" (Hoffmann 1997: 25–30, Young 1994).

Remarkably, two German initiatives cut across the official freeze of relations: the Socialist Youth (*Sozialistische Jugend*, SJ), loosely affiliated with the Social Democratic Party and the church initiative *Aktion Sühnezeichen Friedensdienste* (Initiative Symbol of Atonement, Service for Peace). In organizing (partly reciprocal) visits by German youths to the sites of genocide and war crimes, both forged transnational networks and fostered exchange.

A first delegation of the Socialist Youth—irritatingly, given their pacifist commitments, nicknamed the Falcons—travelled to Poland in March 1958. Ostensibly, the aim was to defy the vilification of the enemy in the Cold War's ideological standoff, and to send a signal of German remembrance and acknowledgement of guilt as a means of opposing backsliding and authoritarianism. Polish party youth group Union of Socialist Youth (ZMS) paid a return visit a year later, paving the way for a larger excursion. In November 1959, 450 Falcons boarded sixteen buses emblazoned with a greeting "to the Polish people" in West Berlin and set out for Auschwitz and Cracow. During a five-hour visit to the concentration camp site, the Falcons laid a wreath and emphasized their commitment to remember the victims and their country's guilt. The next year, seven hundred Socialist Youth members travelled East, and there were four further trips similar in scope and participation until 1967.

In that year, Aktion Sühnezeichen also began organizing visits to Auschwitz. The group itself was older. Its initial impulse had been to rebuild churches, homes, and cultural icons destroyed during the war in the lands of Nazi Germany's enemies and victims. While the physical ruins were by and large a thing of the past by the mid-1960s, the moral work of atonement (*Wiedergutmachung*) remained very much to be done. The first group of Aktion Sühnezeichen volunteers, fourteen in number, stayed on the former camp grounds for two weeks. Their days were devoted to study and commemorative contemplation, but above all to rituals of atonement, none more poignant than the eight hours spent in silence pulling weeds and working to restore the camp grounds. In 1973, five hundred young Germans volunteered in Auschwitz through AS, and a decade later the organization facilitated the visits of fifty groups per year, by far numerically the most important group of German visitors to Cold War Poland (Huener 2001: 516–26).

Both Falcons and Aktion Sühnezeichen faced a complex political landscape and were at times at risk of being pulled into the logic of Cold War confrontation. During the very first larger-scale visit to Poland in November 1959, the Polish host and ZMS general secretary Adamski used his speech at the Auschwitz commemoration to attack West Germany and applaud the GDR and the Soviet Union. This openly political utilization of the celebration and concomitant media attention was a provocation to the Falcon delegation, who, while acknowledging Germany's historic guilt and deploring authoritarian tendencies in the FRG, had carefully steered clear of Cold War mudslinging. Now they felt unable to respond (not wishing to compromise the occasion), and some advocated curtailing the visit in protest and returning home that same evening. More conciliatory voices prevailed, and at the next commemoration, in Cracow's Slovacki Theatre the following evening, Falcons leader Ristock mixed criticism of the FRG and applause for Poland's "people's democracy" with pointed criticism of the abuse of the concepts of socialism and democracy in the GDR.

Despite the exchange of some barbed language, the echo of the visit was overwhelmingly positive. Even allowing for an element of self-congratulation, there is little reason to doubt the Falcons leadership's assessment that the trip had succeeded in furthering the organization's goals. By going to Poland, the group had raised awareness of Germany's historic responsibility for Polish and Jewish suffering and death, and mobilized opposition to those who would gloss over or bury the past. The group also defied the official diplomatic freeze. Moreover, this success stemmed precisely from privileging remembrance of past guilt and suffering rather than getting drawn into Cold War confrontation. That the éclat between Adamski and Ristock, which some had feared failed to materialize, and that in fact the Falcons-ZMS exchanges went from strength to strength in the following years suggests that the memorialization of Auschwitz and genocide defied an easy incorporation into Cold War point-scoring.

At the height of the ideological confrontation, "grassroots *Geschichtspolitik*" (Huener 2001) thus trumped, at least to an extent, the memory freeze others have diagnosed. In demonstrating this, the Falcons and to a lesser extent Aktion Sühnezeichen played a pioneering role. From the success of the (East German branch of) Aktion Sühnezeichen in lobbying the German public broadcasting company to drop a weather map using 1937 borders ("a nightly affront to the Polish people") to the collaboration of German and Polish prosecutors in making possible the site visit of the Frankfurt *Landgericht* to Auschwitz during the eponymous 1963 trial, these were stepping stones en route to Brandt's famous gesture at the Warsaw ghetto memorial. Moreover, Aktion Sühnezeichen in particular was an ostensibly European endeavor, with volunteers also visiting France, Hungary, the Soviet Union, and Israel, among others.

In France, the nationalization of camp memory is even clearer than in the case of the official Polish Auschwitz memorial. After initial use as an internment camp, Natzweiler-Struthof was declared the French "national necropolis" for the victims of deportation (the categorization which Jews were invited to assume in France). Whereas other camps commemorated—at least initially—the multinational composition of their prisoner populations, in Struthof it was in some ways the reverse. A commemorative plaque for the international victims of deportation notwithstanding, the primary goal was to make Struthof—located in Alsace and thus in a region where patriotism was perennially in need of disambiguation—a national monument. To this end, ashes or soil from the burial grounds of other concentration camps were brought to Struthof. Not (as in the case of Buchenwald) to give the remains of foreigners a piece of home in which to rest, but rather to bring home the remains of deported Frenchmen.[2] The hierarchies of victims were likewise determined along criteria laid down by the national narrative of heroic resistance. The deported were either categorized *de résistance* (and especially honored) or *de travail*—forced laborers with a whiff of collaboration. Jews had no separate category.

From these (necessarily) limited observations, it appears that a number of qualifications may be made to the argument that the Cold War froze and de-nationalized memory of the war. The Cold War did act as a catalyst for suppressing some and emphasizing other aspects of the wartime experience, as Judt, Diner, Lagrou, and Assmann have argued; certainly, a waning of the internationalism and the idea of a united Europe emerging from the camp experience is evident. But did the "Cold War's chemistry" really act as "the great neutralizer of the substrate of nationalism and the particularistic memories bound up with it" (Diner 2003)?

In fact, the experience of National Socialist occupation and persecution, while subjecting at least a great number of victims to homogenous (and terrible) experiences regardless of their nationality, did not feed directly into a unified European consciousness. On the contrary, the memory of these experiences was harnessed to bolster projects of national reconstruction, as well as being utilized by both East and West in the emerging Cold War confrontation, as Pieter Lagrou has demonstrated for the memory regimes of postwar Belgium, France, and the Netherlands:

> The dominating collective experience was not heroism: it was, rather, economic hardship, individual suffering, humiliation and arbitrary persecution. The liberated societies of Europe were traumatized, and their now fragile national self-consciousness was in urgent need of the kind of patriotic epic that only the resistance could deliver. In this context, persecution as a more fundamental experience was unacceptable, something not to be spoken of.

Groups such as resistance veterans, forced laborers, and victims of persecution were "united less as citizens of different states and more by the shared experience of resistance, forced economic migration or Nazi persecution." Nonetheless, the straitjacket of heroic postwar memory regimes insisted on recasting their experiences in *national* discourses of remembrance, so that "the memories they engendered were quite divergent" (Lagrou 2000: 2–6, 11, 301).

As a Europeanizing agent, much more important than the rather vague conception of a new Europe entertained by Henselmann and others was the anti-German feeling engendered by Nazi occupation. As Dutchman Ian Buruma puts it, it

> was comforting to know that a border separated us from the nation that embodied the evil. They were evil, so consequently we must have

been good. The fact that we grew up in a country which had suffered under the German occupation meant, to us, that we were on the side of the angels. (Buruma 1994: 11)

Tony Judt speaks of a "European consensus" regarding this question, and Peter Esterhazy expresses the idea even more radically: "To conceal one's own guilt by referring to Germany's crimes is a European habit. Hatred for the Germans is the foundation of the post-war period" (Esterhazy 2004). In that sense, the main Europeanizing function of camp memorialization may have been to sustain this habit and consensus, its Europeanizing effect thus quite independent of overt political utilization. A paradoxical Europeanization, turning as it did the memory of German guilt at the same time as Western Germany was rearmed and integrated into NATO, and as the country emerged as one of the central participants in the Europeanization of Western Europe. This paradox may in part explain the depth of sentiment and alarm during the Bitburg affair, alarm at what was perceived (probably rightly) as an attempt to rewrite the basic script of memory of German guilt and Europeanization. It may also explain why in today's Europe, with German historical guilt undisputed but now also remote, the search for a Europeanized and a Europeanizing Holocaust memory is definitely on.

Conclusion

In concluding, I would like to survey a few features of post-1989 memory politics. It should first of all be said that it is in this period that the trend towards Holocaust memorialization has been most pronounced. Many of the features of the memorialization landscape that we take for granted were contested and/or inaugurated only in the mid-1990s: the Berlin Holocaust memorial, for instance, or the introduction of a memorial day (27 January) honoring the victims of Fascism are of such recent vintage, as is the memorialization of the *Rafle*. Jan Gross's book on the Jedwabne pogrom, the apology by the Polish government for the crimes of Poles against their Jewish neighbors and the debate this precipitated are further cases in point. Outside Germany, national narratives have thus become more nuanced to reflect the ambiguities of the wartime experience and even, perhaps, instances of complicity in Germany's genocidal violence. At the same time, scholars have begun to question whether the status of the Holocaust as the dominant paradigm for the contemplation of Europe's twentieth century has

37

been obscuring as well as enlightening. In France, for example, intellectuals have debated whether remembrance of the Nazi genocide has unduly eclipsed the engagement with Stalinism's crimes and victims (to which critics reply that memory is not a zero-sum game). In Eastern Europe generally, scholars diagnose a sense that the Holocaust paradigm is too narrow to allow for adequate expression of wartime and postwar experiences with Communist as well as Nazi oppression (Delanty and Rumford 2005: 99–101.

One factor that stands out in post 1989 Holocaust memorialization is the drive toward restitution after the collapse of Communism. Dan Diner argues that:

> growing awareness concerning the Holocaust we do observe in Europe since 1989 seems to be a phenomenon largely moored in a basic anthropological assumption—the obvious, indeed organic interconnection between restituted private property rights and the evocation of past memories, or vice versa: Restitution of property as the result of recovered memory. This intriguing anthropological conjunction between property and memory can help explain why World War II and the Holocaust may well enjoy a long future in an emergent common European memory. (Diner 2003: 39–40; also see Rousso 2007: 30–2)

Regula Ludi and especially Jan Surmann have fleshed out this hypothesis with important empirical work. The latter describes the Clinton administration's "crusade for justice" as changing complexion dramatically over the years. From an effort to restitute property and acknowledge abuses after the fall of Communism in Eastern Europe, it turned into a much broader moral-political project in which Holocaust remembrance serves as a cornerstone of efforts to resist gross human rights abuses. Stuart Eizenstat has described this shift as a move "from money to memory," and in fact, Eizenstat's own career corroborates Diner and Surmann's thesis *in nuce*. From the US President's "special envoy for property claims in Central and Eastern Europe," Eizenstat's role was redefined as "special envoy for Holocaust issues" (Surmann 2011). The very definition of the scope of restitution as "Holocaust era assets" is further illustration of just how (literally) era-defining the memory of the Nazi genocide has become since the early 1990s (I have commented on the significance of legal discourse and restitution for both Europeanization and the Stockholm and Washington conferences and the Holocaust Task Force elsewhere).

Holocaust memory has not been the driver of a simple, unidirectional process of Europeanization. *Coming to terms* with the divisive potential and the incompatibility of national narratives, the discourse in various national contexts and across national boundaries, however, may well be such a driver. Holocaust memory may be one of the subjects of the "transnational public sphere" postulated rather grandly by Eder and Spohn. By fostering awareness of the historical self-image of European neighbors, it may allow us to negotiate the sticking points, to identify where and why national narratives clash and to reconcile them—or, at the very least, to agree to disagree.

Notes

1. See Hoffmann 1997: 100–2: The date of the town council meeting where Henselmann presented his ideas is erroneously given as 16 January 1945: it was actually on that date in 1947.
2. http://www.struthof.fr/en/la-memoire-du-campbr-apres-guerre/remembrance-of-the-camp-after-the-war/. 4 September 2008.

References

Assmann, Aleida. 2007. "Europe: A Community of Memory?" *GHI Bulletin* 40 (1): 12–25.

Buruma, Ian. 1994. *Erbschaft der Schuld. Vergangenheitsbewältigung in Deutschland und Japan.* München: Carl Hanse.

Confino, Alon. 2006. *Germany as a Culture of Remembrance. Promises and Limits of Writing History.* Chapel Hill: University of North Carolina Press.

Delanty, Gerard and Chris Rumford. 2005. *Rethinking Europe. Social Theory and the Implications of Europeanization.* London: Routledge.

Dewandre, Nicole and Jacques Lenoble. 1994. *Projekt Europa. Postnationale Identität: Grundlage für eine europäische Demokratie.* Berlin: Schelzky und Jeep.

Diner, Dan. 2003. "Restitution and Memory: The Holocaust in European Political Cultures." *New German Critique* 90: 36–44.

Esterházy, Peter. 2004. "Alle Hände sind unsere Hände." *Süddeutsche Zeitung* (11 October).

Evans, Richard. 2011. "The shackles of the past." *New Statesman* 140 (24 November), 23–5.

Herf, Jeffrey. 2002. "The emergence and legacy of divided memory: Germany and the Holocaust after 1945." In *Memory and Power in Post-War Europe: Studies in the Presence of the Past,* ed. Jan-Werner Müller. Cambridge: Cambridge University Press.

Hoffmann, Detlef. 1997. "Einleitung." In *Das Gedächtnis der Dinge: KZ-Relikte und KZ-Denkmäler 1945–1995,* ed. Idem. Frankfurt a.M.: Campus.

Huener, Jonathan. 2001. "Antifascist Pilgrimage and Rehabilitation at Auschwitz. The Political Tourism of Aktion Sühnezeichen and Sozialistische Jugend." *German Studies Review* 24: 513–32.

Hutton, Patrick. 2008. "The Memory Phenomenon as a Never-Ending Story." *History and Theory* 47: 584–96.

Jarausch, Konrad. 2001. "Living with Broken Memories: Some Narratological Comments." In *Divided Past: Rewriting Post-War German History*, ed. Christoph Klessmann. Oxford: Oxford University Press.

Judt, Tony. 2002. "The Past is another country: Myth and Memory Making in Postwar Europe." In *Memory and Power in Post-War Europe: Studies in the Presence of the Past*, ed. Jan-Werner Müller. Cambridge: Cambridge University Press

Kansteiner, Wulf. 2002. "Finding Meaning in Memory: A Methodological Critique of Collective Memory Studies." *History and Theory* 41(2): 179–197.

Karlsson, Klaas-Goran. and Ulf Zander. 2003. *Echoes of the Holocaust. Historical Cultures in Contemporary Europe*. Lund: Nordic Academic Press.

Knigge, Volkhard. 1997. "Buchenwald." In *Das Gedächtnis der Dinge: KZ-Relikte und KZ-Denkmäler 1945–1995*, ed. Detlef Hoffmann. Frankfurt a.M.: Campus.

Lagrou, Pieter. 2000. *The Legacy of Nazi occupation. Patriotic Memory and National Recovery in Western Europe, 1945–1965*. Cambridge: Cambridge University Press.

Lenz, Claudia and Harald Welzer. 2007. "Opa in Europa. Erste Befunde einer vergleichenden Tradierungsforschung." In *Der Krieg der Erinnerung. Holocaust und Widerstand imeuropäischen Gedächtnis*, ed. Harald Welzer. Frankfurt a.M.: Fischers.

Ludi, Regula. 2006. "The Vectors of Postwar Victim Reparations: Relief, Redress and Memory Politics." *Journal of Contemporary History* 41 (3): 421–50.

Müller, Jan-Werner. 2002. *Memory and Power in Post-War Europe: Studies in the Presence of the Past*. Cambridge: Cambridge University Press.

Olick, Jeffrey. 1998. "Introduction." *Social Science History* 22 (4): 377–88.

Osiel, Mark. 1995. "Ever Again: Legal Remembrance of Administrative Massacre." *University of Pennsylvania Law Review* 144(2): 463–704.

Patel, Kiran and Ulrike von Hirschhausen. 2010. "Europeanization in History: An Introduction." In *Europeanization in the Twentieth Century: Historical Approaches*, ed. Martin Conway and Kiran Patel. New York: Routledge.

Raulff, Ulrich. 1998. "Der Augenblick Danach" *Frankfurter Allgemeine Zeitung*, 8 July 1998.

Rousso, Henri. 1986. "The Reactions in France: The Sounds of Silence." In *Bitburg in Moral and Political Perspective*, ed. G. Hartmann. Bloomington: Indiana University Press.

Rousso, Henri. 2007. "Histories of Memory, Policies of the Past: What For?" In *Conflicted Memories. Europeanizing Contemporary Histories*, ed. Konrad Jarausch and Thomas Lindenberger. New York: Berghahn.

Schrafstetter, Susanna. 2003. "The Diplomacy of Wiedergutmachung: Memory, the Cold War, and the Western European Victims of Nazism, 1956–64." *Holocaust and Genocide Studies* 17 (3): 459–79.

Spohn, Winfried. 2005. "National Identities and Collective Memory in an Enlarged Europe." In *Collective Memory and European Identity. The Effects of Integration and Enlargement*, ed. Klaus Eder and Winfried Spohn. Aldershot: Ashgate.

Surmann, Jan. 2011. "Restitution Policy and the Transformation of Holocaust Memory: The Impact of the American 'Crusade for Justice' after 1989." *Bulletin of the German Historical Institute Washington* 49: 31–49.

Uhl, Heidemarie. 2005. "Vom Opfermythos zur Mitverantwortungsthese: NS-Herrschaft, Krieg und Holocaust im Österreichischen Gedächtnis." In

Transformationen gesellschaftlicher Erinnerung: Studien zur Gedächtnisgeschichte der Zweiten Republik, ed. Christian Gerbel et al. Vienna: Turia + Kant.
Wolfgram, Mark. 2006. "The Holocaust through the Prism of East German Television: Collective Memory and Audience Perceptions." *Holocaust and Genocide Studies* 20(1): 57–79.
Young, James. 1994. *The Texture of Memory: Holocaust Memorials and Meaning.* New Haven: Yale University Press.

2

Appeasement Analogies in British Parliamentary Debates Preceding the 2003 Invasion of Iraq

Joseph Burridge

Introduction

We would do well not to take too literally the provocative claim that "metaphors can kill" (Lakoff 1991a: 1); not if we wish to retain a clear sense of human agency and responsibility. Nevertheless, it is very clear that symbolic processes can be extremely important in shaping the understanding of military conflict—in relation to historical conflicts, and those that are ongoing, as well as those that are proposed for the future.

It is a matter of some consensus that metaphorical thinking necessarily highlights some features of any context while suppressing others (Lakoff and Johnson 2003), and that the elements of a historical source domain, to some extent, guide how we understand the features of its more contemporary target domain. The availability of various different historical analogies, which can offer very different evaluative possibilities, means that a lot can be at stake when one is used to make sense of the present. Their selection can therefore involve a highly strategic dimension (Toye 2008).

Historical analogies can, and often do, play a particularly powerful role in attempts to frame (and orientate) the discursive context within which attempts to justify military action take place. Such "orientational metaphors" (Stuckey 1992) can fulfill important roles in facilitating and undermining proposed military actions—depending upon the varying, and often contested, symbolic resonances of the specific conflict(s) that are invoked.

This chapter explores the significance of one such historical analogy as it was used in a relatively contemporary context. Specifically, it considers the ways in which World War Two (henceforth WWII) was invoked in the debate that preceded the 2003 invasion of Iraq. It analyses material from British Parliamentary debates, looking at two main, interlinked, aspects of analogical discourse: the assertion that Saddam Hussein was another Hitler, and the associated implication that those against the proposed invasion wanted to engage in appeasement. Various recent contributions have noted the continued relevance of aspects of WWII to European social, cultural, and political life (see for example Pakier and Stråth 2010; Wodak 2008; Lebow 2006). By exploring the operation of analogies of WWII this chapter engages with one aspect of the "presence of the past in the present" (Karner and Mertens present volume: 1).

Metaphors and Historical Analogies

In a recent critique of neoliberal foreign policy, Record (2008) has advocated that the appeasement analogy be retired from all American national security debates. Of course, it is all very well to suggest such a thing if we assume that its invocation is somehow purely strategic. However, this particular analogy has considerable and continued cultural force in line with the extent to which WWII and its wider context continue to impinge upon us.

Painful examples of national failure or misguided martial action often necessitate that repeated processes of comparison and denial are undertaken when proposed wars are discussed. For instance, the United States' failure in Vietnam has had intense cultural influence ever since—the so-called Vietnam syndrome, with its accompanying "never again" imperative. Any military action proposed subsequent to that—including the First Gulf War—has had to deal with the question of whether or not it will be another Vietnam (see Simons 1998; Hackett and Zhao 1994; Stuckey 1992; Voss et al. 1992).

While the Suez crisis has a similar significance in Britain (Varble 2003), generally speaking, WWII has a much more positive set of resonances. This is in part due to the successful construction of the Holocaust as an absolute evil in recent European history (Müller 2010: 32), such that WWII is widely perceived as a successful and just war, or so goes the "*hegemonic* national narrative" (Wodak 2008: xiii) regarding Britain's involvement (also see Berger 2010: 124). At the same time, the positive valuation of Britain's contribution to WWII is accompanied by a very negative evaluation of much of the decade prior to that war—including the engagement in a policy of appeasement during the 1930s, with the Munich Agreement of 1938 serving as a metonym of that policy. Overall, there is arguably an entrenched negative moral evaluation of the failure to undertake military action earlier than was the case, which is expressed as a national mistake (albeit usually personalized through the figure of the then Prime Minister Neville Chamberlain—see Toye 2008: 366), and as a matter of deep and longstanding national regret. This extremely negative moral evaluation of this period of British and European history is a shadowy accompaniment to the triumph of WWII itself, and is used quite commonly to dismiss or undermine opposition to proposed military action. It has its own redemptive imperative, a "never again" narrative akin to that associated with Vietnam in the United States. Appeasement is put forward as something of which we must never be found guilty again. From the experience of WWII, we need to show that we have learned the lessons of history.

According to many arguments made in favor of war, the ongoing Iraq crisis was to be understood as analogous to Europe in the 1930s—it was WWII again. Those arguing against war were constructed as the equivalent to those advocating appeasement of Hitler's expansionist agenda, and as in the 1991 conflict, where he was first allocated the role, Saddam Hussein was cast as Adolf Hitler.

Throughout the literature on both Gulf conflicts, there is a degree of consensus identifying a specific historical theme as being central in representations of Saddam Hussein—the drawing of analogies between himself and Joseph Stalin and/or Adolf Hitler. Reinforcing some of the ideas above, Aburish (2001: 288) claims that the latter representation comes in part from a British attitude that became a "national trademark since the failure to appease Hitler in the 1930s."

In his analysis of the metaphoric frameworks that facilitated the conduct of the First Gulf War in 1990–91, Lakoff (1991b: 2) wrote of the mythical qualities of the Saddam is another Hitler analogy:

> The Hitler analogy . . . assumes that Saddam is a villainous madman. The analogy presupposes a Hitler myth, in which Hitler too was an irrational demon, rather than a rational self-serving brutal politician. In the myth, Munich was a mistake and Hitler could have been stopped early on had England entered the war then.

45

The relatively entrenched idea that the WWII could and should have been fought earlier means that accusing an opponent of war of wanting to engage in appeasement has become quite a powerful way of attempting to undermine their position—both culturally and strategically. Associated with this discourse is a "never again" imperative akin to that which operates in relation to the Vietnam analogy in American contexts (see Hackett and Zhao, 1994). The "never again" imperative associated with the analogy as a definition of a situation attempts to foster a preference, for a particular type of activity. Most uses of the analogy mobilize a specific teleology—being associated with a very clear end: war, and sooner rather than later. Record (2008: 1) reinforces this interpretation of the analogy's significance: "if the enemy really is another Hitler, then force becomes mandatory, and the sooner it is used the better."

The logic of the workings of the analogy in the context of the debates preceding the 2003 invasion of Iraq can be captured, in an ideal-typical sense, by recognizing a series of moral evaluations, and asserted equivalences between the source and target domains, as follows:

- Saddam Hussein is another Hitler—that is: Hitler's analogue
- Continuing weapons inspections without full compliance is failing to deal with him properly (and is therefore appeasement equivalent to that of the 1930s)
- Military action is the only option (and always is the only option with "a Hitler")
- Anyone arguing against military action is therefore an appeaser
- Appeasement is morally abhorrent and did not work in the 1930s
- Appeasement delays the inevitable, and made WWII more difficult
- Since war is inevitable, we should fight it before it gets more difficult (a form of cost-benefit analysis that has been identified by others in relation to the first Gulf War—Operation Desert Storm—see Lakoff, 1991a and b; Voss et al., 1992; also see Record 2008)
- Given what we know of the 1930s, appeasers should know better—and are therefore ignorant in historical knowledge, or willfully immoral (pacifists but without the principles)

Of course, all of these elements are not articulated together in an explicit way in every attempt to mobilize the broader analogy, as will become clear. Before presenting an analysis of five different contributions to the UK Parliamentary debates preceding the invasion of Iraq, and a discussion of a small amount of newspaper content, I now turn to some very brief methodological reflections.

Methodological Reflections

Although the appeasement analogy received widespread use throughout the broad public debate, here I focus upon its use in four important debates in the UK Parliament—two each from the House of Commons and the House of Lords.

The data analyzed consist of extracts from five contributions to the debates that took place within the UK House of Commons and the House of Lords on 26 February 2003 and 18 March 2003 as the controversies over the continuation of United Nations weapons inspections, and the prospect of military action against Iraq, were debated and voted upon. Specifically, the data has been extracted from the official records kept of the debates (Hansard 2003a; 2003b; 2003c; 2003d), rather than recordings of the utterances that were actually made by speakers. These official records omit the prosodic features of speech—hesitation, intonation—and therefore provide an "idealized model" of the debate that took place (Chilton 2004: 94).

I approach the analogy through a focus upon the pragmatic or strategic role it played in arguing for war, and how that was resisted by opponents of war. The interest here is therefore firmly upon what connective possibilities the analogy opens up, and how its use undergoes contestation. I will therefore not consider whether the analogy does, or does not, accurately capture the reality of the situation in 2003. As will become clear, the politics of the usage of the analogy itself became a theme in the debate, undergoing substantial problematization by those at whom it was directed—opponents of military action.

Analysis of Examples

Accusations of Appeasement

As already stated, one of the most common ways in which the source domain of WWII was made relevant within the wider public debate, and in parliament in particular, was through construction of a desire to avoid military action and continue weapons inspection as being consistent with the appeasement of the 1930s. Many of the accusations proceed in a rather nebulous manner—with rather vague statements being made about appeasement's presence in the public debate, without clarity about who is accused, or how precisely appeasement is defined.

In his speech delivered on 17 March 2003, ostensibly directed toward giving Saddam Hussein forty-eight hours to leave Iraq and avoid war, US President George W. Bush (2003) referred to the continuation of inspections without full compliance as "a policy of appeasement." Of course, his was certainly not his first allusion to the context of WWII. In his address to the United Nations General Assembly earlier on in the process, Bush (2002) had challenged the UN to ensure that it did not suffer the same fate as its predecessor, the League of Nations, by failing to act with conviction in relation to Iraq's violation of UN Resolutions.

A prime example of this process of accusation in the UK parliament, invoking various aspects of the context of WWII, and the 1930s before it, comes from Julian Lewis (Conservative), as follows:

> Plenty of people argued that it was wrong to take action against the Nazis, until it became so late that the action that had to be taken proved much more costly than that which could have been taken earlier. Had such action been taken earlier, it would have been denounced as unwarranted and pre-emptive.
>
> [. . .] Those who said, in advance of the action that was eventually taken against the Hitlerite regime, that no action was justified get a bad press, because they are now regarded as having no reasonable arguments. Let me assure you, Mr. Deputy Speaker, that if we could revisit the debates that took place in this House in the 1930s, we would hear arguments for appeasement just as sophisticated as those put forward today. Those arguments were wrong then, and they are wrong now. It will be a grave mistake if people think that the cause of peace is served by always avoiding conflict. Sometimes the only way to bring peace is to face up to the need for conflict, and this is one of those occasions. (Hansard 2003a: 333)

Many of the arguments made against war are here portrayed as having been heard before—in the 1930s—and Lewis seems to be suggesting that just because "plenty" of people take a view against war now, that does not mean that they are right—precisely because the corresponding people from the 1930s have been shown to have been wrong by history. For Lewis, the people making such arguments are unreasonable and their arguments wrong, despite being sophisticated, since they are equivalent to those made against war with Hitler, the makers of which are now regarded as "having no reasonable arguments." Lewis's sense of moral certainty, inspired by the analogy, is palpable—something that chimes with Müller's (2010: 33) observations about the extent to which: "summoning the past appears to furnish the participants in political debates with a moral certainty."

Lewis's claims about action becoming more costly the longer it is postponed resonates with Record's (2008) account of the appeasement analogy, and the sense of urgency that it tries to mobilize via a cost-benefit logic. That is, Lewis is suggesting that the longer that the (inevitable) military action is delayed, the worse it will be. Implicitly, therefore, appeasement is not only known to have been wrong and counterproductive, but those who engage in it are partly responsible for that higher cost—whether in money or lives. Such assertions pose discursive difficulty for those on the other side of the argument, who often responded by engaging critically with the process of accusation involved, as will become clear.

Because of the average age of members of the House of Lords being closer to seventy years than the fifty years of the House of Commons, speakers in the Lords were able to invoke rhetorically their own personal memory of the 1930s and 1940s as part of their arguments—claiming a form of category entitlement in Potter's (1996: 132) sense. They were there back then, and could therefore construct themselves as bearing witness to any parallels that they claimed existed between the present context and that of WWII. For instance, Baroness Sharples (Conservative) made the following contribution regarding our knowledge of Saddam Hussein, connecting him indirectly with Hitler:

> The present situation brings memories flooding back. In 1939, I do not believe that we were universally aware of the dangers facing the world because of the aspirations of one man, Hitler, who was an appalling tyrant. Now, things are vastly different. With constant television and the media generally, Saddam Hussein has been shown to be evil and dangerous. (Hansard 2003d: 194–195)

Here Baroness Sharples claims that the current context is directly connected to that WWII in that it resonates to the extent that her memories (conceptualized as liquid) come "flooding back," something suggesting that the connection is so powerful that the recall (the flow of that liquid) is not under her control. Without stating directly that Saddam Hussein is another Hitler, she moves from discussing Hitler to Hussein in consecutive sentences where she makes claims about the information sources available in 2003. Her suggestion here seems to be that we could have been forgiven for not fully understanding the seriousness of the situation in 1939, because of it being less easy to access information, but also, by contrast, that the greater availability of media sources now (in 2003) robs us of any excuse involving lack of knowledge about the character of Saddam Hussein. Arguably, one implication of this is that given the asserted lack of availability of ignorance as an excuse, opponents of war are willfully ignoring the seriousness of the situation.

Although Baroness Sharples is implicitly equating Hitler and Hussein, she does so in a relatively nuanced and indirect way—emphasizing our ability to know about the morality of Saddam Hussein and the seriousness of the situation. The important issue at stake is therefore our level of knowledge and our willingness to access the information available now—to understand the morality of, and danger posed by, Saddam Hussein. The full range of aspects of the analogy is not articulated clearly, but they are not all necessary to pose discursive difficulty for opponents of war. Her partial use of the analogy omits reference to several portions of it. Others, including the next extract discussed, deliberately and actively attempted to control which aspects were and were not mobilized. Such examples clarify clarifying in an explicit way those parts of the source domain that were, and were not, considered appropriate for making sense of the current context. Again such contributions tended to focus upon our shared historical knowledge, and its relevance as a guide to action.

Strategic Selectivity

Early on in his speech to start the debate about UN Resolution 1441 and the decision to engage in military action in Iraq, a speech described by Charteris-Black (2011: 248) as "perhaps the most important political speech he made," the then British Prime Minister Tony Blair addressed aspects of the appeasement analogy in a relatively nuanced but of course strategic way:

> There are glib and sometimes foolish comparisons with the 1930s. I am not suggesting for a moment that anyone here is an appeaser or does not share our revulsion at the regime of Saddam. However, there is one relevant point of analogy. It is that, with history, we know what happened. We can look back and say, "There's the time; that was the moment; that's when we should have acted." However, the point is that it was not clear at the time—not at that moment. In fact, at that time, many people thought such a fear fanciful, or worse, that it was put forward in bad faith by warmongers. . . .
>
> Now, of course, should Hitler again appear in the same form, we would know what to do. But the point is that history does not declare

the future to us plainly. Each time is different and the present must be judged without the benefit of hindsight. (Hansard 2003c: 767)

Here, Blair tries to draw upon the appeasement analogy very carefully and selectively, trying to construct himself as not mobilizing certain elements of it, amounting to an argument that only part of the source domain (WWII) resonates with its target (Iraq 2003).

Blair first suggests that the analogy with the 1930s is superficial and foolish, before going on to specify exactly which bit of it he wants to mobilize, the small part that he wants to be considered resonant with the current situation. He claims that he is not constructing opponents of war as appeasers, nor is he suggesting that they are pro-Saddam Hussein. Simultaneously, he nevertheless wants to mobilize the idea that we should have learned from history. Blair suggests that our hindsight about the 1930s should result in us being less wary about militarizing the situation than people were then. Although we do not have hindsight about the present, we can, or have to, use the past to infer it. The logic here is something akin to conducting a risk assessment: using the past or a version thereof to infer the future.

Blair is suggesting to his opponents that they should not take risks in relation to Saddam Hussein, but also in relation to how they will be judged by history: They are incited to not risk that their position now will be seen as the equivalent of that of the appeasers prior to WWII, that they not risk that history will show them to have been terribly wrong in their opposition to action, that they not allow themselves to be judged in the future as having been misguided. Of course, looking at this now with the benefit of a degree of hindsight, there is a certain irony about Blair encouraging others to act in such a way as to avoid future moral condemnation. Nevertheless, he was attempting to foster a degree of difficulty for his opponents at the time by mobilizing elements of the past, as well as tapping into the redemptive imperative already discussed.

As with Lewis's contribution, these sorts of claims and accusations using historical analogies create discursive problems for opponents, who cannot afford to be directly lined up with the appeasers of the past—given their moral evaluation. With that in mind, I will now discuss two contributions that engage critically with the assertion that the Iraq Crisis could and should be understood via an analogy with WWII—demonstrating the contested, and therefore not straightforwardly deterministic character of the analogy.

Problematization of the Accusation

In one of many speeches by her that were consistent in their opposition to war, and one of several critical engagements she made with the appeasement accusation specifically, Baroness Turner of Camden (Labour) stated the following:

> I do not believe that those in this country who are in favor of war fully understand the revulsion that many of us feel of the reasons for it. We are accused of supporting Saddam Hussein, or else of appeasement, as if a minor dictator of a broken, battered country that has been reduced to third-world level can somehow be compared with Hitler! Those who make such comments are too young to have experienced those days or else know no history. (Hansard 2003d: 211–212).

Here Baroness Turner engages with the appeasement analogy, via a limited process of comparison and denial. She trivializes the threat posed by Saddam Hussein, who is categorized as only a "minor" dictator—in contrast to Hitler—and makes deprecatory comments about the level of development and capability of Iraq in 2003, after the first Gulf War and many years of UN sanctions ("a broken, battered country . . . reduced to third-world level"). This attempts to undermine the idea that the threat posed by Iraq in 2003 can be considered equivalent to that offered by Germany in, and before, WWII.

Like Baroness Sharples's contribution discussed earlier, Baroness Turner constructs herself as an eyewitness to the 1930s—the source domain of the analogy. She constructs herself as an eyewitness to WWII, and therefore also asserts her category entitlement to adjudicate the existence or absence of any parallels between WWII and the present. She constructs those who invoke parallels as their being ignorant of history, or as a product of the fact that they, in contradistinction to her, are too young to have had first-hand knowledge of Hitler—with whom Saddam Hussein cannot be accurately compared.

Another similar contribution directed toward problematizing the applicability of appeasement as a description of opposition to war, was provided by Lord Morgan (Labour):

> As a historian, I worry about the crude use of history, particularly our old friend the 1930s. Time and again we hear that this crisis is the 1930s come again—what nonsense. Saddam is not another Hitler. Where is his *Mein Kampf*? Where is his dream of universal conquest? George Bush is certainly no Churchill; it would be a calumny on the reputation of that great man to suggest it. It is a facile argument, and

it disturbs me that Downing Street produces it, all the more because I taught one or two of them. My efforts were clearly somewhat in vain. (Hansard 2003b: 332).

Here Saddam Hussein avowedly not "another Hitler," because he has neither written an equivalent to *Mein Kampf*, nor expressed expansionist ambitions akin to those of Hitler. Lord Morgan also denies strongly the validity of comparing George W. Bush to Churchill, another implicit but rarely articulated entailment of the wider WWII analogy (suggesting that the comparison is insulting to Churchill). He asserts his authority to speak on all of these matters by mentioning that he is a historian, yet another form of category entitlement that constructs him as entitled to adjudicate the validity of the appeasement analogy, which he characterizes as both "crude" and "facile," and implicitly overused. Moreover, he makes a joke about his lack of success as a teacher by noting that he was responsible for teaching some of the people in government in Downing Street who have been involved in mobilizing this (according to him, incorrect) historical analogy.

Taken together, the incompatibilities that Lord Morgan invokes amount to an argument that the whole analogy does not fit. Morgan is claiming that too many of the important elements from the source domain of the metaphor do not connect up with elements in its target—if Saddam is not Hitler, and Bush is not Churchill, then the analogy does not fit successfully. The implication is that the analogy breaks down if one or several parts of it fail to fit.

In his work on political discourse, Chilton (2004: 52) argues that the entailments of a metaphor tend to work in a holistic fashion such that "if one part is accepted other parts follow" in a relatively automatic way. In Tony Blair's attempt to appropriate the appeasement analogy selectively we have seen evidence that partiality is possible, but also that effort is perhaps required to engineer it. At the same time, a reasoned evidential comparison and denial of its validity or part thereof does not appear to be sufficient to undermine the workings of the analogy, since contributions such as Baroness Turner's and Lord Morgan's did not cause talk of appeasement to evaporate.

In his exploration of how the Saddam=Hitler analogy was utilized in media coverage of the first Gulf War, Link (1991) draws a distinction between structural and interactional analogies. Structural analogies involve a comparison of Iraq and Germany in terms of Empire, expansionist intentions, and technological development, the types of comparison (and denial) undertaken by Turner and Morgan as well as others. Interactional ones involve comparison on the level of character, morality, and motives, facilitated by the personalization of the conflict. While Link argues that a systematic structural comparison of Hussein's Iraq and Hitler's Germany would identify that parallels could not be sustained, the more interactional aspect of the analogy—the portrayal of the character of Hussein as a madman, a criminal, a megalomaniac, as evil—is much more resistant to being undermined by any sort of evidence-based comparison. Therefore it can continue to resonate, and continue to pose difficulty for opponents of war, even if structural parallels are problematized successfully. In that respect, in being characterized as interactionally similar to Hitler, Saddam Hussein is still a candidate for appeasement, as are others who can be similarly characterized.

Reversing the Accusation

In his work on uses of metaphor in political speeches, Charteris-Black (2011: 37) argues that skilled rhetoricians are able to "draw on different aspects of the source domain to extend the metaphor to generate a different inference from the one intended by the person who first used it." Practices akin to extending the metaphor of appeasement had some presence in the wider public debate over the Iraq Crisis, and were prominent in newspaper opinion pieces during early 2003.

Rather than trying to undermine the historical analogy with the 1930s as illegitimate, some contributions asserted the relevance of appeasement but as part of arguments *against* war, a reversal of its more conventional application. Here contributors accepted the relevance of the analogy but argued that it was not being applied to the correct people, reversing the direction of the accusation to apply it to the UK government or Tony Blair in particular. Some such contributions accused George W. Bush of a degree of hypocrisy in his use of the appeasement analogy given the United States of America's "late" entry into WWII (Robert Fisk, *The Independent*, 27/1/03: 5). Others expressing opposition to war asserted that appeasement was at stake, but in the opposite direction (see Seumas Milne, *The Guardian*, 13 February 2003: 22), or in the case of John Pilger (*Daily Mirror* 29 January 2003: 4), Tony Blair was accused not merely of appeasement of George W. Bush and the United States, but, with Pilger's characteristic intensity, of the "most dangerous appeasement humanity has known since the 1930s."

Richard Dawkins also accused the British government of being guilty of appeasement in their orientations toward US policy, as follows:

> The distorting mirror of Munich and appeasement is held up with irritating regularity. . . . Jack Straw warns that Washington would abandon the UN and NATO if Europe refuses to fall into line: "What I say to France and Germany and all my other EU colleagues is take care, because just as America helps to define and influence our politics, so what we do in Europe helps to define and influence American politics . . . And we will reap a whirlwind if we push the Americans into a unilateralist position in which they are the center of this unipolar world." If that is not appeasement, I'd like to know what you call it. (*The Guardian*, 6/3/03: 27)

Here Dawkins notes the metonymic significance of Munich, and its place in accusations of appeasement, claiming that they are "irritating" distortions. He utilizes a statement made by Jack Straw (then UK foreign secretary), regarding the relationship between Europe and the United States—that a certain nonconfrontational approach should be adopted so that the EU does not "reap a whirlwind" of US unilateralism—and argues that this constitutes appeasement of the US.

Examples of this type, reversing the accusation, serve to sustain or reaffirm the negativity of appeasement (or other aspects of WWII) by making use of some of its connotations in order to redirect the process of accusation. As such, they contribute to the continued cultural relevance of appeasement as a technique or analogy for understanding orientations to war in the future. Such reversals do little to undermine the general utility of accusations of appeasement for marginalizing opposition to war in general, since the illegitimacy of appeasement is left intact; indeed reversal is reliant upon that illegitimacy for its efficacy.

The possibility of such reversal lies in the lack of directional specificity in terms of appeasement's meaning, along with agreement about the moral evaluation of appeasement as an approach. If the direct link made between appeasement and opposition to a specific war can be broken, then a much wider pool of people can be an appeaser or be appeased (including George W. Bush) and condemned on that basis. Of course, some less mainstream contributors to the debate explicitly equated Bush with Hitler, but that equivalence is not formulated directly here by Dawkins, although it is, of course, potentially available as an inference. The appeasement analogy always affords the possibility of identifying a Hitler, but also more importantly always acts as a form of condemnation—a use of WWII, and lessons from history, to direct action in the present.

Conclusion

In summary, this chapter has explored some of the ways in which aspects of WWII were invoked, reconstructed, and used analogically, for specific rhetorical purposes in 2003 in the context of the then proposed invasion of Iraq. It has contributed to our understanding of the continued cultural significance of that period of European history, and its strategic instrumentalization as a reference point—an orientational metaphor—in a more contemporary politically charged context, as well as articulating some of the complexity of its usage and contestation.

In arguments in favor of military action, the apparent need for redemption—the need to never appease again—can be harnessed to create discursive obstacles for those opposed to war. Opponents of war then have to spend time engaging with and trying to undermine the value of the analogy rather than making their arguments against military action. If the perceived need for redemption persists, and if the problematizations of the accusation of appeasement merely deny its applicability in this specific case, or continue to reinforce the importance of not engaging in it, or reinforce that via reversal, it would seem unlikely that appeasement will be reduced in its significance as a technique for causing such difficulty for those opposed to future potential wars.

It would be unwise to assert too strong a set of conclusions on the basis of this evidence, but it is fair to claim that the legacy of the appeasement of the 1930s continues to have a hold over the culture and politics of Britain, and especially in relation to situations in which military action is undergoing consideration. The redemptive imperative associated with the failure of appeasement is such an entrenched part of the repertoire used for making sense of war, and for strategic use in its justification, that its usage seems to be unlikely to diminish. In fact, to the extent that it works on a moral and mythical level, rather than in relation to detailed comparison between source and target domains, it may be rather unlikely to diminish in significance when there are no longer any eyewitnesses around to problematize it using their direct experience. The extremely negative esteem in which appeasement is held as a policy, and the extent to which it continues to be central to our understanding of war, and to the justifications offered for proposed wars, certainly merit more extensive exploration elsewhere.

Because of the problems that were confronted by the Coalition forces following the invasion and occupation of Iraq, the 2003 invasion of Iraq has its own rather different and rather negative analogical affordances, rather different to those of WWII and appeasement. Indeed, the Iraq analogy has already been mobilized in order to problematize and undermine military action proposed in relation to Libya, with current British Prime Minister David Cameron engaging in much comparison and denial that the establishment of a no-fly zone over Libya in March 2011 could lead to "another Iraq" (see for example Hansard 2011: 709). It will be interesting to see how the legacy of the invasion is made sense of as its history is written and rewritten, as well as which elements of it are used as a source domain, and precisely for which purposes—for like each new war, it has become another in the repertoire of orientational metaphors.

References

Aburish, Saïd K. 2001. *Saddam Hussein: The Politics of Revenge*. London: Bloomsbury.

Berger, Stefan. 2010. "Remembering the Second World War in Western Europe, 1945–2005." In *A European? Contested Histories and Politics of Remembrance*, eds. Malgorzata Pakier and Bo Stråth. Oxford: Berghahn.

Bush, George W. 2003. *Message to Saddam*, 17 March 2003, available from www.presidentialrhetoric.com/speeches/03.17.03.html, retrieved 20 June 2012.

Bush, George W. 2002. *Remarks at the UN General Assembly*, 12 September 2002, available from www.presidentialrhetoric.com/speeches/09.12.02.html, retrieved 20 June 2012.

Charteris-Black, Jonathan. 2011. *Politicians and Rhetoric: The Persuasive Power of Metaphor* (2nd edition). Basingstoke: Palgrave MacMillan.

Chilton, Paul A. 2004. *Analysing Political Discourse: Theory and Practice*. London: Routledge.

Hackett, Robert A. 1993. *Engulfed: Peace Protest and America's Press During the Gulf War*. New York: NYU Center for War, Peace and the News Media.

Hansard. 2003a. *Official Report of the House of Commons*. 400 (51), 26/2/03: 265–372.

Hansard. 2003b. *Official Report of the House of Lords*. 645 (52), 26/2/03: 244–379.

Hansard. 2003c. *Official Report of the House of Commons*. 401 (65), 18/3/03: 760–911.

Hansard. 2003d. *Official Report of the House of Lords*. 646 (66), 18/3/03: 138–232.

Hansard. 2011. *Official Report of the House of Commons*. 525 (136), 21/3/11: 700–807.

Karner, Christian and Bram Mertens. Present Volume. "Introduction: Memories and Analogies of World War Two." In *Nation States between Memories of World*

War Two and Contemporary European Politics, eds. Christian Karner and Bram Mertens. New Jersey: Transaction.

Lakoff, George. 2003. "Metaphor and War, Again." Available from: www.alternet.org/story/15414

Lakoff, George. 1991a. "Metaphor and War: The Metaphor System Used to Justify the War in the Gulf (Part 1 of 2)." *Vietnam Generation Journal and Newsletter*: www2.iath.virginia.edu/sixties/HTML_docs/Texts/Scholarly/Lakoff_Gulf_Metaphor_1.html

Lakoff, George. 1991b. "Metaphor and War: The Metaphor System Used to Justify the War in the Gulf (Part 1 of 2)." *Vietnam Generation Journal and Newsletter*: www2.iath.virginia.edu/sixties/HTML_docs/Texts/Scholarly/Lakoff_Gulf_Metaphor_2.html

Lakoff, George and Mark Johnson. 2003 [1980]. *Metaphors We Live By* (2nd edition). Chicago: University of Chicago Press.

Lebow, Richard N. 2006. "The Memory of Politics in Postwar Europe." In *The Politics of Memory in Postwar Europe*, eds. Richard N. Lebow, Wulf Kansteiner and Claudio Fogu. London: Duke University Press.

Link, Jürgen. 1991 "Maintaining Normality: On the Strategic Function of the Media in Wars of Extermination." *Cultural Critique* 19: 55–65.

Müller, Jan-Werner. 2010. "On 'European Memory' Some Conceptual and Normative Remarks." In *A European Memory? Contested Histories and Politics of Remembrance*, eds. Malgorzata Pakier and Bo Stråth. Oxford: Berghahn.

Pakier, Malgorzata., and Bo Stråth. 2010. "A European Memory?" In *A European? Contested Histories and Politics of Remembrance*, eds. Malgorzata Pakier and Bo Stråth. Oxford: Berghahn.

Potter, Jonathan A. 1996. *Representing Reality: Discourse, Rhetoric and Social Construction*. London: Sage.

Record, Jeffrey. 2008. "Retiring Hitler and 'Appeasement' from the National Security Debate." *Parameters* 38 (2): 91–101.

Simons, Geoff. 1998. *Vietnam Syndrome: Impact on US Foreign Policy*. Basingstoke: MacMillan.

Stuckey, Mary E. 1992. "Remembering the Future: Rhetorical Echoes of World War II and Vietnam in George Bush's Public Speech on the Gulf War." *Communication Studies* 43 (4): 246–256.

Toye, Richard. 2008. "The Churchill Syndrome: Reputational Entrepreneurship and the Rhetoric of Foreign Policy since 1945." *British Journal of Politics and International Relations* 10 (3): 364–378.

Varble, Derek. 2003. *The Suez Crisis 1956*. Oxford: Osprey.

Voss, James F., Joel Kennet, Jennifer Wiley, and Tonya Y. E. Schooler. 1992. "Experts at Debate: The Use of Metaphor in the US Senate Debate on the Gulf Crisis." *Metaphor and Symbolic Activity* 7 (3–4): 197–214.

Wodak, Ruth. 2008. "Preface to the First Edition: 'How History is Made'—the Origins and Aims of the Project." In *The Discursive Construction of History: Remembering the Wehrmacht's War of Annihilation*. eds. Hannes Heer, Walter Manoschek, Alexander Pollak, and Ruth Wodak. Basingstoke: Palgrave.

3

How Deeply Rooted Is the Commitment to "Never Again"? Dick Bengtsson's Swastikas and European Memory Culture

Tanja Schult

The (Non-)Incident and European Memory

During Sweden's EU presidency, Foreign Minister Carl Bildt invited his colleagues from the other EU member states to a two-day meeting, to be held at the Moderna Museet in Stockholm in September 2009. The EU's Foreign Ministers assembled for an informal meeting to discuss their possible support for Afghanistan and the peace process in the Middle East, as well as the membership applications of Croatia, Turkey, and the Former Yugoslav Republic of Macedonia. Before the conference, the museum was asked by the head of the Secretariat for the EU meetings, Mårten Grunditz, to remove two particular paintings by the well-known Swedish artist Dick Bengtsson (1936–1989), *Hat- and Cap-factory* and *Edward Hopper: Early Sunday Morning*, for the duration of the meeting. The EU Secretariat feared that the swastikas displayed in the two paintings might cause offense and draw attention away from issues relevant to the meeting (Sveriges Radio, 10 September 2009; Benholm 2009). The museum's leadership agreed to the request and the paintings were temporarily taken down, as reported by the TV program *Kulturnyheterna* (Svenska Television, SVT, 10 September 2009). Criticized by the media, Mårten Grunditz and the then head of the museum,

Lars Nittve, accounted for their decision by quoting a lack available of pedagogical resources explaining the paintings (Klasson and
Benholm 2009; SVT 10 September 2009). The media reacted with
more criticism: the whole museum was closed to the public for a
whole week, from 31 August to 8 September, and booked exclusively for the EU meeting, so why could the staff not have given
guided tours and explained the paintings? That, as the SVT's journalists pointed out, would have been easy to do, given that two
texts explaining the use of the swastika in Bengtsson's work already
existed on the museum's homepage (Castenfors 2006; Widenheim
2006). All that was needed was to translate these texts for the
ministers of the EU member states. While some journalists—and
even some artists who were ardent admirers of Bengtsson's work—
agreed with the museum's decision and did not consider Bengtsson's paintings suitable in the context of such a meeting (Arndtzén
2009; Sveriges Radio 2009), the dominant impression conveyed by
the media was that the country's most prestigious institution for
modern art had given in to political demands and that this decision
was not merely motivated by financial profit, but also spurred by
other motives, revealing a great deal about the Swedish unwillingness to come to terms with its past or the mendacity of the Swedish
self-image (SVT 2009; Wolodarski 2009).

What most media reports did not stress or mention at all, however,
was that the whole museum was turned into a high-security conference center for the duration of the meeting. Asked about the decision
in 2012, Ann-Sofie Noring, codirector at the Moderna Museet, did not
recall Grunditz request (Noring 2012); according to her, even though
the meeting itself lasted only two days, the museum had to close for
the public for an entire week because the whole building needed to be
refurbished with a security apparatus, seating, and equipment for the
interpreters. Staff did not have access to the museum and were thus
not able to give guided tours. Furthermore, it was not Bengtsson's
work alone that was removed; the museum was essentially stripped
of its art and converted into a conference center. This decision was
motivated partly by conservational reasons (see Hyresavtal 2009), given
that the galleries were used as meeting places where people would eat
and drink, thus potentially jeopardizing the art. And while it is true
that the museum received 1.2 million Swedish crowns for hosting the
event, Noring pointed out that it hardly profited economically from
this agreement, contrary to speculations in the media.

Thus the incident, while interesting to the backdrop of Swedish memory culture and practice, seemed to involve little more than a canard. The scandal was no longer about hidden motives, or the censorship of art works that critically reflected on Sweden's role during World War II, it was simply about a state institution's compromising, but to some extent understandable decision not to bite the hand that feeds it. It seemed questionable why the Moderna was chosen as a conference venue when the inclusion of art in the conference program was not given any priority. But, according to the museum, this happens regularly when it is booked for external conferences (Mendoza Brackenhoff 2012). One can certainly argue that there are many other conference centers in Stockholm that could have been used instead. However, the Moderna's prestige, its unique location on a small, easily securable island, and the fact that the unfurnished rooms made them easy to refurnish, as well as the high technical standards provided, seem to provide explanation enough. Rafael Moneo's architecture served as a magnificent container to this top political meeting. Was there really an incident to write about? And if so, was it an incident which could illuminate facets of Swedish, or even European, politics of memory?

In one aspect the media was right: there clearly was the request by the EU Secretariat to take down the two specific paintings by Dick Bengtsson, and the museum's leadership agreed to this request without hesitation (Sveriges Radio 10 September 2009). Consequently, this raises the question as to what these two paintings represent in Swedish memory culture, and what their potential meaning to wider European memory culture—had they been included in the conference program—could have been taken to be. Therefore, I will discuss these works of art and their removal, as presented in the media, in order to reflect on Swedish memory culture and on how deeply rooted the so-called Europeanization of Holocaust memory really is. Before examining the bones of contention, *Hat- and Cap-factory* (1969) and *Edward Hopper: Early Sunday Morning* (1970), I will give a short introduction to Bengtsson's art, focusing on his so-called "swastika period."

Dick Bengtsson's Art and the Swastika Within

Bengtsson's art is highly appreciated by the art establishment, and since at least the 1990s it has been commonly regarded as being amongst the most distinguished Swedish art production of the twentieth century. However, even if Bengtsson's work is recognized as canonical and widely appreciated, it is also commonly described as mysterious, enigmatic, and difficult to comprehend (Karlsson, Lindgren, and Svensson 2005: 152; Nittve 2005: 10). Furthermore, many critics—even if they like Bengtsson's art—express some ambivalence toward his work, which often causes resentment, at least at first sight. Many experience it as unpleasant, perilous, threatening, and even repulsive, or at least uncertain (see, for example, Springfeldt 1983; Karlsson, Lindgren, and Svensson 2005: 21–23)—especially the works of his swastika-period. Over four years, between 1968 and 1972, swastikas kept appearing in Bengtsson's work, subtly at first, in paintings displaying seemingly idyllic scenery, appearing in the bushes around wooden houses or on window frames, but becoming much more visible with time.

Although the paintings containing a swastika were regarded both as ambiguous and unclear, or as too explicit and shallow, it would have been possible to provide satisfactory explanations for the EU politicians, given that the literature on Bengtsson is comprehensive, and many authors deal with the use of the swastika in his art. In fact, it was the Moderna itself, which featured Bengtsson's work many times throughout the years and contributed to it being appraised as high art. It also played an important role in mediating his work to the public: for the duration of 2012, an entire room was devoted to Bengtsson's work, including the two paintings in question.

The year 1968, when Bengtsson first took up swastikas, was of course a year of rupture in Europe and elsewhere. It is remembered as a year when the second generation no longer accepted their parents' silence, and demanded that the latter faced up to what they had done during World War II. Many authors have pointed out that Bengtsson was critical of the popular Swedish idea of the *folkhem*, arguing that his paintings pointed at parallels between *folkhemmet* and the Nazi's idea of a *Volksgemeinschaft* (Karlsson, Lindgren, and Svensson 2005: 151). Despite the fact that these parallels were minimal (Götz 2001), Bengtsson had grown up in a rather authoritarian society that was in many ways fundamentally different from the more transparent and egalitarian society that Sweden is today. The *folkhemmet's* ideal was that of a healthy, though not necessarily ethnically pure, community, an ideal that was pursued using forced sterilization and the detention of people who were regarded as unfit for society. These measures were used throughout Bengtsson's childhood and went on until the 1950s. It is crucial to remember that Dick Bengtsson belonged to the generation who had experienced the war; some members of his family and people in his surroundings had sympathized with Nazi Germany.

Furthermore, as in Germany, many former teachers or classmates simply "forgot" their former convictions as soon as the war was over (Karlsson, Lindgren, and Svensson 2005: 24).

Some critics argue that Bengtsson was not a political artist in the first place, but interested mainly in formal art discourses and the limits of mediating messages; they regard his art as meta-art—art about art. Further, there are indications that Bengtsson was interested in the possibility to once again change the meaning of the loaded symbol that is the swastika. However, the mere attempt to regain that symbol's original meaning arguably demonstrates that Bengtsson was not interested in formal aspects only—otherwise he could simply have avoided the swastika—but Bengtsson never became a constructivist. Of course, Bengtsson was right when he stated that even the meaning of the swastika is not written in stone: "The symbol stood, in 1940, according to many, for law, order and ideology. Today, it stands, according to many, for historically demarcated horrors. Both interpretations are equally 'temporary'" (Feuk 2005: 104). Bengtsson was not the first artist to highlight the symbol's dependence on context. During the 1920s, Paul Klee had already reflected on the construction of the swastika. Bengtsson's contemporaries also dealt with the possible reconstitution of the misused symbol, as the German painter Jörg Immendorf had done during the 1960s and as Helmut Federle and Rosemarie Trockel did in the 1980s. According to Heinz Schütz, the artistic preoccupation with the swastika was most dominant during the 1980s (Schütz 1988), but artists' fascination with the symbol has not abated, as evidenced in more recent works, such as in *Hitler's Cabinet* by Mischa Kuball (1990) or Peter Freudenthal's series of paintings on the Warsaw Ghetto Uprising in 1943 (2012).

The image that probably best embodies the idea of meta-art in Bengtsson's work is his *Without title* (exact date unknown; painted during the 1960s). In this painting, swastikas are arranged on top of each other and connected in such a way that they build a vertical frieze. The swastikas do not reveal themselves immediately, but become part of a new structure. This is reminiscent of Martin Kippenberger's abstract composition *No matter how hard I try, I just can't make out a swastika* (1984) (Friese 2004: 62–63), the title of which is redolent of the kind of statement often used to downplay racism or anti-Semitism. As a result of the title, the beholder imagines a swastika that is actually not there. By contrast, Bengtsson's work may have an unspecified title, but it cannot hide the model upon which his frieze is built. Consequently, I also regard *Without title* as a comment on the impossibility to change the meaning of the swastika.

Efforts to represent the swastika as a "paradigm of pure auto-reflexivity" were actually rarely successful (Schütz 1988: 70–71), despite the many artistic attempts since the end of the war to reduce it to form only (Schütz 1988: 67; Friese 2004: 64). To this day, and arguably increasingly, given the dominance of the Holocaust in memory discourse, the swastika remains closely connected to Hitler's Third Reich and its crimes against humanity, at least in the Western world (Schütz 1988: 64). The swastika remains stigmatized, regardless of the argument that it is in fact one of the oldest signs in human history, used in Buddhism, Hinduism, Germanic mythology, and Christianity, and that it has also appeared in the Kabbalah and in Islam; a sign that had multiple and complex meanings, both as a sign of good fortune and protection, as well as of violence (Schütz 1988: 69–72). However, after being desecrated by the Nazi regime, all former meanings have lost their relevance in a Western context, although it can of course refer to Fascism more generally, or simply be a marker to indicate that the powers that be are experienced as totalitarian, authoritarian, or imperialistic.

In Bengtsson's work, the swastika forces us to look at the painting in a different way (Karlsson, Lindgren, and Svensson 2005: 9), and the political allusions to the Third Reich's ideology simply cannot be ignored. However, in contrast to John Heartfield's work from the 1920s onwards, which clearly displays the swastika as an incitement to political action, one might not find the same imperative in Bengtsson's work. His critique is more subtle and without the same urgency. While we may not know immediately what it is all about, we may easily say what it is not: Bengtsson's use of the swastika is obviously not the expression of a National Socialist spreading his or her ideology. Douglas Feuk reminds us how far away Bengtsson's aesthetics with its "muddy, raw and corroded colours are from the anxious and slimy art style which had possessed such status in Nazi Germany. The politically burdened is not the 'manner' but rather the motive" (Feuk 2005: 88). It is through the use of the swastika that the scene portrayed is stigmatized, as in *Edward Hopper: Early Sunday Morning*. Bengtsson's painting is very close to Hopper's original from 1930, but where Hopper's painting expresses human loneliness (or, as some would have it, refers to the looming economic depression of the early 1930s), Bengtsson's version has a rather perilous atmosphere. What makes the difference is the use of the colors and, especially, the patina.

Figure 1
Dick Bengtsson, *Edward Hopper: Early Sunday Morning* (1970), oil on masonite, 90 cm × 152 cm © Moderna Museet, Stockholm

Covert Threat

While many of Bengtsson's motifs are borrowed from other works of art or illustrations from encyclopedias, and therefore could actually be regarded as a kind of "quotation art" (Feuk 2005: 16), it is the patina that is characteristic of his work. Bengtsson achieved this by ironing the paintings immediately after they were finished and before putting on the glaze. He also often harmed his paintings by scratching the surface. Using these methods, he achieved an expression of originality and timelessness.

If one were to describe the essence of Bengtsson's art, one could say that not all is quite as it appears: do not trust your first impressions; there is a hidden threat behind the idyllic scenery (Karlsson, Lindgren, and Svensson 2005: 15; Olvång 1983). Here, the patina plays an important role because it creates distance (Karlsson, Lindgren, and Svensson 2005: 11). An unpleasant feeling emanates from Bengtsson's works, but still we are fascinated, in part due to the artistic quality of the patina, and want to discover the hidden meaning underneath the shiny surface. Bengtsson's paintings are not political pamphlets, but rather evoke conflicting sentiments that the observer has to endure. Typical of Bengtsson is his ability to "dimly evoke visceral conflicts into life" (Feuk 2005: 17). In fact, as Feuk has shown, duality is one of the main topics in Bengtsson's work, most obviously displayed in his diptychs. A figurative motif appears twice, with one of the images reversed. What holds the pictures together is the use of an emblem that appears in both paintings (Feuk 2005: 36), as in the diptych *Hat- and Cap-factory*, where everything is inverted except for the swastika, which in both images is turned to the right, exactly as it was used by the Nazis. These diptychs are reminiscent of pictures in children's puzzle books, where one is supposed to spot five differences in two seemingly identical pictures. The observer keeps looking for what is wrong in the scenes presented by Bengtsson. The red color of the upper floor in *Edward Hopper: Early Sunday Morning* is reminiscent of the National Socialist flag, but in Bengtsson's painting, the red is not bright and pure but appears dirty, as if consciously contaminated. Through his use of both the specific coloring and patina, Bengtsson creates distance and uncertainty—the added swastika in the lower left-hand corner reinforces this impression.

As Bengtsson himself said, with reference to another of his swastika paintings, he wants us to feel insecure about the meaning of his paintings. That is why he makes use of the swastika: "A symbol is meant to help decipher the meaning in a picture. But it can also impede and obstruct an interpretation, and that was precisely my intention. I chose the swastika because it stood in as much contrast as possible from the rest of the picture" (Karlsson, Lindgren, and Svensson 2005: 14). As demonstrated previously, the swastika is not simply an eye-catcher or a tool to create distance, it also acts as a signifier in Bengtsson's paintings. This symbol, in the same way that the cross stands for Christianity, is familiar to a wide audience as a mark of a totalitarian regime and its inhumane ideology. I would argue that Bengtsson's main concern is to remind us of the ideology that built the foundation for this regime. This thesis gains further strength when we understand that even when the swastika disappears from his imagery, Bengtsson is preoccupied with themes related to the ideology of the Third Reich, as in *Hitler and the dream kitchen* (1974), which was painted during the heyday of the Swedish Welfare state (Karlsson, Lindgren, and Svensson 2005: 36). This painting can be seen as an ironic comment on the functionalist belief in social engineering (mostly associated with Alva and Gunnar Myrdal), with Bengtsson linking, in a rather humorous way, the Swedish model of an ideal kitchen to the petty bourgeois dreams of the Fascist leaders, thereby reminding us of the implications of the ideal of a pure society (Jahnsson-Wennberg 1998: 36); a warning to be cautious of any fanatical attempts to construct a perfect society.

Figures 2 & 3
Dick Bengtsson, *Hat- and Cap-factory* (1969), oil on panel, 122 cm × 91 cm (each) © Moderna Museet, Stockholm

European Holocaust Memory in a Nutshell:
Bengtsson's *Hat- and Cap-factory*

The associations triggered by *Hat- and Cap-factory* (1969) are alarming: the building is variously described "as a piece of sharp-edged brutal architecture against the night sky in an artificial green colour, with an icy blue moonlight over the roof" (Feuk 2005: 73), and as a "threatening machine" (Karlsson, Lindgren, and Svensson 2005: 27). The building's uncanny appearance, not least due to the added swastika, reminds critics of a concentration camp, a crematorium, or of the ovens of an extermination camp, or even its gas chambers (Karlsson, Lindgren, and Svensson 2005: 24). The critics were aware that Bengtsson's painting was inspired by a real building, as the point of departure for *Hat- and Cap-factory* was a photograph published in the Swedish Encyclopedia, showing a dye works in a hat factory (Nylén 1998). The roof, with its characteristic ventilation system, actually resembled a hat. This building was designed by German-Jewish architect Erich Mendelsohn (1887–1953), known for his expressionist and functionalist buildings; Mendelsohn's mother actually was a hat maker. His hat factory in Luckenwalde, fifty kilometers south of Berlin, was completed in 1923 and became one of the city's landmarks. It is regarded as one of Mendelsohn's and modern architecture's masterpieces.

Bengtsson's painting acts as a metaphor for the brutal Nazi regime and is an apposite illustration of modern European history. Mendelsohn, along with the Jewish owners of the factory, was forced to emigrate in 1933 when the Nazis came to power. Just a year later, his famous building was used as an armaments factory, which also led to comprehensive conversions that caused the building to lose its characteristic appeal. Only at the beginning of the new millennium was the building restored to its former glory in order to once again pay homage to Mendelsohn's genius, and in 2003 a permanent exhibition was set up, dedicated to Mendelsohn's life and work (Nathan 2005; "Hutfabrik Luckenwalde" 2011).

I regard the building and its history as the key for possible readings of Bengtsson's painting that would have been relevant to EU politicians. Within just one year of coming to power in 1933, the Nazis had completely transformed German society, ideologically and structurally. What this meant in practice is illustrated by the exile of Mendelssohn and the factory owners, as well as by the fact that the factory was then made to serve the purpose of war. What the eleven years that followed meant for Europe can be illustrated by the deterioration of the building during and after the war. Similarly, its restoration within the last few years is symptomatic of European history, even if Bengtsson could not possibly have known this, given that he died in 1989, before German reunification, which would be so decisive for contemporary European memory.

However, Bengtsson certainly was aware of the fact that he changed the famous architect's building in a significant way: he left out what is so characteristic for Mendelsohn, namely the typical shape of the corners. By taking away this detail, the building's appeal is changed entirely from a modernist, progressive structure into one of closeness and defense, a building representing a totalitarian system. With the elimination of the corners, Bengtsson reminds us that "the devil is often in the detail" and that nothing can be taken for granted. Mendelsohn, today an icon of modernist architecture, was a representative of another Germany, a progressive country with a reform movement and a flourishing intellectual environment. Bengtsson's painting can be seen as a critical reflection on what the other modernist project embodied by the National socialists implied and on the human and intellectual losses it caused. The dominant feeling the painting evokes is arguably a kind of demonized, dark pathos and anger about those losses (Feuk 2005: 78).

Sweden as a Precursor of a European Memory Based on the Holocaust

An evaluation of the journalists' interest in the removal of Dick Bengtsson's paintings requires a short summary of the Swedish memory discourse of the last thirty years. For decades, narratives centered on Swedish neutrality had dominated the national mythscape. Although never occupied or allied in the war, during the 1980s Sweden nevertheless began to be confronted with its responsibility in the genocide, although it was not until the late 1990s that the Holocaust finally entered the political agenda. Part of the now accepted national narrative was a new acknowledgement of Sweden's economic and political dealings with Nazi Germany. Sweden's restrictive immigration policies during the war, especially toward Jews, and its concomitant responsibility for the fate of the European Jews, were finally acknowledged (Åmark 2011), and the commemoration of the Holocaust became institutionalized (Schult 2012; Schult 2013). In 2003, the Living History Forum, which had begun its work in 1997, became a public body. Its purpose is to work toward promoting tolerance and human rights and strengthening democracy, with the Holocaust as its point of departure. However, after the change from a social democratic government to a conservative coalition in 2006, Communist crimes became part of the Forum's agenda as well.

With its focus on strengthening Swedish democracy by facing the Holocaust, and belief in the idea that knowledge of this particular past can create a better present and future, the Living History Forum can be seen as a prime example of what Bickford and Sodaro call a new "future-orientated paradigm" (2010: 67–68). In many ways, Sweden can be seen as a precursor for a trend that has now become common practice, not only in Europe but in many parts of the world. In general, political decision-making, as it developed during the last twenty years, is based on the belief that we have to confront our dark pasts in order to build a better future.

The memory of the Holocaust is no longer confined only to the nations most immediately involved in the genocide of European Jewry, but also includes those that recognize a less direct involvement in the Holocaust as part of their history. With the founding of the Living History Forum, Sweden acknowledged its own moral responsibility to remember the Holocaust and affirms "its 'universal significance'" (Müller 2010: 31). According to Jan-Werner Müller, a nation can confront its dark past more easily when it is an integrated part of a supranational context, such as the European Union. The engagement in the Task Force for International Cooperation on Holocaust Education, Remembrance and Research, in the conference *The Stockholm International Forum on the Holocaust* in 2000 (and its successors), as well as in the Living History Forum, all seemed to have helped Sweden to find its role in this process (Kroh 2006). Sweden became a key actor on the European scene and a forerunner for Holocaust education, not least with respect to educating Eastern European states aiming to become EU members. Much has happened on the national level as well, as in 1999, when 27 January became an official national commemoration day in Sweden. Fifty-four years earlier, the Red Army had liberated the death camp Auschwitz-Birkenau—a site that has become synonymous with the genocide committed against the European Jews. Today, the Holocaust is part of the main curriculum in Swedish schools, and more than three thousand Swedish school children travel to Auschwitz each year. The Holocaust plays indeed an important role in Swedish politics and education, and it is present in the country's public debates, rhetoric, and popular culture (Kingsepp and Schult 2012).

European Memory between Media Hype and the Media's Responsibility

The journalists' interest in the request to remove Bengtsson's paintings must be seen against this background of the last three decades of coming to terms with Sweden's past. Their reactions can therefore be seen as evidence of "an increasing recognition of a European responsibility for the Holocaust" (Pakier & Stråth 2010: 11). The media's outcry over the removal of Bengtsson's paintings also focused on the politicians' demands to remove the paintings not as an attempt to avoid conflict with other EU member states, but rather as an attempt to avoid any kind of uncomfortable debate about Sweden's role during World War II. This certainly stood in strong contrast to the officially accepted maxim during former Prime Minister Göran Persson's social democratic leadership (1996–2006) of coming to terms with the past, a tendency which, as highlighted before, had also become common practice in other European countries. We will never know whether the European politicians would have been offended by Bengtsson's paintings, but given growing historical awareness of the issues concerned, it seems rather questionable.

Interestingly, there was an earlier incident involving one of Bengtsson's paintings that then illustrated growing interest in Sweden's role during World War II. Bengtsson's painting *Kumla Prison Auditorium* (1971) was vandalized by another artist, the expressionist painter Olle Carlström, who considered it as an unreasonable demand to raise his glass at a reception given by the Moderna in 1986 in the presence of a painting that displayed a swastika. So he pressed a plate of potato salad onto the swastika (Gmelin 1996: 20). Carlström's reactions can be seen as a symptom or result of a new memory discourse gaining momentum then, the call to come to terms with the country's dealings with Nazi Germany. These historical issues were already highly sensitive during the 1980s, before acquiring political recognition and becoming institutionalized. While the potato salad incident showed how morally charged the debate already was back in 1986, it also revealed that the consequence of this is not necessarily a deeper knowledge of the Holocaust or its memory, but can also entail overreaction and misunderstanding of these art works that deal with Fascism as a hidden threat.

Another example shall illustrate how this morally charged debate influenced the perception of Bengtsson's art. While many critics regard his paintings, especially those displaying a swastika, as conveying a subliminal critique of the glossy image of the Swedish welfare state, art critic Ronald Jones goes so far as to interpret the appearance of the swastika in the following way:

> Bengtsson's use of the swastika . . . poignantly rakes at Sweden's claim to neutrality during World War II. The gift of hindsight charitably amended Sweden's role to that of self-interested noncombatant, an

assessment closer to, but still at arm's length from full acceptance of the truth, and so Bengtsson's swastikas continue to provoke animosity. (Jones 2006)

As convincing as Jones's statement sounds, he surely reads too much into the painting. Here we see what art *became* as a consequence of the memory discourse, and not what it meant when it was created. This kind of reinterpretation of Bengtsson's work reflects wider discussions concerning Swedish cooperation with Nazi Germany rather than helping to comprehend the artwork itself. We are thus confronted with a typical post-Holocaust-memory perspective, reflecting the fact that since the late 1980s the Holocaust has become the dominant focus for memory discourse—also in Sweden. Bengtsson's work is today commonly associated with this highly charged memory discourse, as Jones's statement makes clear (see also Lomfors 2009). It is important to understand that this perspective is still the dominant one, because this also explains the media's strong criticism of the removal of Bengtsson's paintings: The journalists regarded themselves as critical observers who would not let Swedish politicians once again hide behind a mask of neutrality or moral superiority as had happened for many decades. Their reactions must be understood against this background (as much as they also advocated the autonomy of art, an aspect not discussed in any detail here). However, Bengtsson was not alluding to the Swedish reluctance to deal with the past in the first place, at least not in the two paintings discussed here; other paintings such as those with the swastikas in the window frames or added to idyllic landscapes may be better suited to this purpose, as would his film *The Crime of Year* from 1969.

There are indeed other artists contemporary to Bengtsson who have dealt with these topics more explicitly, such as Peder Josefsson in his *Transit* from 1970. Josefsson portrays a young hippy family in front of the image of a German troop transport through Sweden in Swedish trains. As the soldiers in the painting are unarmed, it is most likely that he alludes to the *Permittenttrafiken* during 1941–43, which transported German soldiers on the way to their furlough. Josefsson also added the famous poster of the Swedish Tiger, which was created during the autumn of 1941 and intended to remind Swedes to be careful and not to jeopardize Swedish neutrality by acting too critically of Nazi German politics. The Swedish expression "En svensk tiger" also meant "a Swede keeps quiet." The painting is thus a critical reflection on the Swedish politics of appeasement during World War II and the censorship of the Swedish press that went hand in hand with it. Furthermore, it reflects the moral dilemma of how to live with this responsibility after the national narrative of Swedish neutrality fell apart, as expressed in the troubled faces of the little family in the front.

While Josefsson's work is not in the collection of the Moderna, the museum owns images that deal with the question of repressed memories and Swedish sympathies for Nazi Germany, such as Ann Böttcher's *Ryamatta* (2008), bought the year before the EU meeting and displayed in the permanent exhibition. The long-pile rya rug has as its starting point a postcard from the 1930s displaying a rising swastika in the place of the sun, sent out as a Christmas card by the extreme right party *Nationalsocialistiska Blocket*. The swastika rises behind two spruces standing to attention like soldiers. The swastika remains unknotted in the rug, but is there, ready to be knotted again, by which Böttcher illustrates the mechanisms of displacing history and history's recurrence (Johannesson 11 May 2008). It is one of many examples of Swedish art dealing with Sweden's role during World War II and the influence of Nazi ideology on parts of Swedish society.

In summary, then, the media's strong criticism of the storing away of Bengtsson's paintings displaying swastikas can be explained as follows. Many of the journalists were quite familiar with Bengtsson's work, which they understood first and foremost as anti-totalitarian (Wolodarski 2009). Even more important was the fact that Bengtsson's art had become associated with the memory discourse of the last twenty years. The journalists regarded it as their duty to act as reminders that the commitment to Holocaust memory should not fall into oblivion under the conservative government.

The Power of Images and the Implementation of a European Memory

Moderna Museet's then director Lars Nittve's response to the media was that the politicians had not come to see art. Nevertheless, they booked Sweden's leading museum of modern art. In fact, from the beginning the opportunity to present Moderna's "activities to an assembled world press" was one reason why the Moderna agreed to host the EU meeting (Klasson and Benholm 2009). Originally, the plan had been for Lars Nittve himself to act as a guide for the ministers (Lönnebo 2009). Furthermore, the Swedish Culture Ministry had sent a circular to all cultural institutions of Sweden announcing the coming EU presidency as an opportunity to present the best that Swedish culture had to offer (Regeringskansliet 2008). So when asked to remove Bengtsson's paintings, Nittve could have resisted and insisted that Bengtsson's paintings should be left on the wall, given that they are acknowledged as high Swedish art, and given the prominence and importance of Holocaust memory.

By borrowing from the American painter Hopper and the German-Jewish architect Mendelsohn, Bengtsson also leaves the sphere of the nation state. These two paintings are in fact not about a Swedish unwillingness to come to terms with the past, but deal with the historical context to the founding of the later European Union, making them highly relevant to an EU summit. The EU was born out of the memory of the war, its large-scale violence and atrocity:

> The EU itself has always been a peculiar kind of monument to the Second World War—not a monument that commemorates battles, but an institutional edifice whose foundations contain the very lessons learned from the experience of totalitarian war, subjugation and European-wide genocide. (Müller 2010: 30)

The discrepancy between the commitments expressed by politicians on certain occasions, such as the anniversaries commemorating the end of World War II or Holocaust Remembrance Days, and their commitments to practice what they preach when the opportunity arises is disconcerting. Bengtsson's works had to face censorship when they could have potentially brought up important issues and contributed to the way that decisions were made. The feeling of uncertainty which Bengtsson's art creates may be hard to endure—but is a deep uncertainty about human nature not the very legacy of the Holocaust? It was the land of the *Dichter und Denker*, which was responsible for one of the worst crimes in human history. These crimes proved once again that all codes of civilization are learned and not stable. In the aftermath of World War II, and as late as the 1990s, we reached a consensus to build future societies on the commitment to lessons learned from the Holocaust. Artists dealing with the subject have often regarded it their duty to act as reminders of both uncertainty and of the commitments we have made. Disputes over works of art dealing with these memories do not necessarily have to be counterproductive, they can be a reminder that the memory of this past still matters and can in fact lead to commonly held values.

If the EU secretariat had, with the help of Moderna, decided to actively integrate Bengtsson's paintings and other works—such as those of Josefsson's or Böttcher's—into the program of the summit, Sweden would not only have had the chance to demonstrate that the country practices a self-critical *Vergangenheitsbewältigungswille*, in Jan-Werner Müller's words (the will to come to terms with the past) by addressing its specific past, but that Sweden also trusts the EU to be a community of shared values based on a shared history. The paintings could have been an opportunity for an open debate on Europe's past and thereby motivated careful decision-making for the future (Levy 2010: 29).

Is it reasonable to conclude that the incident at the Moderna Museet confirms that a genuinely rooted European memory based on World War II and the Holocaust is still not part of political practice? Or alternatively, given the omnipresence of World War II and the Holocaust, was it really necessary to be reminded yet again of Europe's negative founding myth? Unfortunately, Bengtsson's paintings are still relevant, especially at a time when extreme right-wing parties are in government again in several European states, and the economic crisis leads to a profound EU skepticism. In the words of Mårten Castenfors, the tainted Nazi symbol in Bengtsson's works "breaks up the stillness of the paintings and alludes to the darker undercurrents that are a constant threat to our democratic societ[ies]" (Castenfors 2006).

Sources and References

Archives

-Kungliga bibliotekets arkiv för audiovisuella medier
Kulturnyheterna. 7 September 2009. SVT 1, 19:00–19:15
-Moderna Museet arkiv
Copies of e-mail correspondence and the agreement between the *Regeringskansliet* and the Moderna Museet, only cited material is listed here:
Hyresavtal. 2009. mellan *Regeringskansliet* och Moderna Museet
Lovisa Lönnebo's e-mail containing a memo regarding the planned EU meeting (15 May 2009).
Regeringskansliet. 2008. "Kulturaktiviteter under Sveriges ordförandeskap i EU hösten 2009"
Interviews and e-mail correspondence during May and June 2012 with the following persons
Oskar Anesten, reporter at *Kulturnyheterna*, SVT

Sofia Benholm, editor at *Kulturnyheterna*, SVT
Ulf Eriksson, curator at the Moderna Museet
Susana Mendoza Brackenhoff, authority of registrar at the Moderna Museet
Ann-Sofie Noring, Codirector and Chief Curator at the Moderna Museet
I tried to contact Lars Nittve and Mårten Grunditz, but the first cannot remember the details of the case and the second did not respond.

Internet Sources

Arndtzén, Mårten. 2009. "Rätt att ta ned Bengtssons hakkors." *Sveriges Radio*, 11 September, http://sverigesradio.se/sida/artikel.aspx?programid=478&arti kel=3093803. Accessed 4 June 2012.

Benholm, Sofia. 2009. "På tal om Modernas bristande resurser." Svenska Television (SVT), 8 September, http://svt.se/2.27170/1.1682741/pa_tal_om_modernas_ bristande_resurser. Accessed 28 May 2012.

Castenfors, Mårten. 2006. "Varför målade Dick Bengtsson svastikor?" Moderna Museet's homepage, http://www.modernamuseet.se/sv/Stockholm/Utstall-ningar/2006/Dick-Bengtsson/Varfor-malade-Dick-Bengtsson-svastikor/. Accessed 28 May 2012.

"Hutfabrik Luckenwalde." 2011. Deutsche Stiftung Denkmalschutz's homepage, http://www.denkmalschutz.de/hutfabrik.html. Accessed 29 May 2012.

Johannesson, Sune. 2008. "Att gräva fram historien." *Kristianstadsbladet*, 11 May, http://www.kristianstadsbladet.se/kultur/article1008272/Att-graumlva-fram-historien.html. Accessed 21 June 2012.

Jones, Ronald. 2006. "Dick Bengtsson: Moderna Museet." *Artforum* 2006, http://findarticles.com/p/articles/mi_m0268/is_10_44/ai_n26911698/. Accessed 19 June 2012.

Klasson, Isak and Sofia Benholm. 2009. "Konst för laddat för ministermöte." SVT, 7 September, http://svt.se/2.27170/1.1681455/konst_for_laddat_for_minister-mote. Accessed 28 May 2012.

Lomfors, Ingrid. 2009. "Hakkors i museitaket." *Expressen*, 11 September, http://www.expressen.se/kultur/hakkors-i-museitaket/. Accessed 21 June 2012.

Nathan, Carola. 2005. "Hüte unterm Hut. Meisterwerk von Medelsohn hat wieder eine Zukunft." *Monumente Online.* Magazin der Deutschen Stiftung Denkmalschutz. http://www.monumente-online.de/05/01/streiflicht/hutfabrik_ luckenwalde.php. Accessed 30 May 2012.

Sveriges Radio. Studio Ett, 10 September 2009. (Guests: Mårten Grunditz, Lars Nittve, Peter Wolodarski, Ernst Billgren), http://sverigesradio.se/sida/artikel. aspx?programid=478&artikel=3093803. Accessed 30 May 2012.

Svenska Television (SVT). 2009. "Chef: Ministrarna kom inte för att titta på konst," 10 September, http://svt.se/2.27170/1.1685638/chef_ministrarna_kom_inte_ for_att_titta_pa_konst. Accessed 28 May 2012.

Widenheim, Cecilia. 2006. "Varför målade Dick Bengtsson svastikor?" Moderna Museet's homepage, http://www.modernamuseet.se/sv/Stockholm/Utstall-ningar/2006/Dick-Bengtsson/Varfor-malade-Dick-Bengtsson-svastikor/. Accessed 28 May 2012.

Wolodarski, Peter. 2009. "Censur: Olustig konstdiplomati." *Dagens Nyheter*, 10 September, http://www.dn.se/ledare/signerat/censur-olustig-konstdiplomati. Accessed 4 June 2012.

Literature

Åmark, Klas. 2011. *Att bo granne med ondskan. Sveriges förhållande till nazismen, Nazityskland och Förintelsen*. Stockholm: Bonniers.

Bickford, Louis and Amy Sodaro. 2010. "Remembering Yesterday to Protect Tomorrow: The Internationalization of a New Commemorative Paradigm." In *Memory and the Future: Tansnational Politics, Ethics and Society*, eds. Gutman, Yifat, Adam D. Brown, and Amy Sodaro. Basingstoke: Palgrave Macmillan.

Feuk, Douglas. 2005. "Ironi, fobi, demoni." In *Dick Bengtsson*, eds. Mårten Castenfors, Moderna Museet, and Sveriges Almänna Konstförening. Stockholm: Atlantis.

Friese, Peter. 2004. "Nach-Bilder als Bildstörungen." In *After Images: Kunst als soziales Gedächtnis*, ed. Neues Museum Weserburg, Bremen. Frankfurt am Main: Revolver/Archiv für Aktuelle Kunst.

Gmelin, Felix. 1996. *Art Vandals*. Stockholm: Riksutställningar.

Götz, Norbert. 2001. *Ungleiche Geschwister: Die Konstruktion von nationalsozialistischer Volksgemeinschaft und schwedischem Volksheim*. Baden-Baden: Nomos.

Gutman, Yifat, Amy Sodaro and Adam D. Brown. 2010. "Introduction: Memory and the Future: Why a Change of Focus is Necessary." In *Memory and the Future: Tansnational Politics, Ethics and Society*, eds. Gutman, Yifat, Adam D. Brown, and Amy Sodaro. Basingstoke: Palgrave Macmillan.

Jahnsson-Wennberg, Bengt. 1998. "Om ironi och sentimentalitet." In *Tema: Dick Bengtsson*. Stockholm: Hjärnstorm.

Karlsson, Bo A., Per Lindgren and Joel Svensson. 2005. *Här bor Dick Bengtsson. Ett besök hos konstnären*. Göteborg: Boart.

Kingsepp, Eva and Tanja Schult, eds. 2012. *Hitler för alle: Populärkulturella perspektiv på Nazityskland, andra världskriget och Förintelsen*. Stockholm: Carlssons.

Kroh, Jens. 2006. *Transnationale Erinnerung: Der Holocaust im Fokus geschichtspolitischer Initiativen*. Frankfurt/New York: Campus.

Levy, Daniel. 2010. "Changing Temporalities and the Internationalization of Memory Cultures." In *Memory and the Future: Tansnational Politics, Ethics and Society*, eds. Gutman, Yifat, Adam D. Brown, and Amy Sodaro. Basingstoke: Palgrave Macmillan.

Müller, Jan-Werner. 2010. "On 'European Memory': Some Conceptual and Normative Remarks." In *A European Memory? Contested Histories and Politics of Remembrance*, eds. Małgorzata Pakier, and Bo Stråth. New York/Oxford: Berghahn.

Nittve, Lars. 2005. "Försvunnet: målning och mening." In *Dick Bengtsson*, eds. Mårten Castenfors, Moderna Museet, and Sveriges Almänna Konstförening. Stockholm: Atlantis.

Nylén, Leif. 1998. "Hatt- och mössfabrik." In *Tema: Dick Bengtsson*. Stockholm: Hjärnstorm.

Olvång, Bengt. [1983] 1994. "En moralist i svensk konst." Review published first in *Arbetet*, 21 April 1983. Republished in *Dick Bengtsson (1936–1989). Dokumentation*, ed. Lunds konsthall.

Pakier, Małgorzata and Bo Stråth. 2010. "A European Memory?" In *A European Memory? Contested Histories and Politics of Remembrance*, eds. Małgorzata Pakier, and Bo Stråth. New York/Oxford: Berghahn.

Schütz, Heinz, ed. 1988. *Transformation und Wiederkehr. Zur künstlerischen Rezeption nationalsozialistischer Symbole und Ästhetik*. Themaheft. *Kunstforum* 95: 64–98.

Schult, Tanja. 2012. "Susanne, Eva och Anna Berglind. Två konstnärsgenerationer och Förintelsens trauma." In *Från sidensjalar till förintelsekonst. Judarna i Sverige—en minoritets historia*, eds. Lars M. Andersson, and Carl Henrik Carlsson. Uppsala: Opuscula Historica Upsaliensia.

Schult, Tanja. 2013 (forthcoming). "Förintelsemonument i Sverige 1949–2009." *Nordisk Judaistik. Scandinavian Jewish Studies*. New series 1.

Springfeldt, Björn. 1983. *Dick Bengtsson*. Stockholm: Moderna Museet (Exhibition calalogue).

4

Cultural Memories of German Suffering during the Second World War: An Inability *Not* to Mourn?

Karl Wilds

In recent years, the memories of the Second World War that have appeared most captivating to a wide audience in Germany have centered on experiences of German wartime suffering. Over the past decade, the six hundred thousand Germans who died in Allied bombing raids, the twelve to fourteen million who fled or were expelled from Eastern Europe 1944–1948, and the estimated two million German women raped by Red Army soldiers have captured academic, political, and wider public interest. Calls for public days of mourning and the commission of memorials, museums, and exhibitions seek to codify in cultural memory narratives of German wartime suffering which are primarily disseminated and consumed in popular culture. Literary treatments of wartime suffering such as Max Sebald's book *Memories of Air War and Literature* from 1999, Günter Grass's novella *Crabwalk*, published 2002, and the anonymous *A Woman in Berlin*, republished in 2003, stimulated broader public discussion of the topic. Television and film have also popularized the theme, with Guido Knopp's television documentary *The Great Escape* from 2002 and the two redemptive love stories *Dresden*, shown on ZDF in 2006, and *The Escape*, shown on ARD in 2007, each of which attracted more than ten million viewers (Cohen-Pfister 2006: 316–336; Fuchs 2008: 11–16).

The significance of this recent turn in German cultural memory has been much debated and can be viewed as the latest stage in a process of *Vergangenheitsbewältigung* (coming to terms with the past) that stretches back into the postwar period. Historical surveys of West German attitudes toward the Nazi past commonly identify three broad developmental phases: a period of collective silence during the immediate postwar years, followed by the radical confrontation with the Nazi legacy between the 1960s and 1980s, before consciousness of perpetration became integrated into official cultural memory of the Third Reich in post-unification Germany (Rüsen 2001: 279–299). Even a perfunctory review of German memories of the Second World War since 1945 illustrates that *memory* is a historically specific and politically malleable concept whose meaning can only be apprehended in context. In recent years, this process of *Vergangenheitsbewältigung* has been explained with recourse to generational and psychotherapeutic theories of memory that account for the dynamic status of the past in the present with reference to generational turnover and the therapeutic confrontation with repressed past trauma (Rüsen 2001: 145–179; Assmann 2003: 133–142).

The Mitscherlichs' *Inability to Mourn* was first published in 1967 at a time in West Germany when official narratives of Germany's wartime experience began to unravel. The postwar focus on German victims of the war appeared to them an exculpatory defense mechanism that prevented the real task of mourning facing West Germans namely to mourn for the lost "love object" of the *Führer* in a process of "remembering, repeating and working through" the Nazi past (Mitscherlich 2004: 24). While for the Mitscherlichs the inability to mourn reflected West Germans' inability to confront their own complicity and narcissistic infatuation with Hitler, recent discussion of the inability to mourn has focused on the need to mourn German victims of wartime suffering. In this chapter, I wish to consider some of the ways in which this inversion occurred in conjunction with the rise of a wider inability *not* to mourn the passage of history that structures present discussion of German wartime suffering.

Contested Traditions

The development of the social-market economy in the West provided the fledgling FRG with arguably its greatest resource of legitimacy in the Economic Miracle, which saw real incomes treble between 1949 and 1973 (Wehler 2008: 54). Adenauer's 1957 election campaign slogan of *No Experiments!* and Ludwig Erhardt's *Prosperity for All* reflected demonstrably improved standards of living for the mass of the West German population. For Adenauer, the FRG represented the "last bulwark of western civilization" (Günther 1981: 84) as an occidental, anti-Communist democracy. An antitotalitarian state doctrine also underlined the legitimacy of the FRG by effectively quarantining the Third Reich from an otherwise honorable history and ascribing all responsibility for the regime to a small clique of totalitarian fanatics who had seduced the masses and destroyed the nation created by Germany's "last great statesman," Otto von Bismarck (Ritter 1948: 82; Ritter 1950: 169). This reading isolated a minority of major war criminals from the mass of the population for whom Third Reich and Second World War were understood through the prism of German victimhood (Überschär 2000). As the SPD Elder of the *Bundestag* declared during the opening session of parliament in September 1949, Germans had been victims of both Nazi tyranny *and* the Allied campaign to defeat the Reich (Wolgast 2001: 332). Public opinion surveys in the 1950s consistently placed war widows and orphans, victims of bombing raids, generals held in Allied prisons and Germans expelled from the East as the principal victims of the war (Frei 1999: 280). The April 1951 131 Law regulated the reintegration of former state functionaries and the *Lastenausgleich* (Law for the Equalization of Burdens) of September 1952 extended Federal aid to the victims of the air war and expulsions (Frei 1999: 69–100).

During the 1960s, however, the postwar amnesty and reintegration of hundreds of thousands of former functionaries of the Nazi state became increasingly understood as a fundamental *weakness* of West German democracy. For critics such as Walter Dirks and the Mitscherlichs, West Germany's formal commitment to western democracy sustained by anti-Communism, economic reconstruction, and narratives of wartime suffering actually thwarted the cultivation of a *substantial* concept of democratic culture (Dirks 1960: 156; Mitscherlich 1967: 18–24). The Mitscherlichs recognized that the suffering endured by civilian victims of the air war raised the question of how this particular group should be dealt with. Yet they noted that the practice of flying flags at half-mast outside public buildings on the anniversaries of heavy bombing raids contrasted starkly with the absence of remembrance days for the victims of concentration camps, Gestapo, and *Sonderkommandos* (SS Special Forces) (Mitscherlich 2004: 42). For the philosopher Karl Jaspers, the mass reintegration of former élites testified to the fact that West Germany had failed to conduct the "moral-political revolution" required of post-Fascist society to finally break with the authoritarian, antidemocratic traditions that had defined the German political élite

83

since Bismarck's defeat of liberalism a century before (Jaspers 1966: 20, 115, 175).

The juridical and political confrontation with former perpetrators exemplified in the 1958 Ulm *Einsatzgruppen* Trial, the trial of Eichmann in Jerusalem 1961, and the Auschwitz, Belzec, Treblinka, and Sobibor Trials of 1963–1966 cast the postwar policy of amnesty and amnesia in a critical light. Over the following decade, the "discretion towards our past" that had sustained antitotalitarianism (Habermas 1987: 178) became untenable, as the confrontation with National Socialism and wider scrutiny of national traditions was integrated into reformist and radical concepts of democratization. With the election of Brandt as chancellor of the social-liberal coalition in 1969, under the slogan of "daring more democracy," leftist politicians and intellectuals began to cultivate a distinctly antinational, republican heritage of the FRG that celebrated liberal and social democratic traditions of German history. The development of Critical Historical Social Science in the 1960s paralleled this political shift and examined the roots of National Socialism in the specific route to modernity (*Sonderweg*) taken by the nineteenth-century nation. On this reading, National Socialism did not result from the totalitarian seduction of the masses but rather sprang from the authoritarian, antidemocratic mindset of the German élites. The fact that rapid socioeconomic modernization had been steered politically by a traditionalist, militaristic caste of landowning Prussian aristocrats demonstrated a systemic asynchrony between socioeconomic and political-cultural modernization that exploded in war and revolution in 1914–18, and the overthrow of Weimar democracy in the early 1930s (Wehler 1979: 143).

During the 1970s these debates on national history were refracted through a political climate of impending social crisis in the wake of a global recession, Trade Union militancy, and the terrorist campaign of the RAF that fuelled frenetic discussion of German identity (Wolfrum 1999: 304). Both left- and right-wing intellectuals responded to social-economic crises with increasing skepticism toward the ability of economic production to bind society together with purpose and meaning, as the stalling of growth undermined the positive social visions of Christian and Social Democracy alike. Leftist intellectuals diagnosed the end of the "utopia" of the "work society" and contended that the "paradigm of production" had ceased to serve as a conduit of "emancipatory perspectives" (Habermas 1985:115–116, 123–124; Habermas 1988a: 95–103). Conservative historian Michael Stürmer warned that welfare capitalism alone was incapable of generating the "higher meaning" required by the state in order to harness the emotional loyalties of the citizenry (Stürmer 1983: 84–86). The search for post-material resources of social solidarity and state authority was channeled into two distinct models of collective identity that contested the value of national traditions in West German political culture.

For the philosopher Odo Marquard, although modernity brought many benefits, the constant recreation of the social fabric propelled by accelerated modernization undermined the continuity of traditions inherited by the subject as a particularist identity (Marquard 1982: 102–123). In a world of accelerated modernization, and of the "unintended side-effects" of our actions (Lübbe 1979: 657), the only tenable outlet of agency in history is the preservation of cultural continuities and traditions that function rather like a child's teddy bear: traditions provide modern society with a sense of familiarity and reassurance by reminding us who we are in a modern age growing ever more alien and universal (Marquard 1988: 240). On this view, history compensates the subject by providing breathing space for the modern psyche in the "nostalgia for an innocent yesteryear" (Lübbe 1982: 16). Marquard and Lübbe's reworking of Jacob Burkhardt's late-nineteenth-century anti-Hegelian "law of compensation" that understood history as a process of *loss* (Burkhardt 1978: 267–9) similarly rested on an understanding of man's "anthropological condition" as an essentially "suffering being" rather than the "triumphant victor" of history imagined by Hegel and Marx (Marquard 1982: 112).

For conservative intellectuals and politicians, the roots of social malaise lay in the alienation of wide swathes of West Germans from their national history (Kohl 1996: 26). Incubated during the *Tendenzwende* (change of course) of the 1970s (Wolfrum 1999: 303–316), the appeal to rehabilitate a more positive relationship with national traditions was championed by the CDU-CSU-FDP coalition elected in 1983. Kohl's "spiritual-moral renewal" of West Germany aspired to foster a "proper moral attitude" and consensus on the FRG's "basic values" (Kohl 1987: 36) by inserting West Germany into older continuities of national history. The primary obstacle to this enterprise was the fact that it contained episodes that provoked anything but fond nostalgia. It is in this context that Nolte's interpretation of the "causal nexus" between the "class genocide" of the Bolsheviks and the race genocide of the Nazis (Nolte 1986: 39–47) can be understood: the integrity of this particularist national identity was predicated on a universalization of National Socialism as history. While Nolte was a maverick, his genealogy of twentieth-century "totalitarianism" in the "philosophies of history" which, since the late eighteenth century, had propagated the hubristic illusion of "practical transcendence" or mastery over the human social world conformed to mainstream conservative political philosophy (Nolte 1985: 39–40; Stürmer 1986: 36; Marquard 1988: 72–74).

The reaction of social-democratic politicians and intellectuals in the fractious Historians' Argument of the 1980s (Augstein 1987) was sparked by the fear that "neo-conservative" intellectuals and government sought to reverse the "re-founding" of the FRG as a post-national western democracy, a feat retrospectively ascribed to the impact of the counterculture and Brandt's coalition (Habermas 1988b: 21–28). Constitutional Patriots upheld a post-national definition of West German democracy that was predicated on the self-critical public confrontation with National Socialism through the purview of the *Sonderweg*. After Auschwitz, the naive, reverential cultivation of "inherited" national traditions was simply untenable and the appropriation of traditions in the widest sense was forced to pass through the "consciousness of sin" bequeathed by the Holocaust (Habermas 1988c: 150). This interrogation of national traditions echoed, for Habermas, the "revolutionary consciousness" of "Western Enlightenment Culture" by demonstrating the moral-political necessity of jettisoning "particularist" traditions and cultivating a universalist orientation as a resource of social solidarity (Habermas 1987). For Constitutional Patriots, identity represented more than the passively inherited outcome of our prehistory, but rather described a project that we control and whose content we consciously select (Habermas 1988c: 155–156). Constitutional Patriotism took up Jaspers's demand for a "moral-political revolution" and the Mitscherlichs' plea for a self-reflexive mourning in a model of post-national collective identity anchored in the need to radically discontinue national traditions in defining the "self-understanding" of the FRG.

Cosmopolitan Cultural Memory

West German conservatism was momentarily buoyed by the implosion of the Eastern Bloc as the failure of the "greatest social experiment of the twentieth century" appeared to confirm both the superiority of market society and the "normality" of a unified German nation state (Schwarz 1990: 154). Yet loudly proclaimed fears that Germany was drifting rightward proved unfounded. In key public debates during the 1990s from the Exhibition of *Wehrmacht* crimes, the public reception of Goldhagen's *Hitler's Willing Executioners*, the deployment of military forces in Kosovo, or the construction of a central Memorial to the Jewish Victims of the Holocaust, the confrontation with the Nazi past was established as the only tenable normative reconnection with the national past (Niven 2001). Historical consciousness of German perpetration became codified in official cultural memory as the cornerstone of domestic and international sovereignty. Far from the patriotic "reparation" of national history (Stürmer 1994: 274), post-unification discussion of collective identity has focused on Germany's "broken national identity" (Habermas 1999: 47–59), "perpetrator memory" (Assmann 2006: 219) or "genocide memory" (François 2005: 19).

Since unification, cultural memory has been most successfully developed by leftist politicians and intellectuals divested, however, of any faith in the promise of an emancipated "self-determined future" and who instead "seek *reconnection* with the past" as an anchor of cultural identity (A. Assmann 2003: 62–63). Although the Red-Green government (1998–2005) was at the forefront this new normalization of national history, it describes a project that is remarkably consensual across the political spectrum. This rapprochement between West German left and right, grounded in the mutual exhaustion of national and post-national models of collective identity, has shaped the manner in which the National Socialist past has been drawn into a meaningful relationship with the present. The West German left's, albeit pessimistic, accommodation to market society as the only viable option in a post-utopian world (Fischer 1992: 176–181) coincided with a more or less reluctant acceptance on the right that, since the 1980s, the center-left had effectively won the "higher moral-political ground" in debates on the German past (Busche 2003: 140–142).

As a specific theory and practice of mediating the relationship between past and present, cultural memory emerged from the old West German identity debates and yet at the same time represents an important departure. The most influential theory of cultural memory since the 1990s was developed by Jan and Aleida Assmann. Assmann returned to the interwar sociologist Maurice Halbwachs's 1924 study of the social framework of memory as a useful reminder that ultimately, present social context has the final word in reconstructing the past (Halbwachs 1992: 46–51). Although concurring on this point, Assmann departs from Halbwachs's distinction between the *memories* shared by particular social groups and their later objectification in culture as *history* by arguing that the process through which communicative memories of a past become transformed into history is *constitutive* of group identity. For Assmann, collective identity only emerges after it is "concretized" in cultural memory and history is transformed into a *myth* that functionalizes the past for contemporary political purposes, defining both the "myth of origin" and *telos* of the present with normative force (J. Assmann 1992: 42–45).

In contrast to the memories transmitted in the private sphere, official cultural memory is cultivated by an exclusive caste of "High Priests"— the specialists and experts who have the power to "make society visible to itself" by institutionalizing the past as a "cultural heritage" that can foster "consciousness of social unity and specificity" (Assmann, Czaplicka 1995: 128–133). Taken as a symbol of nation building, the Berlin Holocaust Memorial illustrates how the Nazi past serves to define the social unity and specificity of post-unification society: the act of memorializing a thoroughly shameful past is constitutive of a curious postconventional pride rooted not in past glory but rather in the successful confrontation with a totally discredited national history. It was in this sense that Habermas and others understood the function of the memorial as a symbol of united Germany's moral-political sovereignty (Habermas 1999: 136; Rüsen, Jaeger 2001: 418).

This postconventional pride in the FRG's successful confrontation with the Nazi past reflects the transformation of *Vergangenheitsbewältigung* from a critical to an affirmative cultural resource. Now concluded, *Vergangenheitsbewältigung* can be applied to other periods of German history (most notably the former GDR) and, indeed, other states. Thus the *Bundestag* passed a motion in 2005 censuring Ankara's refusal to commemorate fittingly the "mass murder and expulsion" of Armenians in 1915. Observing that the *Bundestag* knew only too well how difficult it was for a people "to face up to the darkest periods of its history," German politicians upheld the working through of traumatic pasts as a benchmark of European values and demanded a more thorough engagement with the "expulsion and extermination" of Armenians in 1915 in the context of the "history of ethnic conflicts in the twentieth century" as a means of "reconciling" Muslims and Armenians (Antrag 2005: 1–3). This recontextualization of the Holocaust as a paradigm of twentieth-century ethnic conflict continues the universalizing reflex of antitotalitarianism but no longer out of fealty to traditional nationalism.

On the contrary, the universalization of the Holocaust as the "signature of the twentieth century" (François 2005: 20) has been most forcefully pursued by post-national thinkers as an important cultural resource of cosmopolitanism. Equally skeptical toward compensatory traditions and the prospect of emancipation, cosmopolitan thinkers argue that the answer to the alienation produced by the globalized market is the globalization of feelings of empathy with the suffering of "distant victim others" which trump national cultures and state sovereignty (Sznaider, Levy 2001: 204–206; Beck 2002: 83). This is a cosmopolitan vision grounded not in a potential, emancipated future but rather in the "barbaric twentieth century" marked by the devastation wreaked by Stalinism and National Socialism for which the Holocaust stands as "paradigm" (François 2005: 19–20; Assmann 2006: 202–203). The rewriting of the history of the twentieth century as a narrative which pitted "gruesome perpetrators" against "hapless victims" appeals to politicians and cosmopolitan thinkers throughout the west because it appears to offer an absolute moral category in a Western culture dominated by relativism (Sznaider, Levy 2001: 234).

The post-mural preoccupation with memory is shaped by the eclipse of "traditional master narratives" of the past as well as the "breakdown of the grand utopias of the future" during a period in which history is experienced as an unremitting maelstrom of accelerating social, political, economic, and cultural transformation (Francois 2005: 19–20). Ulrich Beck observed in this vein that globalized modernity refutes the premise of both traditional Marxist *and* functionalist sociology: we are experiencing a radical transformation of modern society without, however, having to endure a revolution (Beck 1996: 29–30). Beck's influential sociology of risk holds that we cannot anticipate, let alone plan, the future consequences of present technological, industrial, and scientific developments. On this view, the motor of history is no longer conscious human endeavor but rather the "unintended side-effects" of the process of modernization itself (Beck 1996: 40–55). For Beck, the ensuing condition of "reflexive modernity" does not mean that individuals will experience "an increase of mastery and consciousness" and an enhanced awareness of the social context in which they lead their lives, but rather "a heightened awareness that mastery is impossible" (Beck & Bonβ 2001: 19). Beck's response to the "shock of a closed future," which condemns us "to live in the world as it is" (Furet 1999: 502), is to downgrade subjective agency in a theory that recasts men and women as the *victims* of the historical process.

This abstract recreation of the subject as victim informs Jörn Rüsen's fusion of history and memory through the concept of mourning. Rüsen follows Burkhardt's reading of history as a process of loss that must be mourned with an important modification: after the twentieth century we are compelled to mourn the loss of meaning in history itself (Rüsen 2001: 301–302). On this view, only mourning history's victims allows a fragile reconnection with the past that eschews reassuring teleological continuities as history appears to us rather like "a shattered mirror," the shards of which cut us when we try to piece them together (Rüsen 2001: 178–179). This search for ethical-political orientation from history does not rediscover the symbolic teddy bears of a nostalgia-inducing past nor the utopian potential of liberation from tradition, but rather "acting perpetrators," beguiled by the hubris of making history and responsible for the horrors of the twentieth century (Sznaider, Levy 2001: 236). The conservative philosopher Lübbe's view of the twentieth century as a reciprocal process of accelerated modernization and politically motivated mass murder meets seamlessly with the cosmopolitan sociologist Beck's conclusion that the "brutal and bloody" history of the twentieth century's "collective systems of insanity" demonstrate that modernization and the modernization of barbarism go hand-in-glove (Lübbe 1997: 143; Beck 1996: 61). Although constructed on the basis of a horrific past, this founding myth of cosmopolitan cultural memory is coordinated by a deep pessimism toward the future or potential *telos* of western modernity. Thus for Rüsen we emerge from the twentieth century chastened by the experience that utopian visions of the future society activated a dormant "will to extermination" that may also return to haunt our own *futures* (Rüsen 2001: 332–334).

Mourning German Victims

Most recently, cultural memory has focused on mourning the suffering of a group who appear to challenge cosmopolitan perpetrator memory: German victims of the Second World War. Claims that discussion of the air war, German expulsions, and mass rapes represents the breaking of a "last taboo" that prohibited mourning German victimhood (Röhl 2002), or the final chapter of an "unmastered past" (Nawratil 2003), obscure the discussion of these topics during the postwar period. Röhl and Nawratil's claims of taboo-breaking are firmly embedded in post-1960s national-conservative criticism of *Vergangenheitsbewältigung* as an assault on memories of German victimhood. Schmitz articulated a representative critique of commemorating

German wartime suffering in arguing that the principal problem was that it "happens at the expense of, and in competition with, remembrance of Nazi victims" (Schmitz 2006: 108). Such interpretations respond to the potential of narratives of German wartime suffering to "undermine awareness of German perpetration" (Niven 2006: 4–5) by resurrecting the neat distinction between Nazi perpetrators and German victims that characterized the immediate postwar discussion (Welzer, Moller, Tschuggnal 2003: 79–80).

The striking mimesis of linguistic and conceptual terms associated with the history and memory of the Holocaust fuels suspicion that narratives of German victimhood aim to equate German suffering with that of the Nazis' victims. Jörg Friedrich's *Der Brand* (2002) (*The Fire*) graphically portrayed the German experience of Allied bombing raids, selling several hundred thousand copies within the first few months (Huyssen 2006: 184). What made *The Fire* problematic for many critics was that Friedrich's emotive, thick historical reliving of the air war sacrificed historical context for the empathetic reconnection with German victims (Berger 2006: 220). Although Friedrich emphasized that the air war was initiated by Germany, the ductus of *The Fire* appeared to imply a moral equivalence between Hitler, Churchill, and Roosevelt (Friedrich 2002: 432). Particularly striking in Friedrich's account is the framing of German victimhood through Holocaust terminology; the cellars in which civilians met their death "functioned as crematoria" (Friedrich 2002: 194, 377), the air war is repeatedly described as an act of *Vernichtung* (extermination) (Friedrich 2002: *passim*) conducted by *Einsatzgruppen* (Friedrich 2002: 311) that effected a "rupture of civilization" (Friedrich 2002: 169).

A similarly problematic language is employed in claims for public recognition of the suffering endured by the expellees. Since 1998, the *League of Expellees* has been led by the CDU politician and spokeswomen on human rights for the CDU-CSU faction in parliament, Erika Steinbach. Steinbach's descriptions of the violent expulsion of Sudeten Germans in the Death March of Brno (Steinbach 2005) or of the internment camp in the town of Gakovo, in which Danube Swabians were held, as the "Gakovo extermination camp" (Steinbach 2005) seem to confirm suspicion that underpinning this discourse is an attempt "by the ultimate perpetrators" to gain entry to the "global community of victims" (Sznaider, Jacob 2003). Steinbach's thick description of the expulsions that relives this history through the purview of individuals subjected to traumatic suffering is clearly intended to silence critical dissent, and she dismisses the need for a new "historians' argument," claiming that "it suffices to listen to the testimony of eye-witnesses" (Steinbach 2005).

The case of the expellees is particularly controversial, as this influential West German lobby long upheld a revanchist understanding of national unification that envisaged a return to Germany in its pre-1937 borders. Paradigmatic of postwar narratives of wartime suffering, the expellees' 1950 Stuttgart Charter claimed that of all those who had suffered during the war, the expellees had "suffered the most" (Charta 1950). For Brumlik, the League's continuing adherence to the charter, of whose signatories approximately one-third had been active functionaries of the Nazi state and military, betrays a revisionist agenda that cleaves to the memory politics of the 1950s (Brumlik 2005: 88, 106–108). While this analysis of the charter as a historical document is valid, the reinvention of the *BdV* as a "victims' league" concerned to promote rapprochement in Europe through empathetic mourning (Steinbach 2004) represents more than a PR exercise or political camouflage. Despite the propensity of expellee representatives to inflame tensions with Germany's eastern neighbors, the wider meaning of this cultural memory of the expulsions is not to sustain a traditional, revanchist concept of nation.

Significantly, many prominent leftist politicians and intellectuals have promoted public discussion of German victimhood. As with Friedrich, the revisionist label does not fit intellectuals and politicians such as Otto Schily, Joschka Fischer, Peter Glotz, Günter Grass, WG Sebald, and Daniel Cohn-Bendit, who have all contributed to public discussion of the topic. The cofounder of the Center against Expulsions proposed by the League in 2000, the late Social Democrat politician Peter Glotz, remained a staunch advocate of Holocaust memory and skeptical about the use and abuse of "national identity" up until his death (Glotz 2005). The former RAF lawyer, Otto Schily, earned the praise of the League for a speech delivered in 1999 in which he condemned the dismissive attitude of the '68 generation toward their parents' suffering during the war. Cohen-Pfister observes that the academic and public discussion of the mass rapes changed between the 1990s and 2000s as political questions of the relationship between German victimhood and perpetration ceded to discussion of the authenticity of witness testimonies of this past (Cohen-Pfister 2006: 322–324).

The popular resonance of the personalized, emotive retelling of the air war and German expulsions has been interpreted as evidence of the "clear gap" that separates official memory culture and the communicative memories which structure family narratives of the past (Welzer 2006: 292). Welzer's study of the generational transmission of memories of National Socialism in families identified a tendency of grandchildren to rewrite the biographies of their grandparents in a process of "cumulative heroization" which, even when contradicted by historical fact and personal testimony, could transform fellow travelers into resistance fighters, active executioners into critical dissidents, and those who profited from the regime into its victims (Welzer, Moller, Tschuggnal 2003: 207). Others have also interpreted the resonance of victim narratives as indicating the discrepancy between official remembrance of the Holocaust and the private remembrance of German suffering (Cohen-Pfister 2006: 323–324), as "an invasion of the public realm by private memory" (Niven 2006: 20) or as "private family memories standing up to official historical consciousness" (Berger 2006: 223).

Historians have criticized the marginalization of historical scholarship in public discussion of wartime suffering that is primarily promoted through media and film portrayals as a "felt history" communicated via witness testimonies that stimulate empathetic rather than analytical responses to the past (Jarausch 2002: 9–24). The potential of the "pathos of memory" to transform history into myth should be taken seriously when contextualizing witness accounts (Sabrow 2007: 2). Yet explaining the vitality of victim narratives as an assertion of family memories against official cultural memory obscures the real relationship of power and the extent to which cultural memory actively seeks to integrate communicative memories as a means of reconnecting past with present. Cultural memory is the dominant partner in this relationship that selects and filters communicative memories in accordance with the normative historical and political precepts that it enforces.

For Assmann, family memories of wartime suffering should not be dismissed, as the integrity and authenticity of cultural memory in fact *rests upon* the testimony of historical witnesses (A. Assmann 2007: 1–18). The answer to the potential dissonance between public and private memory of wartime suffering lies, for her, in integrating family narratives systematically into a hierarchical cultural memory that privileges memory of German perpetrators and their victims. Providing that this hierarchy is upheld, other memories of victimhood can be integrated into the structure without upsetting the normative coordinates of the system (Assmann 2003: 121–122; Assmann 2006: 202–204, 256–258). Despite formally respecting the autonomy of historical scholarship and private family communication, this theory transforms both into auxil-iary resources to be drawn upon to provide intellectual legitimacy and emotional authenticity for a normatively endowed cultural memory of the twentieth century. The purpose of cultural memory to codify con-sciousness of "unity and specificity" inevitably overrides the subtleties of historical scholarship or the autonomy of family memories so that the past is valued primarily as a potential resource of social consensus. Thus recent narratives of wartime suffering appear to Assmann as a much-needed "emotional bracket" as "a new national myth that binds East and West together" (Assmann 2006: 193).

Cultural memory is more than a theory, and perhaps the greatest challenge to historians' role in shaping society's understanding of the past has come neither from media nor private family narratives but from a political class more convinced than ever of the need to "take responsibility, strengthen the reappraisal of the past and deepen com-memoration" as the Commissioner for Culture's 2008 paper on the centralization of commemorative sites declared (Unterrichtung 2008:1). Frei was one of the few to question the right of the Chancellor's Office to conduct "memory politics" and lay down "official" narratives of German history (Frei 2009: 20–21). Although this official joint com-memoration of National Socialism and the GDR understands both regimes as totalitarian dictatorships, despite surface similarities with old West German anti-Communism, it is committed to preserving the memory of the Nazi genocide in all its facets. The meaning of both National Socialism and GDR in contemporary cultural memory is to strengthen the "anti-totalitarian consensus" of the present by keeping memory of the "human suffering of the victims" alive in east and west (Unterrichtung 2008: 1–19).

This model of reconnecting with the past in an official cultural memory of human suffering at the hands of perpetrators unites not only National Socialist and GDR Germany but, since 2008, also includes Ger-man victims of the expulsions. The foundation *Flight, Expulsion Rap-prochement*, chaired by Commissioner for Culture Bernd Neumann, stands under the patronage of the German Historical Museum and is directed by the historian Manfred Kittel. "Communicative memories" of individual victims of this traumatic experience are central to the permanent exhibition that documents the expulsions through authen-tic testimonies and objects, with the aim of fostering an empathetic reconnection with this past (Neumann 2008; Kittel 2010: 17). Despite the controversial topic of the former "German east," this state-led and financed foundation's stated aim is to preserve memories of the expulsions as an essential component of German national identity, while promoting European rapprochement by commemorating the abuse of Human Rights in Europe's "century of expulsions" (Kittel 2010: 4).

Kittel's 2010 framework paper for the permanent exhibition stresses the immediate prehistory of the expulsions in Nazi Germany's war of extermination in the east, differentiates between genocide and expulsion, and recognizes the commitment to mourn the Nazis' victims. Yet the Holocaust itself has been recontextualized in an older European history of mass expulsions and ethnic nationalism that began, at the latest, with the Ottoman expulsion of Armenians in 1915 and continued into the Balkan Wars of the 1990s (Kittel 2010: 23–24). This certainly removes both the expulsions and Holocaust from their specific historical context, yet this recontextualization bears closer resemblance to the cosmopolitan transformation of the Holocaust into the paradigm of national modernity than it does revanchist nationalism. Rather than revisionist reflex, this reconnection with the past through the prism of universalized victimhood corresponds to a historical sensibility which appears less concerned with the circumstances in which an individual perished—be it Death Camp or cellar—but rather with the moral imperative to recognize the traumatic suffering of individuals and expose the perpetrators—be they German "desk perpetrators" or "British Air Marshalls" (Sabrow 2009a: 14–21).

Critics have noted that recent narratives of wartime suffering frequently invoke the Mitscherlichs' *Inability to Mourn* but exchange the focus on German perpetration for the perspective of German victims (Brumlik 2005: 113–114; Fuchs 2008: 14). Unlike the Mitscherlichs' West Germany, contemporary victim discourse is the product of a society fluent in mourning the lost "love object" of the *Führer* at the same time as the terms in which this past is made meaningful to the present have changed radically. Sabrow contextualizes the recent interest in victim narratives with reference to a factor that lies external to the dynamic of remembering and forgetting, namely the normative models of orientation that determine whether individuals experience the passage of history as a painful loss or unremarkable renewal, as a destruction of the past or as an adjustment to the future (Sabrow 2007:5). Since the end of German and European division, this subjective negotiation of the experience of social change has been channeled through official cultural memory of the "totalitarian twentieth century" as a vital resource of orientation in an age of globalized risk. The recent valorization of German wartime suffering can be understood as the particular expression of a much broader shift in the way in which the past is drawn into a meaningful relationship with both present and future that has also transformed memories of National Socialism and the GDR. Sabrow noted a curious characteristic of sites of memory of the former GDR in that they offered the opportunity of dialogue with a past that we "neither wish to repeat nor do without" (Sabrow 2009: 24–25). It is this sensibility of historical stasis, of being stuck in the present at a time of accelerated modernization that shapes the reconnection with the past through mourning past trauma and is codified in a cultural memory that cannot countenance a future history that would not need to be mourned.

References

Antrag der Fraktionen SPD, CDU/CSU, BÜNDNIS 90/DIE GRÜNEN und FDP. 15. 06. 2005. *Erinnerung und Gedenken an die Vertreibungen und Massaker an den Armeniern 1915 – Deutschland muss zur Versöhnung zwischen Türken und Armeniern beitragen.* Deutscher Bundestag Drucksache 15/5689 15. Wahlperiode.

Assmann, Aleida. 2003. *Errinerungsräume: Formen und Wandlungen des kulturellen Gedächtnisses.* München: Beck.

Assmann, Aleida. 2006. *Der lange Schatten der Vergangenheit. Erinnerungskultur und Geschichtpolitik.* München: Beck.

Assmann, Aleida. 2007. "Die Last der Vergangenheit." *Zeithistorische Forschungen/ Studies in Contemporary History, Online-Ausgabe,* 4. H. 3

Assmann, Jan. 1992. *Das kulturelle Gadächtnis: Schrift, Erinnerung und politische Identität in frühen Hochkulturen.* München: Beck.

Assmann, Jan and John Czaplicka. 1995. "Collective Memory and Cultural Identity." *New German Critique* 65: 125–133.

Augstein, Rudolf, et al. 1987. *"Historikerstreit": Die Dokumentation der Kontroverse um die Einzigartigkeit der nationalsozialistischen Judenvernichtung.* München: Piper.

Beck, Ulrich. 1996. "Das Zeitalter der Nebenfolgen und die Politisierung der Moderne." In *Reflexive Modernisierung: Eine Kontroverse,* eds. Ulrich Beck, Anthony Giddens, and Scott Lash. Frankfurt: Suhrkamp.

Beck, Ulrich, Wolfgang Bonß and Christoph Lau. 2001. "Theorie reflexiver Modernisierung – Fragestellungen, Hypothesen, Forschungsprogramme." In *Die Modernisierung der Moderne,* eds. Beck, Ulrich and Wolfgang Bonß. Frankfurt: Suhrkamp.

Beck, Ulrich. 2002. *Macht und Gegenmacht im globalen Zeitalter.* Frankfurt: Suhrkamp.

Berger, Stefan. 2006. "On Taboos, Traumas and Other Myths: Why the Debate about German Victims of the Second World War is not a Historians' Controversy." In *Germans as Victims,* ed. Bill Niven, New York: Palgrave.

Brumlik, Micha. 2005. *Wer Sturm sät. Die Vertreibung der Deutschen.* Berlin: Aufbau.

Burckhardt, Jacob. 1978. *Weltgeschichtliche Betrachtungen.* Stuttgart: Kröner.

Busche, Jürgen. 2003. *Die 68er: Biographie einer Generation*. Berlin: Berlin Verlag.

Charta der deutschen Heimatvertriebenen. 1950. http://www.bund-der-ver-triebenen.de/derbdv/charta-dt.php3

Cohen-Pfister, Laurel. 2006. "Rape, War and Outrage: Changing Perceptions on German Victimhood in the Period of Post-Unification." In *Victims and Perpetrators: 1933–1945. (Re)Presenting the Past in Post-Unification Culture*, eds. Laurel Cohen-Pfister and Dagmar Wienroeder-Skinner, New York: de Gruyter..

Dirks, Walter. 1960. "Unbewältigter Vergangenheit - demokratische Zukunft." *Frankfurter Hefte/ Zeitschrift für Kultur und Politik* 15 (3): 153–158.

Fischer, Joschka. 1992. *Die Linke nach dem Sozialismus*. Hamburg: Hoffman und Campe.

Frei, Norbert. 1999. *Vergangenheitspolitik: Die Anfänge der Bundesrepublik und die NS-Vergangenheit*. München. dtv.

Frei, Norbert. 2009. *1945 und Wir: Das Dritte Reich im Bewußtsein der Deutschen*. München: dtv.

François, Etienne. 2005. "Meistererzählungen und Dammbrüche: Die Erinnerung an den Zweiten Weltkrieg zwischen Nationalisierung und Universalisierung." In *Mythen der Nationen. 1945-Arena der Erinnerungen*, ed. Monika Flacke, Berlin: Deutsches Historisches Museum.

Friedrich, Jörg. 2002. *Der Brand: Deutschland im Bombenkrieg 1940–1945*. München: Propyläen.

Fuchs, Anne. 2008. *Phantoms of War in Contemporary German Literature, Films and Discourse*. Hampshire: Palgrave Macmillan.

Furet, François. 1999. *The Passing of an Illusion: The Idea of Communism in the Twentieth Century*. Chicago: University of Chicago Press.

Glotz, Peter. 2005. "Auf das Pferd steige ich Ihnen nicht!" In *Junge Freiheit*, www.jungefreiheit.de 05/05, 28 January.

Günther, Rolf. 1981. *Politische Reden in der Bundesrepublik Deutschland*. Berlin: Diesterweg.

Habermas Jürgen. 1985. "Die Krise des Wohlfahrtsstaates und die Erschöpfung utopischer Energien." In *Die Moderne - ein unvollendetes Projekt*, Jürgen Habermas, Leipzig: Reclam.

Habermas, Jürgen. 1987. "Geschichtsbewußtsein und posttraditionale Identität. Die Westorientierung der Bundesrepublik." In *Die Moderne - ein unvollendetes Projekt*, Jürgen Habermas, Leipzig: Reclam.

Habermas, Jürgen. 1988a. *Der philosophische Diskurs der Moderne*. Frankfurt: Suhrkamp.

Habermas, Jürgen. 1988b. "1968 - Zwei Jahrzehnte danach." In *Die nachholende Revolution*, Jürgen Habermas, Frankfurt: Suhrkamp.

Habermas, Jürgen. 1988c. "Grenzen des Neohistorismus." In *Die nachholende Revolution*, Jürgen Habermas, Frankfurt: Suhrkamp.

Habermas, Jürgen. 1990. *Die nachholende Revolution. Kleine politische Schriften VII*. Frankfurt: Suhrkamp.

Habermas, Jürgen 1992. *Die Moderne - ein unvollendetes Projekt: Philosophisch-politische Aufsätze 1977–1992*. Leipzig: Reclam.

Habermas, Jürgen. 1999. "Der Zeigefinger. Die Deutschen und ihr Mahnmal." In *Zeit der Übergänge*, Jürgen Habermas, Frankfurt: Suhrkamp.

Halbwachs, Maurice. 1992. *On Collective Memory*. Chicago: University of Chicago Press.

Hallmann, Hans, ed. 1972. *Revision des Bismarckbildes: Die Diskussion der deutschen Fachhistoriker*. Darmstadt: Wissenschaftliche Buchgesellschaft.

Huyssen, Andreas. 2003. "Air War Legacies: From Dresden to Baghdad." In *Germans as Victims*, ed. Bill Niven, New York: Palgrave.

Jarausch, Konrad H, Martin Sabrow, eds. 2002. *Verletztes Gedächtnis: Erinnerungskultur und Zeitgeschichte im Konflikt*. Frankfurt: Campus.

Jaspers, Karl. 1966. *Wohin treibt die Bundesrepublik?* München: Piper.

Kittel, Manfred 2010. "Eckpunkte für die Arbeit der Stiftung Flucht, Vertreibung, Versöhnung und die geplante Dauerausstellung." http://www.dhm.de/sfvv/docs/Eckpunkte.pdf

Kohl, Helmut. 1987. *Preserving Creation, Mastering the Tasks of the Future: Government Policy 1987–1990*. Bonn: Press and Information Office.

Kohl, Helmut. 1996. *Ich wollte Deutschlands Einheit*. Berlin: Propyläen.

Lübbe, Hermann. 1979. "Zur Identitätspräsentationsfunktion der Historie." In *Identität. Poetik und Hermeneutik VIII*, eds. Odo Marquard, Karlheinz Stierle, München: Fink.

Lübbe, Hermann. 1982. *Der Fortschritt und das Museum: Über den Grund unseres Vergnügens an historischen Gegenständen*. London: Maney and Son.

Lübbe, Hermann. 1997. *Modernisierung und Folgelasten: Trends kultureller und politischer Evolution*. Berlin: Springer.

Marquard, Odo. 1982. "Universalgeschichte und Multiversalgeschichte." In *Zukunft braucht Herkunft*, Odo Marquard, Stuttgart: Reclam.

Marquard, Odo. 1988. "Zukunft braucht Herkunft." In *Zukunft braucht Herkunft*, Odo Marquard, Stuttgart: Reclam.

Marquard, Odo. 2003. *Zukunft braucht Herkunft. Philosophische Essays*. Stuttgart: Reclam.

Mitscherlich, Alexander and Margarete Mitscherlich. 2004. *Die Unfähigkeit zu trauern: Grundlagen kollektiven Verhaltens*. München: Piper.

Nawratil, Heinz. 2003. *Schwarzbuch der Vertreibung 1945 bis 1948: Das letzte Kapitel unbewältigter Vergangenheit*. München: Universitas.

Neumann, Bernd. 2008. "Sichtbares Zeichen gegen Flucht und Vertreibung." Ausstellungs-, Dokumentations- und Informationszentrum in Berlin. http://www.dhm.de/sfvv/beschluss.html.

Niven, Bill. 2002. *Facing the Nazi Past: United Germany and the Legacy of the Third Reich*. London: Routledge.

Niven, Bill. ed. 2006. *Germans as Victims: Remembering the Past in Contemporary Germany*. New York: Palgrave.

Nolte, Ernst. 1985. *Deutschland und der Kalte Krieg*. Stuttgart: Klett.

Nolte, Ernst. 1986. "Vergangenheit, die nicht vergehen will. Eine Rede, die geschrieben, aber nicht gehalten werden konnte." In *"Historikerstreit,"* eds. Rudolf Augstein et al., München: Pieper.

Ritter, Gerhard. 1948. "Europa und die deutsche Frage." In *Revision des Bismarckbildes*, ed. Hans Hallmann. 1972. Darmstadt: Wissenschaftliche Buchgesellschaft.

Ritter, Gerhard. 1950. "Das Bismarck Problem." *Revision des Bismarckbildes*, ed. Hans Hallmann. 1972. Darmstadt: Wissenschaftliche Buchgesellschaft.

Röhl, Klaus-Rainer. 2002. *Verbotene Trauer*. München: Universitas.

Rüsen, Jörn. 2001. *Zerbrechende Zeit: Über den Sinn der Geschichte*. Köln: Böhlau.

Rüsen, Jörn and Friedrich Jaeger. 2001. "Erinnerungskultur." In *Deutschland-Trendbuch. Fakten und Orientierungen*, eds. Karl-Rudolf Korte, Werner Weidenfeld, Opladen: Leske+Budrich.

Sabrow, Martin. 2009a. "Den Zweiten Weltkrieg Erinnern." *Aus Politik und Zeitgeschichte* 36–37, 31 August.

Sabrow, Martin, ed. 2009b. *Erinnerungsorte der DDR*. München: Beck.

Schmitz, Helmut. 2006. "The Birth of the Collective from the Spirit of Empathy: From the 'Historians' Dispute' to German Suffering." In *Germans as Victims*, ed. Bill Niven, New York: Palgrave.

Schwarz, Hans-Peter. 1990. "Das Ende der Identitätsneurose." In *Historiker betrachten Deutschland: Beiträge zum Vereinigungsprozeß und zur Hauptstadtdiskussion*, ed. Udo Wengst. 1992. Bonn-Berlin.

Steinbach, Erika. 2004. "Empathie – Der Weg zum Miteinander. 60 Jahre Warschauer Aufstand. Rede in der Französischen Friedenskirche. Berlin. 19 Juli." http://www.bund-dervertriebenen.de/download/Steinbach.pdf.

Steinbach, Erika. 2005. "60 Jahre Kriegsende - Vertreibung als Teil deutscher Identität." Sonntag, 1 Mai 2005. http://www.erika-steinbach.de.

Stürmer Michael. 1983. "Kein Eigentum der Deutschen" In *Die Identität der Deutschen*, ed. Werner Weidenfeld, München: Hanser.

Stürmer, Michael. 1986. "Geschichte in geschichtslosem Land." In *"Historikerstreit,"* eds. Rudolf Augstein et al., München: Pieper.

Stürmer, Michael. 1994. *Die Grenzen der Macht*. Berlin: Siedler.

Sznaider Natan, Günther Jacob. 14. 08. 2003. "Die Lust am eigenen Leid." *Die Tageszeitung* Nr. 7130.

Sznaider Natan, Daniel Levy. 2001. *Erinnerung im globalen Zeitalter: Der Holocaust*. Frankfurt: Suhrkamp. Überschär, Gerd, ed. 2000. *Der Nationalsozialismus vor Gericht: Die alliierten Prozesse gegen Kriegsverbrecher und Soldaten 1943–1952*. Frankfurt: Fischer.

Unterrichtung durch den Beauftragten der Bundesregierung für Kultur und Medien. 19.06.2008. *Fortschreibung der Gedenkstättenkonzeption des Bundes Verantwortung wahrnehmen, Aufarbeitung verstärken, Gedenken vertiefen*. Deutscher Bundestag Drucksache 16/9875. 16. Wahlperiode.

Wehler Hans-Ulrich. 1979. *Krisenherde des Kaiserreichs 1871–1918: Studien zur deutschen Sozial- und Verfassungsgeschichte*. Göttingen: Vandenhoeck und Ruprecht.

Wehler, Hans-Ulrich. 2008. *Deutsche Gesellschaftsgeschichte: Bundesrepublik und DDR 1949–1990*. München: Beck.

Welzer, Harald, Sabine Moller and Karoline Tschuggnall. 2002. *"Opa war kein Nazi": Nationalsozialismus und Holocaust im Familiengedächtnis*. Frankfurt: Fischer.

Welzer, Harald. 2006. "The Collateral Damage of Enlightenment: How Grandchildren Understand the History of National Socialist Crimes and Their Grandfathers' Past." In *Victims and Perpetrators*, eds. Laurel Cohen-Pfister and Dagmar Wienroeder-Skinner. New York: de Gruyter.

Wolfrum, Edgar. 1999. *Geschichtspolitik in der Bundesrepublik Deutschland: Der Weg zur bundesrepublikanischen Erinnerung 1948–1990*. Darmstadt: Wissenschaftliche Buchgesellschaft.

Wolgast, Eike. 2001. *Die Wahrnehmung des Dritten Reiches in der unmittelbaren Nachkriegszeit (1945/46)*. Heidelberg: Winter.

5

From Perpetrators to Victims and Back Again: The Long Shadow of the Second World War in Belgium

Bram Mertens

To anybody with a passing interest in the history of the Low Countries, the statement that the memory of the Second World War in Belgium has always been contested would not come as a great revelation. Nor would it appear to make Belgium particularly unique, as attested by a growing corpus of research on contested memories and mythologies of the Second World War in Europe, from Henry Rousso's *Le Syndrome de Vichy* (1987) to Chris van der Heijden's *Grijs Verleden: Nederland in de Tweede Wereldoorlog* (2001) and beyond. Every European state has its own particular narratives and their contestations, and in every European state, the construction and contestation of these narratives is "infused by politics" (Lebow 2006: 4). However, what makes Belgium unusual is that, unlike its immediate neighbors or indeed any of the European nations directly involved in the Second World War, Belgium is (or was) a "consociational democracy," a term coined by Arend Lijphart to define the kind of political regime which seeks to give democratic stability to countries divided along ethnic, religious, or linguistic lines (Huyse 2003; Deschouwer 2006: 895; Peters 2006). As mythmaking processes are so closely linked to issues of identity—be they individual, or collective, regional, or national (Lebow 2006)—it would be only rational to expect to find a different memory pattern in a country where the concept of identity itself is that little bit less straightforward. In this chapter, I will investigate how the structure of Belgium as a consociational democracy has affected the construction of national and regional narratives of the Second World War, and how the development and evolution of these narratives in turn affected the consociational structure of the country. In this context, I will look at the emergence of a Flemish counternarrative of the Second World War and its aftermath between 1944 and 1970 as a symptom of the changing social, cultural, and political landscape in Belgium. Research on this area in English, insofar as it deals with the issue at all, is very sparse indeed (Conway 1997, Witte and Van Velthoven 1999, Huyse 2000 and Lagrou 2000 touch on aspects of the question), and although the topic has been addressed by scholars writing in Dutch and, to a lesser degree, French, these studies have also tended to concentrate on certain aspects of it only, rather than seeking to provide a comprehensive overview within a theoretical framework.

A Consociational Nation

Consociational democracy is defined as "government by élite cartel to turn a democracy with a fragmented political culture into a stable democracy" (quoted in Deschouwer 2006: 895). According to this particular definition, Belgium appeared to qualify as a consociational state, if not a democracy, from its very inception in 1830. After all, it was the so-called Monster Union of the ideologically opposed Catholics and Liberals that sustained the Belgian revolt as well as the Belgian state from 1830 to 1846 (Witte, Craeybeckx, and Meynen 2010). Nor did the emergence of the Flemish Question fundamentally threaten the stability of the country throughout the nineteenth century or even until the eve of the Second World War. Naturally, a couple of major caveats apply. Firstly, throughout the long nineteenth century, it was the lack of democracy that allowed the élite cartels to maintain stability in their fragmented state, particularly where linguistic or social issues were concerned. Secondly, as attested by the years of majoritarian single-party government between 1846 and 1917, consociationalism was not a permanent feature of Belgian politics, but was deployed in times of acute crisis when added pressure on the internal divisions threatened the system itself (Deschouwer 2006: 898). When Belgium was first analyzed as a consociational democracy in 1971 by the sociologist Luc Huyse, he did not comment on the first 114 years of Belgium's existence, due to a lack of data, limiting his analysis to the period between 1944 and 1961. During this period, coinciding with the long aftermath of the Second World War, Belgium could be seen as a consociational democracy, but also saw off consociationalism as an accurate descriptor, as one of its perennial divisions would begin to dominate the political landscape and eventually lead to the federalization of the country.

Looking at the state of affairs when Belgium entered this short period of consociationalism proper, Huyse identified three divisions, namely religious, economic, and ethnolinguistic. However, these divisions often cut across and thus effectively neutralized one another, guaranteeing the stability of the country, as no one single division ever came to dominate the political agenda to the total exclusion of all others (Deschouwer 2006: 897). A further segmentation which cut across the religious, economic, and ethnolinguistic divisions was an ideological "vertical pluralism" or "pillarization," which Huyse identified as another powerful brake on the centrifugal potential of the other divisions (Huyse 2003: 119). This vertical pluralism entailed the division of the country and its population across three "pillars"—hence segmentation rather than division—each composed of a number of organizations covering practically every aspect of daily life, from nurseries, sports clubs, and cultural centers to newspapers, unions, and even undertakers. The resulting pillars—the Catholic, the Socialist, and the considerably smaller Liberal—were thus not monolithic entities, but derived all of their strength from the organizations of which they were composed (Huyse 2003: 41–43). It is easy to see how this segmentation has every potential to cut across the ethnolinguistic division, and the existence of a unitary party for every one of the three pillars appears to confirm as much. However, between 1968 and 1980, these unitary party structures all disappeared and made way for what we would now call federal, but are in essence (ethno-)linguistic, party structures. The Christian-Democrats were the first to divide into the *Christelijke Volkspartij* and the *Parti Social Chrétien* in 1968, the Liberals became the *Partij voor Vrijheid en Vooruitgang* and the *Parti de la Liberté et du Progrès* in 1971, and the Socialists were the last ones to divide into the *Socialistische Partij* and the *Parti Socialiste* in 1980 (Sanders, Devos et al. 2008). Leaving the ethnolinguistic division to one side, the potential for pillarization to cut across the economic and religious divisions appears much less straightforward. In terms of religion, pillarization appears simply to replicate the division, with the "godless" socialists and anticlerical liberals diametrically opposed to the Catholic pillar, a common pattern throughout the nineteenth century. Matters are slightly more complex where the economic division is concerned, as it pits labor against capital, and thus the Socialist pillar along with the christian-democratic, left wing of the Catholic pillar one the one hand against the Liberal pillar and the more conservative, right-wing elements of the Catholic pillar on the other hand. However, looking at the relative sizes of the pillars, both nationally and regionally or ethnolinguistically, a clear pattern emerges that complicates the notion that the vertical pluralism of pillarization cleanly cuts across and neutralizes the other divisions. After the introduction of universal (and compulsory) male suffrage in 1919, the Socialists established a very firm power base in the South of the country, dominating almost every Wallonian city and maintaining an absolute majority in two out of the four Wallonian provinces, whereas the Catholic pillar acquired a similar balance of power in the North (Huyse 2003: 38). The elections in 1939 gave the Catholic Party 32.7 percent of the vote nationally and 41 percent in Flanders, whereas the Socialist BWP (*Belgische Werklieden Partij*) gained 30.2 percent of the vote nationally and 38.6 percent in Wallonia (Van den Wijngaert et al. 2004: 253–254). The Liberal pillar, conversely, may have cut across the ethnolinguistic division to a much greater extent, but as the smallest and least well-organized of the three pillars, it had been reduced to an auxiliary role after the First World War and the party only acquired 17.2 percent of the vote in the 1939 elections (Van den Wijngaert et al. 2004: 255).

The best example of an instance where the majority effect of pillarization actually reinforced the ethnolinguistic division is without a doubt the *Koningskwestie* or Royal Question, which brought the country to the edge of revolution between 1944 and 1950, and was, appropriately, closely linked to the issue of wartime collaboration. Already in conflict with his government on the policy of Belgian neutrality, King Leopold III remained in the country after the German invasion in May 1940 and offered the unconditional surrender of the Belgian army eighteen days later, whereas the government went into exile and wanted to continue the war. After a complete breakdown of trust, neither side recognized the legitimacy of the other, and King Leopold sought a rapprochement with the German occupier, convinced that the geopolitical map of Europe had changed forever. The day after the D-Day landings, the Germans deported the king to the Reich, where he wrote his controversial political will, in which he accused his government of betrayal, maintained his own blamelessness, and announced drastic changes to the Belgian parliamentary democracy (demanding rather less of it, in fact). Yet the king had completely misjudged both the extent to which some of his own subjects had turned against him over the course of the war, and the lack of enthusiasm of Britain and the US in particular to see him back on the throne (Verhoeyen 1993; Lagrou 1995; Lagrou 2000; Van den Wijngaert, Dujardin, and Dumoulin 2001). The issue was eventually resolved after a referendum, held by the majoritarian Catholic government of Gaston Eyskens in 1949, resulting in a narrow victory for the Royalists with 57.86 percent of the votes in favor of the king's return (the minimum required for a decision had been set at 55 percent). The regional divisions were extremely telling, as the king commanded the support of a large majority in Flanders (72 percent), but no majority at all in Brussels (48 percent) and Wallonia (42 percent) (Van den Wijngaert and Dujardin 2006: 15). The results by electoral district show an even greater divergence, with yes-votes in excess of 84 percent in Turn-hout, Roeselare-Tielt, and Tongeren-Maaseik, and no-votes between 65 percent and 69 percent in Mons, Soignies, Charleroi, and Liège (*Parl. St.* Kamer 1949–1950: 316). In direct contravention of the unwritten consociational rules, the homogenous Catholic government of Jean Duvieusart decided to enforce its majority and call the king back to Belgium in July 1950, a move that brought the country to the edge of civil war with a wave of strikes, riots, and the death of four protesters in Grâce-Berleur near Liège. Order was restored after the government returned to the consociational model of a negotiated compromise, which meant that Leopold would abdicate in favor of his son Boudewijn I (Huyse 2003: 33–34), but the Belgian consensus model had come under greater pressure than ever before (Deschouwer 2006: 898). Between the end of the second School War in 1958 and the general strike of 1961, the end date of Huyse's investigation, the ethnolinguistic conflict gradually came to overshadow Belgium's ideological divisions, and the days of the classic consociational model were numbered.

Liminality and Legitimacy

When Belgium was invaded in May 1940, the country had already been through a protracted crisis of its parliamentary democracy, see-ing it challenged by a number of antidemocratic and (proto-)Fascist parties and movements. French-speaking Belgium had been shocked after the 1936 elections by the meteoric rise of Léon Degrelle's fiercely anti-Communist and authoritarian Rex. On a 10.7 percent share of the vote, Rex managed to win twenty-one seats in parliament and a further eight in the senate, all from a standing start. In Flanders, it was Staf De Clerq's VNV (*Vlaams Nationaal Verbond*) that challenged the traditional parties, winning sixteen seats in parliament and a further five in the senate, representing just over 7 percent of the vote. Previously a member of the far-right *Action Catholique*, Degrelle recruited most of his voters from the right wing of the Catholic party, and his targets were what he perceived to be the decadence of the traditional parties as well as the democratic system itself. In this sense, Rex was a model representative of the right-wing populist or Fascist New Order parties and movements that were widespread throughout Europe. The VNV also conformed to this type, but unlike Rex, it was also a nationalist party. An amalgamation of smaller Flemish-nationalist groups, the VNV was also not the first Flemish-nationalist party to send representatives to parliament. That honor went to the *Vlaamsch Nationaal Front*, founded in 1919 and commonly known as the *Frontpartij*, for which Staf De Clerq had himself been a member of parliament until 1932. Although Catholics had always been in a majority, the *Frontpartij* represented the pluralist and moderate tradition of the Flemish Movement, which sought to further the Flemish cause within existing Belgian structures. Throughout the twenties and thirties, however, the party and the Movement gradually shifted to the right, alienating its own left wing. By the time the prominent Flemish nationalist politician Herman Vos left the *Frontpartij* in 1933, it had become dominated by a much more radical, right-wing, and anti-Belgian form of nationalism (Van Causenbroeck 1997; De Wever 1994). Nevertheless, the preexisting tradition of political nationalism may explain in part why the VNV managed to hold on to its seats after the 1939 elections, in fact adding one more member of parliament and three senators to its tally, whereas Rex lost all but four of its seats in parliament and all but one in the senate (Van den Wijngaert et al. 2004).

Almost as soon as the Belgian army had surrendered, VNV and Rex offered their services to the occupier, along with a number of smaller, more marginal, but also more extreme groups such as the *Deutsch-Flämische Arbeitsgemeinschaft* (DeVlag) and the *Algemeene SS-Vlaanderen*. In the case of Rex, this collaboration would be predominantly military, but in the case of the VNV, disposing of a sizeable number of members of parliament and senators, but especially local councilors and mayors, the collaboration would become a veritable attempt at a coup d'état (De Wever 1994; Wouters 2004). Given their political and ideological proclivities, it stands to reason that the VNV and Rex would collaborate with an occupier whose political and social model so closely resembled that of the New Order movements, and whose arrival appeared to offer the opportunity to wield the kind of power which could never be theirs under a representative democracy (De Wever 1992: 57–58; De Wever 1994). The Nazis' *Flamenpolitik*, favoring the Flemish over their francophone countrymen wherever possible, certainly gave the Flemish nationalists hope that this might be their moment, and at the same time bred resentment amongst francophone Belgians (Witte and Van Velthoven 1999: 161–163; Van den Wijngaert et al. 2004: 185). The German military or civilian administrations, however, were only interested in maintaining *Ruhe und Ordnung* in the occupied territories and would invariably defer any decision on the eventual status of those territories until after the war. This we now know with the benefit of hindsight, and over the course of the war it also dawned on all but the most ideologically blinded collaborators. Still, the Second World War, even more so than wars preceding it, was the kind of liminal time and space in which existing social and political structures lose their sense of inevitability and can be made again, it is "the space in which the very distinction between structure and agency ceases to make meaning," and one which appears to offer nothing but opportunity: "Liminality is a world of contingency where events and ideas, and 'reality' itself, can be carried in different directions" (Thomassen 2009: 5). To groups with a revolutionary and apocalyptic bent such as the New Order movements, the sense of being able to change the course of history or make a new reality would obviously be particularly germane. In fact, the very structure of the New Order movements centered around the liminal figures of a leader or a leading élite who are endowed with the power to proclaim and maintain a permanent state of exception, permitting them to reshape society and humanity itself. In the context of the formation of memories and the creation of myths, such periods of liminality are also particularly crucial, not only because the structures of society and indeed reality itself become malleable, but also because the leading élite consequently does not feel constrained by existing laws and structures. When this self-styled élite is confronted with its crimes after the war, they often do not recognize them as such and claim that these were "exceptional times," a claim that appears frequently in former collaborators' memoirs (see for instance Claes 1983).

Immediately after the war, the struggle to gain or regain political legitimacy began across Europe, and with it, inevitably, began the creation and negotiation of the narratives and myths of the war. After their wholehearted collaboration, members and sympathizers of the VNV and Rex naturally found themselves not only excluded from the political process, but also very often in the dock. For those people who, until a few months before, had considered themselves to be part of an élite that was born to lead, the confrontation with an angry mob baying for revenge in September 1944, and with the judicial system thereafter, would prove both shocking and traumatic (Huyse and Dhondt 1991). Again this is an aspect that would often return in their personal narratives of the war. Upon its return to Belgium, the Pierlot government, made up of ministers from the three main parties, found itself challenged by fellow party members who had remained in the country during the occupation, some of whom had been political prisoners, and, as a matter of course, by the resistance. Ideologically, the Belgian resistance was quite diverse, although it was in essence almost as antidemocratic as the collaboration. The largest group was the Independence Front (*Onafhankelijkheidsfront* or *OF*), an umbrella organization of anti-Fascist groups founded and dominated by the Communists, but there was also a right-wing resistance in the shape of the Secret Army (*Geheim Leger*), which consisted mainly of professional soldiers and retired military personnel (Van den Wijngaert et al. 2006: 109). Whereas the Communists of the OF hoped the aftermath of the war would bring the opportunity for them to seize power, the Secret Army contained a substantial Leopoldist element, which hoped to replace Belgium's parliamentary democracy with a strong, authoritarian regime under a more powerful monarchy. The traditional political parties and their postwar governments had to maintain a precarious balance between neutralizing the resistance and using its moral authority to regain legitimacy. For this reason, the first three governments after the liberation were governments of national unity which included both Communists and representatives of the OF, as well as members of the travaillist *Union Démocratique Belge* (UDB), which also had its roots in the resistance (Van Doorslaer 2003: 229). Evidently, these governments also had to promise to deal very quickly and forcefully with the collaboration, and, conversely, give due recognition to the victims of Nazi persecution (Lagrou 2000: 219). As the policy details were hammered out, however, their (un)intended consequences precipitated a battle amongst the three main parties and (between September 1944 and March 1947) the Communists to safeguard both the size and the legitimacy of their electorate. This battle, which coincided with the Royal Question, would chiefly pit the left against the right, but in certain respects it also began to mirror the division between francophone and Flemish Belgium (Huyse 2003: 30–31). The way in which events unfolded and were interpreted over the next six years entrenched this ideological and ethnolinguistic division, hardened opinions on both sides and allowed the emergence and embedding of the Flemish counter-memory of the war.

Postwar Power Games

As the dust settled on the war, and victims and perpetrators were identified, it became clear that the majority of the deportees and political prisoners who were recognized as victims of the Nazi persecution were, predictably, to be found on the left of the political spectrum. Those honored as heroes of the resistance were ideologically more diverse, although the right was proportionally still underrepresented due in no small part to the noncommittal attitude of the Church and the Catholic Party during the war, where segments of the Socialist and Liberal parties and of course the Communists did choose a side and, as time would tell, chose wisely (Van den Wijngaert et al. 2004: 253–256). Even within the same pillar, however, ethnolinguistic differences in approach and attitude were already clearly visible, with the Flemish part of the Catholic pillar being much more tempted by the authoritarian and corporatist ideology of the occupier than its counterparts in Wallonia or Brussels. This led to open conflict in the Catholic Union, when Flemish delegates voted in favor of joining the Nazi-imposed Union of Manual and Intellectual Workers (UHGA/UTMI) in the Autumn of 1940, whereas the Wallonian delegates were categorically opposed to it (Verhoeyen 1993: 130; Van den Wijngaert et al. 2004: 254). A similar pattern emerges when we look at the resistance from an ethnolinguistic perspective, which reveals it to have been numerically much stronger in Wallonia and Brussels than it had been in Flanders, and even there almost 20 percent of resistance fighters came from a francophone household (Van Doorslaer 2003: 231). The profile of the collaboration, on the other hand, showed exactly the same pattern in reverse. The more right-wing profile of the Flemish electorate, the ideological radicalism of the Flemish Movement and its relative size, as well as the German *Flamenpolitik* all meant that especially the political collaboration was overrepresented in Flanders compared to Brussels and even more so to Wallonia. With such an imbalance, the risk that any postwar attempt to deal with the collaboration, or *incivisme* as it was known, would inevitably become politicized was clearly very high. One aspect in particular of the so-called repression would lead to open conflict between the left and the right, and this time it was the left that ignored the unwritten rules of the Belgian consensus model by steering a majoritarian course.

On 6 May 1944, about four months before the Liberation, the government of national unity in London issued a decree that introduced the infamous paragraph 6 of article 123, known as article 123sexies, into the Belgian Penal Code. This paragraph determined that anyone found guilty of any form of collaboration resulting in a prison term of five years or longer would automatically be stripped of some or all of their civil rights, first among them the right to vote or to be elected (Huyse and Dhondt 1991: 25; Horvat 2003: IX). An earlier decree of 17 December 1942 had already defined collaboration in the broadest possible terms as "any deed which, without excuse, constitutes assistance to the enemy," and stipulated a mandatory death penalty for any act of military, economic, or political assistance to the enemy (Huyse and Dhondt 1991: 61). This gave the courts martial responsible for trying and sentencing the collaborators very little room for maneuver, resulting in heavy penalties for those unlucky enough to be tried immediately after the war. The application of article 123sexies would ensure that anyone who had been an active member of any organization deemed to have assisted the occupier in any way would effectively be excluded from society, and it would criminalize every local or national VNV politician, as well as a large number of their fellow travelers. On 19 September 1945, using executive powers specifically designed for matters related to the epuration, Achille Van Acker's left-wing coalition of Socialists, Communists, Liberals, and UDB issued a decree which greatly increased the number of cases in which article 123sexies would apply, including, amongst many others, those who had simply been a member of a long list of suspect organizations or even had allowed their children to become a member of such an organization (Huyse and Dhondt 1991: 142–143; Horvat 2003: XXII). The special executive powers in question had been granted to the previous government of national unity, but Van Acker used them in order to avoid having to debate the matter in parliament. It was certainly not in the spirit of the Belgian consensus model, and arguably constituted the first shot fired in the ideological war that was to follow. The move met with repeated and vocal protests from the Catholic opposition, who saw the size of the right-wing electorate potentially reduced by tens of thousands in one fell swoop ahead of the first postwar elections in February 1946 (Huyse and Dhondt put the number at around sixty thousand [1991: 144]). In a fraught debate in the Senate on 16 October 1945, the Catholic Joseph Pholien accused the government of deliberately partisan and even dictatorial behavior, saying that "it defies common sense for a government . . . to be able to deny certain categories of citizens the vote . . . making a choice between those who could be favorable to them and those who could be hostile to them." The Liberal minister van Glabbeke in turn openly accused the Catholics of wanting to win the upcoming elections with the votes of collaborators, or at least of the wives of collaborators (*Parl. Hand.* Senaat, 50:16/10/1945, 857–862). This last comment referred to Catholic calls to introduce the franchise for women, which the left resisted based on fears that the female vote, especially in Flanders, would predominantly go to the right. The chairman of the BSP, Max Buset, would admit as much in Parliament in March 1947, at the same time suggesting that the very recent Catholic conversion to the female franchise was also born entirely out of electoral expediency: "There is no point in making a mystery about it: we feared the interference of the leopoldist agitation specifically through the female vote. Because of this, we have maybe delayed the accession of women to the electorate by one election. But we see people in this Chamber whom we could actually accuse of having delayed the same electorate by five or by six elections" (*Parl. Hand.* Kamer, 51: 26/03/1947, 12).

The Catholic accusations of partisanship did not appear to be unfounded. When Prime Minister Achille van Acker had announced the upcoming elections to Parliament in August 1945, he had also declared his government's intention to deprive collaborators of the vote, stating that "it would be unjust that those who had doubts about the fate of the country should be allowed to influence its future" (*Parl. Hand.* Kamer, 42: 07/08/1945, 629). By the same token, there is little doubt that the Catholics were prepared to embrace policies, such as the female franchise, and people, such as those who stood accused of collaboration, chiefly for electoral reasons, especially with the Royal Question looming over the political landscape. However, Pholien's rhetorical onslaught in the Senate went further than the accusations of partisan and dictatorial behavior, stating that "political purges at the behest of the government had their precedents in totalitarian countries," and adding: "The Nazis hunted down people under the heading of the 'judaeo-plutocracy'; over here, the terms '*civisme* and *incivisme*' are used for everything, preceding the introduction of the term 'neo-fascist' into the political vocabulary. . . . Nowadays, people are even neo-fascist when they take the liberty of not thinking like some of the extreme left-wing press" (*Parl. Hand.* Senaat, 50: 16/10/1945, 857). The explicit comparison of the government's handling of the collaboration to the Nazi persecution, a mere five months after the end of the War in Europe, may seem both crass and hyperbolic, but it set the tone for kind of apologetic, combative, and accusatory discourse on the collaboration that would gradually become commonplace among large sections of Catholic Flanders. At the time, Pholien's words were as much born out of conviction as they were a signal to the collaborators, their friends, and their families, suggesting that there would still be a home for them in the newly-founded Christian People's Party (CVP/PSC). It also planted the seed of the idea that the repression had been much worse than the collaboration itself, and that those who were sanctioned and punished by it were not just victims of the war as much as those who had suffered under the occupation, but also that their victimhood was in fact much more severe and had much graver consequences. Over the next five years, motivated by ideology as well as by electoral mathematics, the Party continued and even intensified its support for those it called the "victims of the repression," seeking to rehabilitate and legitimize them without putting too great an emphasis, if indeed any, on the recognition of guilt or responsibility. In the eyes of the other parties as well as most of the population, this aligned the Catholic Pillar with the collaboration, the only major party of government in postwar Europe to do so (Van Doorslaer 2003: 233). To howls of outrage from the CVP/PSC benches, the Liberal minister Buisseret stated in the Senate on 13 November 1946: "Gentlemen on the right, since you have taken the pseudonym of the *parti social chrétien*, you appear to me to have come quite a long way. I don't derive any pleasure from saying so. It's a shame for the country and for the system that the successors of a great national party . . . too often appear as the champions and the courtiers of this *incivisme*" (*Parl. Hand.* Senaat, 2: 13/11/1946, 13).

"A Feast of Hatred"

Protected and legitimized to a degree by the patronage of the Catholic pillar, the former collaborators and discredited Flemish nationalists began to regroup almost immediately. Even for those who had not been convicted of *incivisme*, any political engagement as a Flemish nationalist was still very problematic, especially since public opinion in the first year after the liberation was not in a forgiving mood and repeatedly clamored for swift and severe sentences for collaborators (Huyse 1991: 92, 108). Furthermore, article 123sexies explicitly banned those convicted of collaboration from participating in any organization, or being involved in publishing or disseminating material, which had any kind of political character. For these reasons, a large number of "purely" social and cultural organizations and publications saw the light, which would also serve as support networks for convicted collaborators and their families, excluded from most existing organizations. The continuity between these new organizations and publications, both in terms of membership an in terms of ideology, was often blatant. Toward the end of 1944, for instance, a youth organization was founded in Brussels which would become officially known as *De Zilvermeeuwtjes* in the Spring of 1945, but which had been established by the founders of the *Dietsche Blauwvoetvendels*, a division of the now banned National-Socialist Youth of Flanders (NSJV) (Seberechts 1992: 70). The same year also saw the publication of "satirical" and "cultural" periodicals, such as *'t Pallieterke* and *Rommelpot*, which were overtly critical of the repression and sympathetic to its "victims," and which frequently counted these very same "victims" among their contributors, often writing under pseudonyms. With peak circulations of fifty-eight thousand and over ten thousand respectively (De Schryver and De Wever et al. 1998: 2389, 2647), *'t Pallieterke* and *Rommelpot* were very influential and inspired the publication of many similar periodicals, invariably short-lived and with a much smaller print run. These included *Golfslag* (1946), *Wit en Zwart, Branding, Vive Le Gueux!* (1947), *Het Spoor voor de Lage Landen* (1948), *Opstanding* and *De Voorpost* (1949), all of them peddling the same antirepression rhetoric and defending the ideology of the collaboration (Bosman 1990: 2040; De Schryver and De Wever et al. 1998: 1335, 3763, 593, 3306, 2811, 2354–55, 3547). Editors and contributors often moved from one publication to the other, sometimes because a journal sailed too close to the wind and found itself banned by the authorities, and some of them eventually ended up working for national newspapers of journals. Foremost of these was the daily newspaper of the Catholic Pillar, *De Standaard*, taken over in 1947 by a conglomerate that included a number of prominent Flemish nationalists who had been active in the accommodation or even collaboration during the war (Van Doorslaer 2003: 232). All this journalistic activity played a crucial part in the dissemination of counternarratives of the war, the collaboration and the repression, which would gradually become commonplace in right-wing Catholic Flemish circles and reinforce the identification of Flemish nationalism with the right and with Catholicism.

Countless such counternarratives were produced in the immediate aftermath of the war, and they continued to be written and rewritten until the mid-eighties, very often relying on one another for anecdotes, testimonies or facts, which are themselves routinely misquoted or misrepresented. Huyse and Dhondt counted over one hundred books and pamphlets on the repression alone, most of them written by former collaborators or their sympathizers, that rely on only two "source texts" (Huyse and Dhondt 1991: 13). As Joseph Pholien had already done in his Senate intervention in 1946, the counternarratives invariably sought to redefine and reframe the terms of reference. They claimed that the term *collaboration* had been used in too broad a sense, and, conversely, that the term *resistance* had been defined too narrowly. They frequently argued that those who continued or assumed roles in local or national administration under Nazi rule had in fact ensured that the country was saved from chaos or total German domination, even if it had meant finding an accommodation with the occupier (Beyen 2002: 113). In fact, so the argument ran, those who had cooperated fully with the occupier but had kept the interests of the country at the forefront of their mind at all times should surely be seen as part of the resistance within the collaboration, which had been far too broadly conceived (Derine 1983: 15). This interpretation implied a willful blindness to the ideologically and politically motivated collaboration of the VNV, which had constituted, to all intents and purposes, an attempted coup d'état (De Wever 1994). Conversely, the counternarratives sought to redefine, minimize, and discredit the resistance, claiming that its actions had been destructive and counterproductive, both in terms of material damage and German reprisals, that its members had been common criminals or that they were driven by ideological hatred for Catholics and Flemings. The (understandable) intransigence of the Communist resistance in particular on the matter of leniency toward collaborators was taken as further evidence of this and earned them the moniker *the irreconcilables*, which was contrasted to the Christian virtue of forgiveness (De Wever 2004: 22). Another aspect that was common to most counternarratives was their reliance on emotive language or images, ranging from oft-repeated anecdotes of individual suffering and injustice to highly suggestive and often hyperbolic slogans and images. A pamphlet on the repression published in 1966 under the pseudonym Nemrod featured a cover drawing of an old man tied to a stake, with a Bible and a Flemish lion at his feet, clearly intended as a vignette of Flemish Catholic suffering, and carried the title *The Feast of Hatred* (Beyen 2004: 77). The accusation of hatefulness was often leveled at the Belgian establishment which had unjustly and cruelly punished those it considered to be collaborators, and conversely, the latter were often defended as idealists who were motivated only by a deep love for Flanders and its people (Beyen 2002: 115). This appeal to emotion meant that the ideological aspect of the collaboration could be glossed over, as if the authoritarian, totalitarian and racist nature of the Nazi regime was incidental rather than essential to the enthusiasm of the VNV and the other New Order organizations for the occupier. Concealing this ideological divide also served to further blur the distinction between resistance and collaboration, since there had been idealists as well as opportunists in both camps, although the counternarratives invariably suggested there had been more idealists amongst collaborators than amongst members of the resistance. The historian Marnix Beyen sees this "de-ideologisation" as one of the most significant characteristics of the Flemish nationalist discourse (Beyen 2002: 116). In such an ideologically neutralized narrative, it is only the contingency of historical accident that determines whether people end up on the winning or on the losing side.

The counternarratives thus redefined the collaborators from perpetrators to victims, and the real trauma of the war from the German occupation to the Belgian "repression," a term which was also used by the authorities, but always with the rejoinder "of the collaboration" or "of the *incivisme*" (Beyen 2002: 117). The very fact that the counternarratives continued to use the term repression is evidence not just of a moral equivalence, but even of a moral reversal: since the crime is not interpreted as such, any punishment becomes unnecessary, unjust, and worse than the (supposed) crime, or even becomes the crime itself. Chief perpetrator of this crime was obviously the Belgian state, which the anti-Belgian Flemish nationalists had disliked and distrusted from before the war, a feeling that intensified into hatred for many so-called victims of the repression. It became commonplace in the counternarratives for the repression to be portrayed as a conspiracy against the Flemish Movement on the part of the anti-Flemish forces in the Belgian establishment, namely the left, the anticlerical liberals and of course the francophones. It would take until 1991 before this particular myth was finally debunked with the publication of Luc Huyse and Steven Dhondt's study on the collaboration and its repression, *Onverwerkt Verleden*. They concluded that the repression had indeed been used as a political instrument in power struggles between left and right, as illustrated in this chapter, but that there was no evidence that it had been intentionally used to destroy the Flemish Movement (Huyse and Dhondt 1991: 284). However, the counternarratives also frequently identified another perpetrator of the crime against the idealist Flemish nationalists, and this was, perhaps surprisingly, the Flemish people, or more precisely, the Flemish populace, the rabble. Betraying the elitist and authoritarian inclinations which had attracted them to Fascism in the first place, collaborators after the war reproached the Flemish populace for failing to show due recognition and respect for its natural leaders and treating them as criminals (Beyen 2002: 116; Van Doorslaer 2003: 232). This victim mentality, with both a defensive and an aggressive side, would continue to characterize the Flemish Movement for more than forty years after the end of the Second World War, and to this day, marks its (extreme) right wing.

In a country with as many divisions as Belgium already had before the Second World War, and the specific ideological and ethnolinguistic accents of the collaboration, the development of a national patriotic narrative of the war was always bound to be an uphill struggle. As in many other countries that had suffered under German occupation, the first port of call in the quest for both postwar legitimacy and the construction of a national narrative would be the resistance. However, the ethnolinguistic and, to a lesser degree, the ideological make-up of this resistance meant that the political unanimity required for the construction of a national narrative could not be found. Motivated by reasons of ideology and electoral mathematics, much complicated by the very specifically Belgian power struggle that was the Royal Question, the parties of the left aligned themselves with the resistance, whereas the newly-founded Christian Democrats, with their electoral strength based predominantly in Flanders, pursued a policy of appeasement and rehabilitation toward the collaboration. Rather than a unifying factor, the resistance and the repression of the collaboration became a source of political discord, with a specific Flemish counternarrative developing alongside a Belgian narrative that failed to unite the nation.

References

Benvindo, Bruno and Evert Peeters. 2011. *Scherven van de Oorlog: De Strijd om de Herinnering aan WO II*. Antwerpen: De Bezige Bij.

Beyen, Marnix. 2003. "'Zwart wordt van langs om meer de Vlaamsgezinde massa': Vlaamse Beeldvorming over Bezetting en Repressie, 1945–2000." In *Het Gewicht van het Oorlogsverleden*, ed. José Gotovitch and Chantal Kesteloot. Gent: Academia: 106–120.

Beyen, Marnix. 2004. "Der Kampf um das Leid," in *Mythen Der Nationen: 1945 – Arena der Erinnerungen*. 2 vols., ed. Monika Flacke. Berlin: Deutsches Historisches Museum. 67–88.

Bosman, Luc. 1990. "De Vlaamse Beweging na 1945: Actualisering van de Historische Dualiteit." In *Tussen Restauratie en Vernieuwing: Aspecten van de Naoorlogse Belgische Politiek (1944–1950)*, ed. Els Witte, Jean-Claude Burgelman, and Patrick Stouthuysen. 2nd edition. Brussels: VUB Press. 25–261.

Claes, Lode. 1983. *Het Verdrongen Verleden: de Collaboratie, haar Rechters en Geschiedschrijvers*. Beveren: Orbis en Orion.

Conway, Martin. 1997. "Justice in Post-War Belgium: Popular Passions and Political Realities." *Bijdragen tot de Eigentijdse Geschiedenis*. 2: 7–34.

Conway, Martin. 2012. *The Sorrows of Belgium: Liberation and Political Reconstruction, 1944–1947*. Oxford: Oxford University Press.

Deschouwer, Kris. 2006. "And the peace goes on? Consociational democracy and Belgian politics in the twenty-first century." *West European Politics*. 29 (5): 895–911.

Deschouwer, Kris. 2012. *The Politics of Belgium: Governing a Divided Society*. Second edition. London: Palgrave McMillan.

Derine, Raymond. 1983. *Repressie Zonder Maat of Einde? Terugblik of Collaboratie, Repressie en Amnestiestrijd*. Leuven: Davidsfonds.

De Schryver, Reginald and Bruno De Wever et al. 1998. *Nieuwe Encyclopedie van de Vlaamse Beweging*. 3 vols. Tielt: Lannoo.

De Wever, Bruno. 1992. "Het Vlaams-nationalisme tussen Democratie en Fascisme: De Ideologische Karakteristieken en de Sociale Achtergronden van het Vlaams Nationaal Verbond (1933–1945)." In *Herfsttij van de 20ste Eeuw: Extreem-rechts in Vlaanderen 1920–1990*, ed. Rudi van Doorslaer and José Gotovitch. Leuven: Kritak. 47–63.

De Wever, Bruno. 1994. *Greep naar de Macht: Vlaams-Nationalisme en Nieuwe Orde – Het VNV 1933–1945*. Tielt: Lannoo.

De Wever, Bruno. 1999. "Van Wierook tot Gaslucht: De Beeldvorming over de Vlaams-Nationalistische Collaboratie tijdens de Tweede Wereldoorlog." In *Docendo Discimus: Liber Amicorum Romain van Eenoo*, ed. Jan Art and Luc François. Gent: Academia: 607–614.

De Wever, Bruno. 2002. "Goede Belgen, Foute Vlamingen, Grijze Nederlanders." In *Collaboratie in Vlaanderen: Vergeven en Vergeten?*, ed. Eric Corijn. Antwerpen: Manteau. 49–61.

De Wever, Bruno. 2004. "Het Verzet in de Publieke Herinnering in Vlaanderen." In *Tegendruk: Geheime Pers tijdens de Tweede Wereldoorlog*, ed. Paule Verbruggen et al. Brussels: Amsab/ISG-Soma/Ceges. 17–31.

De Winter, Lieven, Marc Swyngedouw and Patrick Dumont. 2006. "Party system(s) and electoral behaviour in Belgium: from stability to balkanisation." *West European Politics*. 29 (5): 933–956.

Horvat, Stanislas. 2003. "Het verloop van de incivismeprocessen voor de militaire rechtbanken in 1944–1949." *SOMA Berichtenblad Dossier Repressie en Gerechtelijke Archieven.* 38: III–XXIII.

Huyse, Luc and Steven Dhondt. 1991. *Onverwerkt Verleden: Collaboratie en Repressie in België 1942–1952.* Leuven: Kritak.

Huyse, Luc. 2000. "The Criminal Justice System as a Political Actor in Regime Transitions: the Case of Belgium, 1944–1950." In *The Politics of Retribution in Europe: World War II and its Aftermath,* ed. István Deák, Jan T. Gros, and Tony Judt. Princeton: Princeton University Press. 157–172.

Huyse, Luc. 2003. *Over Politiek.* Leuven: Van Halewyck.

Lagrou, Pieter. 1995. "US Politics of Stabilization in Liberated Europe: the View from the American Embassy in Brussels, 1944–6." *European History Quarterly* 25 (2): 209–246.

Lagrou, Pieter. 1997. "Welk Vaderland voor de Vaderlandslievende Verenigingen? Oorlogsslachtoffers en verzetsveteranen en de nationale kwestie, 1945–1958." *Bijdragen tot de Eigentijdse Geschiedenis* 3: 143–161.

Lagrou, Pieter. 2000. *The Legacy of Nazi Occupation: Patriotic Memory and National Recovery in Western Europe, 1945–1965.* Cambridge: Cambridge University Press.

Lebow, Richard. 2006. "The memory of politics in postwar Europe." In *The Politics of Memory in Postwar Europe,* ed. Richard Lebow, Wulf Kansteiner, and Claudio Fogu. Durham and London: Duke University Press. 1–39.

Peters, B. Guy. 2006. "Consociationalism, corruption and chocolate: Belgian exceptionalism." *West European Politics* 29 (5): 1079–1092.

Rousso, Henry. 1987. *Le Syndrome de Vichy de 1944 à nos Jours.* Paris: Seuil.

Sanders, Luk and Carl Devos et al. 2008. *Politieke Ideologieën in Vlaanderen.* Antwerpen: Standaard.

Seberechts, Frank. 1992. "Beeldvorming over Collaboratie en Repressie bij de naoorlogse Vlaams-nationalisten." In *Herfsttij van de 20ste Eeuw: Extreemrechts in Vlaanderen 1920–1990,* ed. Rudi van Doorslaer and José Gotovitch. Leuven: Kritak. 65–82.

Thomassen, Bjørn. 2009. "The Uses and Meanings of Liminality," *International Political Anthropology.* 2 (1): 5–27.

Van den Wijngaert, Mark, Michel Dumoulin and Vincent Dujardin. 2001. *Een Koningsdrama: De Biografie van Leopold III.* Antwerpen: Manteau.

Van den Wijngaert, Mark and Vincent Dujardin. 2006. *België Zonder Koning: 1940–1950: De Tien Jaar dat België Geen Koning Had.* Tielt: Lannoo.

Van den Wijngaert, Mark et al. 2004. *België tijdens de Tweede Wereldoorlog.* Antwerpen: Standaard.

Van den Wijngaert, Mark et al. 2006. *België, een Land in Crisis 1913–1950.* Antwerpen: Standaard.

Van der Heijden, Chris. 2001. *Grijs Verleden: Nederland en de Tweede Wereldoorlog.* Amsterdam: Olympus.

Van Causenbroeck, Bernard. 1997. *Herman Vos: Van Vlaams-Nationalisme naar Socialisme.* Antwerpen: Hadewijch.

Van Doorslaer, Rudi. 2003. "Gebruikt Verleden: de Politieke Nalatenschap van de Tweede Wereldoorlog in België, 1945–2000." In *Geschiedenis Maken: Liber*

Amicorum Herman Balthazar, ed. Gita Deneckere and Bruno De Wever. Gent: Tijdsbeeld. 227–249.

Verhoeyen, Etienne. 1993. *België Bezet 1940–1944: Een Synthese*. Brussel: BRTN.

Witte, Els and Harry Van Velthoven. 1999. *Language and Politics: The Situation in Belgium in an Historical Perspective*. Brussels: VUB University Press.

Wouters, Nico. 2004. *Oorlogsburgemeesters 40/44: Lokaal Bestuur en Collaboratie in België*. Tielt: Lannoo.

6

L'Histoire bling-bling—
Nicolas Sarkozy and the
Historians

Paul Smith

In the call for papers for the conference on which this present volume is based, the organizers cited an unnamed British Conservative politician who described the UK Independence Party's use of Winston Churchill in its campaign for the 2009 European parliamentary elections as "inaccurate, thoroughly de-contextualized and historically distorting." It is difficult to think of a better way to describe Nicolas Sarkozy's approach to French history, both before and during his term as president. It has been said of Sarkozy that no president before him provoked such violent reaction—not just disapproval or dislike but visceral animus. And that even goes for the Academy, for one of the sideshows of the *bling-bling* presidency, was the state of more or less open war between Sarkozy and his entourage on the one hand and *les historiens*, academic historians in general, but more specifically the *Comité de Vigilance face aux Usages publics de l'Histoire* (CVUH), a group founded in 2005 by Philippe Noiriel, Nicolas Offenstadt, and Michèle Riot-Sarcey and whose title itself was an echo of *Comité de vigilance intellectuelle antifasciste* of the 1930s, with very obvious connotations. Initially, the CVUH was set up in response to legislation (the law of the 23 February 2005) that represented an official response to the insidious creep of postcolonialism into French education, with a fourth article that instructed *enseignants* (high school teachers and university professors) to teach their students about the positive effects of French colonialism—as if the myth of the *mission civilisatrice* (civilizing mission), for which the colonized peoples are assumed to remain naturally grateful, were not still the dominant discourse in France. The committee's stated aim was to campaign against the instrumentalization of history for political ends. The candidature and presidency of Sarkozy provided matter enough to keep them busy.

Le Roman National

It would be foolish to suggest that any one political culture is more closely tied than another to its own history. Nevertheless, it would also be difficult to find one that makes more ready use of history, or perhaps one might say *mythologies* in Roland Barthes's sense of the word, as a form of historical-cultural shorthand, than France. One anecdotal example will have to suffice here. In May 2009, the author attended a conference at the Maison Française in Oxford, examining relations between presidents and prime ministers in Fifth Republic France (1958 to the present). There, the eminent political commentator Pascal Perrineau, director of CEVIPOF, the center for political research at the Institut de Sciences-Politiques in Paris and a regular contributor to *Le Figaro*, examined the first two years of the Sarkozy presidency by means of a comparison then popular between Sarkozy and Napoleon Bonaparte. Perrineau explored, in particular, the thesis behind Alain Duhamel's *La Marche consulaire*, a book that draws a lengthy comparison between the first two years of *sarkozysme* and the Consular period of the First Republic (1799–1804). Part of the wider popularity of the comparison lay in being able to joke about Napoleon Bonaparte as *Napoléon le Grand* (in French great, but also possibly tall), Napoleon III as *Napoléon le Petit* (the small), and Sarkozy as *Napoléon le Très Petit* (the very small). Such was its appeal to the popular imagination that the writer Patrick Rambuad and illustrator Olivier Grojnowski were able to turn every year of the Sarkozy presidency into a hardback comic-book chronicle, drawn in Consular and Empire style (Rambaud and Grojnowski 2012). Perrineau's paper was both elegant and beguiling, illustrating the French penchant to use historic parallels to explain modern phenomena, in this instance Sarkozian hyperpresidentialism—the propensity to intervene in all levels of government and to be (or seem to be) everywhere. After the paper, during questions, Andrew Knapp, professor of French politics at the University of Reading (UK), remarked that it was a "very French" way of looking at things. If, as seemed likely even back then, David Cameron were to be asked by Her Majesty to form the next government, Knapp doubted if anyone in Britain would draw a serious comparison between Cameron and Pitt the Younger.

After two years in power, Sarkozy had plummeted from very respectable approval ratings in the summer following his election, to a point so low that his prime minister, François Fillon, was scoring better, something never seen before under the Fifth Republic. Elected with 53 percent of the vote in the run-off election against Ségolène Royal, in the summer of 2007 Sarkozy enjoyed an approval rating of very nearly 70 percent. By May 2009 it was barely 40 percent, while the rather austere Fillon was at 50 percent. Sarkozy's gaudy gaucheness antagonized many electors, who quickly tired of his omnipresence and the *président bling-bling*, a reference to his magpie-like attraction to all that glisters, but also to a certain superficiality and lack of gravity, a reputation not always deserved, it should be said, as Sarkozy's handling of the crisis in Georgia illustrated. Rightly or wrongly, the French came to believe that they had installed a nouveau-riche parvenu in the Elysée Palace. In 2012, and at the risk of stretching the historical analogy, they were determined not to allow the Consulate to become the Empire.

While for the general public, the (misborrowed) expression *bling-bling* referred to Sarkozy's taste for expensive watches, the glamorous lifestyle, and the wider *pipolisation* of politics (the process by which politicians began to be treated and act like celebrities, with Sarkozy's own private life being a stand-out example), for historians it became a shorthand for the pathological determination on the part of Sarkozy and his advisors to seize upon the "shining" episodes of French history and ignore the less palatable aspects, to strip historical figures of their context and transform them in turn into historical celebrities. It involved, moreover, an attempt to intervene directly and impose a particular vision of French history into the classroom. It signaled a return to what the French call *le récit/le roman national*. Literally, this translates as "the national story," but signifies a view of French history, bequeathed by the late nineteenth century and the Third Republic, that tells the tale of the immanent and predestined *France éternelle*, from the valiant though ultimately doomed Gauls to the present, a France whose values are good, universal, worth protecting and exporting. De Gaulle was a great advocate of the *roman national*, believing that the French were never stronger than when they forgot their partisan quarrels and remembered what made them great. While popular historians have continued to peddle the *roman national*, their academic counterparts abandoned the notion long ago. Gone are the days, for example, where every French child's history course began with the lesson entitled "Our ancestors, the Gauls," a fact that causes a great deal of chagrin on the right. On 27 August 2011, the ferociously pro-Sarkozy *Le Figaro* published a long and vigorous attack in its Saturday magazine supplement on how teachers and the writers of history primers were failing to teach "your" children the fundamentals and destroying the collective memory, under the unambiguous title: "They are killing the history of France." For Sarkozy, so committed to reviving something called national identity that he even created a ministry dedicated to it, the *roman national* provided the historical underpinning of his presidential campaign, especially given his desire to reach out not only to traditional Gaullist voters but also to grab back from the far right-wing National Front, electors disaffected by the Chirac years.

Le Président-Historien

Ever since de Gaulle set the tone with his "certain idea" that France was not France without rank and grandeur, the French have expected presidents to interpret their history for them, to have something to say about history that extends beyond simple acts of representation in commemoration or celebration. De Gaulle, projecting himself as the "man of destiny," had a particular and peculiar relationship with it. In his writings and in the published versions of his speeches, *Histoire* is always capitalized. His dauphin and successor Georges Pompidou (1969–1974) was less given to acts of grandiose verbosity, but during his time as prime minister under de Gaulle (1962–1968) made regular use of the past, particularly the shortcomings of the Third and Fourth Republics (1870–1940 and 1946–1958), in his verbal duels with the parliamentary opposition. Valéry Giscard d'Estaing (1974–1981), the first non-Gaullist president of the Fifth Republic, though still on the right, was essentially a technocrat and campaigned on the themes of youth (his own) and modernity, into which appeals to history did not fit so easily. Giscard made the mistake, however, of slowing down the pace and changing some of the more bloodthirsty lyrics of the *Marseillaise* and also abolishing the public holiday to mark Victory in Europe. The Socialist François Mitterrand (1981–1995) reversed those decisions and, on the day of his inauguration, after a speech at the Elysée Palace in which he called his election "the victory of hope" and name-checked Jean Jaurès, Léon Blum, and the Popular Front, went to the Pantheon, where the remains of the great men and women of the Republic are kept, in a conscious act of reconnection with mythological figures of the French left: Victor Schœlcher (whose name is a general shorthand for the Abolition of Slavery), Jean Jaurès, and Jean Moulin. The inclusion of Moulin was more controversial, but it was intended to remind the French, lest they had forgotten, of the founder of the National Council of the Resistance, whose program had framed postwar political and social consensus and that there was more to the Resistance than de Gaulle, the call of 18 June 1940 and all that. Like de Gaulle, Mitterrand claimed to be a history lover. He once commented that the difference between himself and his social-democrat rival Michel Rocard was that while he read the work of Fernand Braudel, author of a monumental history of the Mediterranean and, perhaps more significantly, *The Identity of France*, Rocard read the sociologist Alain Touraine. What Mitterrand meant was that he possessed "a certain idea" of France as well, though perhaps not the same one as de Gaulle, while Rocard was too much of a technocrat. In any case, Mitterrand did not mean it as a compliment. The pinnacle of Mitterrand's achievement, in the field of memory, however, was the bicentenary celebration of the French Revolution in 1989.

The *bicentennaire* was a high-water mark in more than one sense. By happy accident it fell, of course, in the year that Communism collapsed across Eastern Europe. The tearing aside of the Iron Curtain and the collapse of the Berlin Wall presaged a period of reconfiguration in Europe from which France would, in fact, never quite recover. With the reunification of Germany, the balance of power and future EU development shifted perceptibly eastward. Just as the postwar certainties began to dissolve, so the French found themselves increasingly confronted with some unexpected and uncomfortable truths about the Second World War and with the official version of events, wherein the French had been victims of German occupation, Nazi oppression, and a small handful of Vichy collaborationists. Postwar *épuration* had been very limited and there was no process of de-Vichyfication. Based on work in German archives, Robert Paxton's *Vichy France—Old Guard and New Order*, published in 1972 and in its translated version in France a year later, had broken new ground in the field and indicated the degree to which Pétain's regime acted on its own initiative. The work was acclaimed in France as well as in the English-speaking world, but even if historians knew of its message and of Henri Amouroux's *Quarante million de pétainistes* (1977), which pointed out that in 1940, most people in France accepted the Marshal's seizure of power, official discourse still pushed the Gaullian line that Vichy was an aberration in the republican continuum and that what happened during the Occupation happened under duress. In 1987, Henry Rousso put his finger right on the sore spot with *Le syndrome de Vichy de 1944 à 198 . . .*, though public awareness of what hitherto seemed like obscure academic arguments was really awakened to the question, inadvertently, by Jean-Marie Le Pen, the leader of the far-right National Front (FN) who, in September 1987, declared that the gas chambers were merely a detail in the general history of the Second World War. The furor generated opened the door to a much wider and very public debate about France, Vichy, the Occupation and the Holocaust than anyone could have imagined. Mitterrand's own personal history and his Vichy past had never been a state secret, but neither had they been much discussed in public, until the publication in 1994, of Pierre Péan's *Une jeunesse francaise*, which explored Mitterrand's career as a young law student, member of various far-right organizations in the late 1930s, his career under Vichy and then his switch to the Resistance. That Mitterrand maintained an inscrutable silence on the matter and also appeared to block all attempts to try Maurice Papon for crimes against humanity, committed when he had been a senior civil servant in the department of the Gironde (Bordeaux) during the Second World War, only made matters murkier.

Mitterrand's successor, Jacques Chirac (1995–2007), was probably the least Gaullian of France's Gaullist presidents and wore his knowledge of history less obtrusively on his sleeve. His presidency nevertheless began with an act that outstripped all Mitterrand's bread and circuses for its deeper significance. Already in 1986, under his stewardship as mayor of Paris, Chirac had overseen the creation of a Place des Martyrs Juifs du Vélodrôme d'Hiver, near the site of the round up of Parisian Jews in 1942. On 16 July 1995, like his predecessor he attended a ceremony at the Vél d'Hiv to remember the victims. But this time, Chirac did something that none of his predecessors had ever done when he recognized the responsibility of the French state for the fate of the victims. At a stroke, Chirac reversed fifty years of orthodoxy and expressed regret and *repentance* for the behavior of the French state machinery. Less dramatically, though no less significantly, also under Chirac, the French army finally issued an apology for its treatment of Captain Alfred Dreyfus and the man at the center of France's best known *cause célébre* was granted a statue of his own.

Hypermnesia

The Chirac years coincided with a gathering pace in the commemoration of memory, what has been described as a process of hypermnesia (Wolf 2011: 9), a reflection of hypermodernity's obsession with remembering the past (Lipovetsky 2004: 82–9; Wieviorka 2010). *Repentance*, apologizing for the past, became acceptable, fashionable even, though there were limits. In 2005 a political storm blew up over government legislation aimed, principally, at recognizing the role of the *harkis*, Muslim soldiers who fought in the French army during the Algerian war. Chirac had fought in Algeria—one of the more emotive arguments he deployed against intervention in Iraq in 2003 was based on his own experience of war in North Africa, experience he pointedly underlined neither Tony Blair nor George W. Bush had ever had. The bill's principal concern was to provide pension rights for the *harkis*. Article four, however, instructed teachers to underline the positive impact of French colonial rule, especially in North Africa. The response among French teachers and lecturers, left-wing voters almost to a man and woman, to say nothing of a section of France's North African immigrant population, first, second, or third generation, can be guessed at. But on the other side of the argument, on the far-right, opposition signified an unacceptable weakening of French moral fiber—just a few months, it will be recalled, before the referendum on the European constitution, a document cast by some as the end of sovereignty and an open door to neoliberal, multinational globalization at the expense of French traditions and values. Intended to give Chirac a much-needed fillip to carry him through to 2007, the referendum was actually unnecessary—it passed through parliament without a hitch and need not have been put to the public. The "no" vote was an unnecessary disaster and left Chirac a lame duck. Before the year's end, rioting broke out in France's more difficult suburbs, especially, though not exclusively those with high immigrant populations. The *fracture sociale*, the broken society that Chirac had promised to mend in his election campaign in 1995, was far from fixed. Into the arena rode his most forthright and robust minister: Nicolas Sarkozy, famously armed with his brand name high-pressure hose (the Kärcher), to clean out the *racaille* (scum).

Sarkozy and Mandel

Few French in 2005 would have thought of Sarkozy as a "History-Man" in the mold of a de Gaulle or a Mitterrand and his reinvention as the *président-historien* came rather late in the day. To be sure, in 1994 he published a political biography of Georges Mandel. That a politician would choose to write a historical biography is not unique to France, but Sarkozy was then an ambitious man who lacked the public profile and weight of right-wing rivals of his generation. To correct that, he set about writing, or perhaps having written for him, a biography of Mandel. According to rumor, the book was in fact largely written by Roger Karoutchi, historian, senator, and one of Sarkozy's closest political circle in the department of Hauts-de-Seine. It has also been suggested that sections of the book resemble very closely another work on Mandel, published twenty-five years earlier. Briefly, Mandel (born Louis Georges Rothschild) was one of a small group of brilliant young men who cut their political teeth during the Dreyfus Affair and emerged as part of Georges Clemenceau's small entourage during the last years of the First World War. Unlike Clemenceau, whose political career had begun among the republican opposition to the Second Empire (1852–1870) and for whom the terms right and left denoted monarchy and republic, Mandel was perfectly at ease—*décomplexé* is the modern French term—with the idea of being a man of the republican right: seeking to build on the wartime *Union sacrée* to bring an end to the standoff between the secular Republic and French Catholics exacerbated by the Dreyfus Affair and the Separation of Church and State (1905), and to introduce a dose of discipline, of authority even, to France's political institutions in the interwar period, in exchange for an end to the endemic instability of the Third Republic. In this regard Mandel had much in common with André Tardieu and Pierre Laval. The regime failed to reform itself and remained unstable and despite his talent and his reputation, Mandel never fulfilled his promise. Unlike other critics of the Republic, however, he rejected Vichy. Minister of the interior in the last republican government of 1940 under Paul Reynaud and alongside de Gaulle, he was unswerving in the pursuit of defeatists on both the far-left and the far-right and led the small group of ministers opposed to the appointment of Pétain, to the armistice and to the creation of the Vichy state. Imprisoned for life in 1941, in July 1944 he was handed over by the German authorities to the French *milice*, who executed him in reprisal for the assassination by the Resistance of Vichy propaganda minister, Philippe Henriot. One does not need to labor the reasons behind the choice of such a political hero by the son of an immigrant whose brilliance also seemed to be misunderstood or undervalued—and one of the few figures on the right of French politics who was perfectly happy to call himself a man *de la droite*. In 1994 Sarkozy was minister for the budget and official spokesman for the Balladur government. A year later he backed the wrong right-wing candidate in the presidential election (Balladur against Chirac), but unlike Mandel, was able to bounce back.

Sarkozy reemerged by sheer force of character. Chirac never forgave him for supporting Balladur in 1995, but Sarkozy's forthright and vigorous contribution to the 2002 victory over Jean-Marie Le Pen in the run-off election, where he tackled Le Pen head-on over immigration and law and order, made his appointment to the government unavoidable. Sarkozy himself hoped to become prime minister, but political need does not equal forgiveness. Instead, Chirac made him minister of the interior. On his appointment Sarkozy declared himself *premier flic de France* (no.1 cop), a nickname first given to Clemenceau, when he had been prime minister and interior minister between 1906 and 1909, years of notable social unrest.

Désaffiliation

This *prima facie* act of plagiarism aside, however, Sarkozy had not seemed particularly concerned to tackle the historical themes associated with French *présidentiables* (candidates for election). Not, at least until late 2005, when it was announced that neither Chirac, nor his prime minister (and Sarkozy's archrival) Dominique de Villepin would attend events to commemorate the two-hundredth anniversary of the Battle of Austerlitz. It seemed an odd, but in many ways laudable decision. Austerlitz is recalled in French culture as a miraculous victory: in everyday French, *le soleil d'Austerlitz*, literally the sun or the dawn of Austerlitz, signifies an unlikely turning point when victory is snatched from the jaws of defeat. Its counterpart, of course, lies in the use of the retreat across the Berezina in 1812 as a synonym for a catastrophe of epic proportion (for example after the victory of the "no" camp in the 2005 referendum). In any case, Sarkozy was handed a stick with which to beat both men, and from that point he did not let it go. He was very ably assisted in his task by the man who became his principal *plume* or speechwriter, Henri Guaino.

A graduate of the Ecole normale supérieure and high-ranking civil servant, Guaino was what is known as a *gaulliste social*. He was politically close to Philippe Séguin, who in the late 1980s and early 1990s had posed a serious challenge to Chirac as leader of the neo-Gaullist *Rassemblement pour la République* (RPR). In 1995, Séguin rallied to Chirac and Guaino is credited as one of the inventors of the slogan of *la fracture sociale*—the broken society, around which Chirac based his successful campaign against fourteen years of *mitterrandisme* and two years of Balladur. After the election, Guaino hoped to be rewarded with a post within the Elysée, but Chirac regarded him as too intellectual and inflexible and appointed him instead to the Planning Commission, a job he then lost when the left won the 1997 general election. He thus had a grudge, and in January 2006, in the aftermath of the Austerlitz row, Guaino approached Sarkozy and warned him that, "You won't get elected just by being a liberal" (Nay 2012: 124). By this, he meant that if Sarkozy wanted, in the first place to win the nomination of his own *Union pour un Mouvement Populaire* (UMP) party and then see off the challenge from the left, he would need to pin down the Gaullist vote and reach out to disaffected voters susceptible to Le Pen's unlikely charms. Sarkozy also had to be mindful that he had supported the "yes" vote over the European constitution and needed, therefore, to reestablish his credentials among Eurosceptic *souverainiste* voters. Above all, if the candidate wanted to look like a president, then he would need some historical gravitas in order to sound like one. Profoundly at odds with academic historians, with the culture of *repentance* and the demise of the *roman national*, Guaino argued that if the candidate was serious about pursuing the theme of national identity as a means of reassuring French voters across the political spectrum that they had nothing to fear from liberal economics and globalization, then he would need to anchor his campaign rhetoric in the realms of memory that they could understand. Sarkozy accepted Guaino's arguments and his help. In fact, never has a presidential candidate's campaign been so drenched in historical references as the campaign Sarkozy set out upon: the shift to historical hypermnesia already evident under Chirac slipped effortlessly into top gear with Sarkozy. In such times, it seems appropriate that the French should have chosen a president who suffered (or benefitted) from clinical hypermnesia (Nay 2012: 78). At times it was all Sarkozy's campaign managers could do to rein in Guaino's flights of rhetorical fancy.

Guaino's thought was guided by *deux Charles*: Charles de Gaulle and Charles Péguy (Nay 2012: 123). Born in 1873, Péguy was a poet and essayist who started out as a disciple of the socialism of Jean Jaurès, before veering toward a Catholic, nationalist point of view. He died on the Front, on the eve of the Battle of the Marne, on 4 September 1914. A pseudo Péguyan synthesis would form the foundation of Guaino and thus of Sarkozy's interpretation of French history. At the core of Guaino's approach lay the notion of *désaffiliation*, of disconnecting left and right from their separate historical traditions and building a new consensus, based on the best of French history as the core of *sarkozysme*, a political project that like so many others claimed to be neither right nor left, but the mythical third way. Thus, in the course of the election campaign, Sarkozy would make repeated use of the phrase "My France is the France of . . ." Between September 2006 and May 2007, he cited de Gaulle ninety-two times in his speeches and Jules Ferry fifty-eight, principally as shorthand for secular, republican education, though also deployable with reference to the civilizing mission of French colonization. The unlikely top of the hit parade, however, was the socialist Jean Jaurès, mentioned ninety-seven times, with Léon Blum enjoying fifty hits (De Cock 2008: 14). Now, while it might be argued that even de Gaulle had a leftist side to him—the claim has even been made that he wanted, after the end of the war, to try to create a French *travailliste* or labor party—the General never tried to claim Jaurès as a posthumous recruit to Gaullism and had very few tender words for Blum, whose lack of decisiveness he found infuriating. Sarkozy, in contrast, manipulated both to justify his opposition to the thirty-five-hour working week and greater freedom of movement among workers.

On the face of it, there is nothing inherently wrong in attempting to de-ghettoize figures and events in history, to break down distinctions of class, race, or political partisanship and attempt to construct a consensus of a shared history. Sarkozy insisted very strongly that he would not tolerate *communautarisme*, the breakdown of the one and indivisible France into separate communities, and he extended this into the telling of French history. It is quite another matter, however, to extract events and people from their context and to claim, for example, that Jaurès and Blum would have been in favor of allowing employees to work more than their allotted thirty-five hours per week as tax-free overtime. Sarkozy's purpose was not to establish a consensus in any case, but to disrupt the line of historical continuity his Socialist opponents traced back to Jaurès, through Blum, himself employed as shorthand for the Popular Front, the forty-hour week and paid holidays. In fact, left-wing rhetoric of the immediate prewar period gave plenty of hostages to fortune, from Communist Maurice Thorez's instruction to the workers in the summer of 1936 that one had to know when to end a strike (*Il faut savoir terminer une grève*), or the Radical premier Edouard Daladier's promise two years later that France would be put back to work (*Il faut remettre la France au travail*), a promise repeated more than once by the triumphant candidate of 2007. But Sarkozy also knew that the collapse of the French Communist Party (PCF) in the

1980s had led to a large slice of the working class electorate defecting not to the Socialists but to the National Front. Paradoxically, in order to reach this electorate, Sarkozy even felt obliged to revive the specter of class struggle, a term not heard in French politics beyond the far-left for nearly three decades.

La Lettre de Guy Môquet

Born in 1955, Sarkozy was the first president of the Fifth Republic who had not lived through the Occupation and might have chosen to let the Second World War alone altogether. He chose, spectacularly, not to. In his presidential campaign in 2007 (and for 2012 for that matter), Sarkozy placed a great deal of emphasis on youth and it was at the annual congress of the UMP youth movement, in early September 2006, that he announced his intention, if elected, that every year, on or close to 22 October, high school students would fall silent and listen while a classmate read out the letter written by Guy Môquet to his mother on the eve of his execution by a German firing squad. (Môquet was executed on 22 October 1941). The idea was Guaino's, but Sarkozy readily bought into the notion of youthful sacrifice in the name of resistance and love of country. And this irrespective of the fact that Môquet was shot not for his resistance activities, but for his political affiliations. He was a Communist and the son of a former Communist deputy, elected under the Popular Front in 1936. Now, the Molotov-Ribbentrop pact placed the PCF in a highly ambivalent position with regard to Nazi Germany between 1939 and 1941. The resistance activity that Môquet was involved in before his arrest in October 1940 was aimed principally against the Vichy regime, not the invader. Sarkozy's aim was twofold: on the one hand to instrumentalize Môquet's youthful revolt against the old guard of Vichy (meaning Chirac and his entourage). On the other, and one should not forget Sarkozy's position as interior minister during the French riots of November 2005, he invited French youth to remember their duty toward the *patrie*, the Fatherland. Revelling in the play on words, Sarkozy insisted that through his act of sacrifice, Môquet showed that love of *patrie* far outweighed commitment to a party. That Môquet makes no reference to *patrie* in his letter, only to his *petite maman chérie* (my darling mother), was neither here nor there. Whatever Môquet's motives, he did not sacrifice himself either for his party or his Fatherland. He was a prisoner handed over by the Vichy authorities to the Germans and shot in reprisal for the assassination

132

of a senior Wehrmacht officer. That is not to belittle the tragedy of Môquet's death, nor the undeniable pathos of the letter.

If the notion that a president could impose this sort of ceremony on the education system seems excessively interventionist, it should be said that French teachers are perfectly used to responding to and acting upon directives and instructions issued by the education ministry. It is a tradition inherited from the nineteenth century, and everyone knows the apocryphal tale of the education minister who boasted to Napoleon III that he could look at his watch at any moment of the day and know exactly what was being taught in any classroom. In 1883, in the wake of the secularization of French education, Jules Ferry wrote a long letter to all teachers giving them very clear instructions regarding their responsibility to inculcate in their charges good republican values and morals with which no honest *père de famille* might find fault. Sarkozy's decree regarding Môquet's letter nevertheless raised more than simple misgivings, but the profession felt he had gone too far when, in 2008, Sarkozy proposed that a program should be introduced whereby schoolchildren aged ten and eleven should "adopt" a child victim of the deportation. The public generally concurred with the view expressed by Auschwitz survivor and former minister Simone Veil that this placed too heavy a burden on young children (Wieviorka 2010: 270). There were other ways to teach and to commemorate the Shoah. The plan was quietly shelved.

Sarkozy's willingness to invent, to reinvent or to appropriate the myths and legends of the Second World War was not limited to individuals. In the week leading up to second-round run-off election on 6 May 2007, even before he had been elected president, in a burst of hyperactive hypermnesia, Sarkozy conducted a series of carefully choreographed public meetings and displays designed to make him look more presidential than his rival, Ségolène Royal, and ready to assume the mantle not of Chirac, but of de Gaulle. Thus, there were visits to all the holy sites of remembrance: to Colombey, the General's country home and last resting place; to Mont Saint-Michel; and to Verdun, an ambiguous choice given its associations not just with stoic defense and sacrifice, but also with Pétain. The last stop on the tour was a rather odd performance. It took place on 4 May 2007, at the Plateau des Glières. Situated in the Haute-Savoie Alpine region of France, the plateau had been taken over by the Secret Army resistance movement, an organization comprised very largely of former soldiers demobilized in 1940. From 1943, the Vichy authorities had begun to tighten their grip in the area, leading to an expansion in the numbers of resistants taking refuge on the plateau. Reinforced by arms drops and believing the Allied landing imminent, the Resistance rose in February 1944. The rising was a heroic failure. Vichy forces were unable to take the plateau, but at the end of March the Germans threw massive land and air forces at the problem. Nevertheless, Glières furnished de Gaulle with a demonstration to the Allies that the French were ready and willing to make the ultimate sacrifices for their liberation. A memorial was built at Glières in the 1970s, largely through the efforts of survivors and veterans organizations, though it was officially opened, in 1973, by former culture minister André Malraux as a national monument. Now, in 2007, Sarkozy chose to renationalize it as a *lieu de mémoire* (site of memory). After a speech revisiting the usual themes—youth, the unity in diversity of the Resistance—he set off alone, a solitary figure disappearing enigmatically into the distance like a penitent following the way of the cross and promised to return every year.

Herein lay the kernel of the dispute between Sarkozy and his supporters on the one hand (including some really quite eminent popular historians such as Max Gallo and Jean Tulard) and the CVUH on the other. For his supporters, Sarkozy was doing no more than reviving and reasserting French identity and sense of difference after two decades in which these had taken something of a battering, both in the wider world in terms of French prestige and rank and from within, from academics focused on micro-histories or even a form of historical *communautarisme*: worse still for the authors of *Le Figaro*'s report, French schoolchildren where learning about "extra-European" cultures. For his opponents, however, the choices were too selective and too obviously political and in the context of the Second World War and the Resistance, oversimplified to the point of being disfigured. As Jean-Marie Guillon explained, in the entry on the Resistance in the CVUH's handbook/manifesto *Comment Nicolas Sarkozy écrit l'histoire de France*:

> The Resistance, then, according to Nicolas Sarkozy, comes straight out of Gaullian legend, with a few sanitised Communist touches. It comprises great heroic figures who have taken their places in the syncretised pantheon of France the Eternal, starting with Vercingetorix [leader of the Gaulish revolt against Caesar]. It can be distilled into a very simple formula. De Gaulle = the Resistance = France; a tortured France, but one united by de Gaulle. (De Cock 2008: 161–2)

But, as Guillon goes on to explain, Sarkozy's Resistance is peopled by a very select crew: de Gaulle of course, Môquet, Mandel, a handful of others. And yet, perhaps the most famous of all Resistance faces, Jean Moulin, he of the trilby and scarf, sent back into France to organize the Resistance, betrayed, captured, and tortured by Klaus Barbie, who then died either by his own hand or was beaten to death by Barbie, is reduced merely to an agent of General de Gaulle. That it was Moulin's genius that succeeded in spite of his capture of pulling together a myriad of movements and organizations separated by ideology and geography into the National Council of the Resistance in the first place, was overlooked. The significance of the 1944 program of the National Council, upon which the entire postwar consensus for reconstruction was founded, was ignored completely, not least because Sarkozy aimed to dismantle many of its provisions. No consideration was given to the Resistance opposition to personalized power, whether wielded by Pétain or de Gaulle. Plurality and diversity are smoothed over and the revolutionary potential of the Resistance is pushed aside.

On several occasions Sarkozy quoted Napoleon, who is reputed to have said, though at a date no one can verify: *De Clovis au Comité public de salut, j'assume tout*: from Clovis, who united the Frankish kingdoms in around the year 500 and is considered the founder of France, to the murderous regime of the Committee of Public Safety, Sarkozy accepted the whole of French history, warts and all. Well, obviously not.

References

Amouroux, Henri. 1977. *Quarante million de pétainistes*. Paris: Robert Laffont.

Badiou, Alain. 2007. *De quoi Sarkozy est-il le nom?* Paris: Lignes.

Buisson, Jean-Christophe and Jean Sévillia. 2011. "C'est l'histoire de France qu'on assassin." *Le Figaro Magazine*, 27 August: 38–49

De Cock, Laurence, Fanny Madeline, Nicolas Offenstadt, and Sophie Wahnich, eds. 2008. *Comment Nicolas Sarkozy écrit l'histoire de France*. Marseille: Agone.

Duhamel, Alain. 2009. *La marche consulaire*. Paris: Plon.

Lipovetsky, Gilles, with Sébastien Charles. 2004. *Les Temps hypermodernes*, Paris: Grasset.

Nay, Catherine. 2012. *L'Impétueux. Tourments, tourmentes et tempêtes*. Paris: Grasset.

Offenstadt, Nicolas. 2009. *L'Histoire bling-bling. Le retour du roman national*. Paris: Editions Stock.

Paxton, Robert O. 1972. *Vichy France. Old Guard and New Order 1940–1944*. New York: Columbia University Press.

Péan, Pierre. 1994. *Une jeunesse française. François Mitterrand 1937–1944*. Paris: Fayard.

Rambaud, Patrick and Olivier Grojnowksi. 5 volumes, 2007–2012. *Les chroniques du règne de Nicolas Ier*. Paris: Grasset.

Rousso, Henry. 1987. *Le syndrome de Vichy de 1944 à 198. . . .* Paris: Seuil.

Sarkozy, Nicolas. 1994. *Georges Mandel, le moine de la politique.* Paris: Fayard.

Wieviorka, Olivier. 2010. *La Mémoire désunie. Le souvenir politique des années sombres, de la Libération à nos jours.* Paris: Seuil.

Wolf, Nelly, ed. 2011. *Amnésies françaises à l'époque gaullienne (1958–1981). Littérature, cinéma, presse, politique.* Paris: Classiques Garnier.

7

The Pasts of the Present: World War II Memories and the Construction of Political Legitimacy in Post–Cold War Italy

Bjørn Thomassen and Rosario Forlenza

In this chapter we want to discuss the particular case of Italy and how World War II in the postwar period came to provide the ground for political legitimacy. However, this ground was interpreted very differently by Catholics and Communists, leading to the notion of a divided nation. Furthermore, the postwar interpretation of the Resistance movement as the foundation of nationhood and democracy was not in congruence with WWII memories among larger segments of the Italian population. Underneath the postwar consensus, therefore, one could find antagonistic notions of the foundations of political legitimacy and national identity. In particular, the paper focuses on how WWII memories were taken up again at the demise of the Cold War, starting a new round of debates that have helped shape Italian political and cultural life during the last two decades. WWII debates have been running high in Europe since the 1990s. However, within a Western European perspective, nowhere as in Italy did the debates question the very existence of the nation as a democratic regime. We will try to explain why this is so. The material discussed consists of political and intellectual controversies over World War II events as these unfolded in the 1990s, with short references also to popular films and books released in the 1990s that stirred heated public debates. We end by indicating the relevance of the Italian case for European debates.

Theoretical Approach: On Narratives, Symbols, and Meaning-Formation in Liminality

Before moving on to the analysis of Italian WWII memories, we would briefly like to make explicit our theoretical approach to the role of memory and myth-making, and to the fundamental importance of periods of political transition for the establishment of political legitimacy. The theoretical inspiration for the analysis offered relies on our understanding of two key concepts, namely *narrative* and meaning-formation in *liminality*. Narrative, as used here, is not a poetic optional extra to the lives we live. In order to have a sense of who we are, we have to have a notion of how we have become, and of where we are going (Taylor 1989: 47). Narrative meaning underlies the structuring of human time, and as such there can be neither personal nor collective identities without it. Narratives are per definition selective: they involve events to the extent that these become registered as meaningful and signifying (Knudsen 1989). Narratives can be competitive and socially divisive; they can also be inclusive and sociologically cohesive.

Our analysis also rests on a more general reading of political transition as a liminal moment. In line with anthropological analysis of liminality in ritual passages (van Gennep 1981; Turner 1967; 1969), such moments are characterized by a high degree of ambivalence, anxiety, and creativity. Liminality is a world of contingency where events and meanings—indeed reality itself—can be carried in different directions. Liminality refers to moments or periods of transition during which the normal limits to thought, self-understanding, and behavior are relaxed, opening the way to novelty and imagination (Thomassen 2009; Szakolczai 2009). It is also in liminal periods that the core symbols and sacred values of a society are brought into play, introducing what Eisenstadt (1995) identified as a new dynamism into the balancing of order-maintaining and order-transforming symbolic forces. Paradoxically, the most emphatically innovative episodes of political transformation likewise appear as the most revealing symptoms of dependence on traditional sources. As discussed also by Arnason, Eisenstadt, and Wittrock (2005), this further roots European political revolutionary ideas in more ancient symbolic constellations and world images of continuity in change, going back to the axial age. It is here worth noticing the parallels in the relationship between memory and power in the period following WWII (1943–1946) and the period following the end of the Cold War (1989–1994). Both periods provoked deep transformations in the political and institutional world: the collapse of Fascism and the double transformation from Monarchy to Republic, and from Fascism to Democracy in the first case; the end of the First Republic, the collapse of the party political system, the birth of new parties, and new electoral laws and institutional procedures in the second case. These transformations at the institutional level were accompanied by equally deep changes in political and social imagery, in people's guiding images of the world. In short, in both periods a dramatic economic and political crisis unfolded together with an existential crisis as acquired universes of symbolic world maintenance dissolved. In this process, political transformation became linked with a foundational rethinking and rediscussing of events and symbols that had provided historical depth and symbolic underpinning of Italy as a political community: the Risorgimento (the period of national unification) after WWII; WWII and the role of the anti-Fascist Resistance as a Second Risorgimento after the end of the Cold War.

The Postwar Configuration: Narratives of the Resistance and Political Legitimacy in the New Republic

Between 1943 and 1947 anti-Fascist forces—Catholics, Communists, Socialists, Liberals, moderates—elaborated and imposed a narrative of the war that was to become the public memory of the Republic. That narrative was based upon the fact of the Resistance. The anti-Fascist front aimed at displaying a sense of a new beginning for the Italian nation. The key features of this narrative were a portrayal of the Italians as victims of Fascism and of a war desired almost exclusively by Benito Mussolini; a re-dimensioning of Italian responsibility in the Axis war, the blame for which was laid entirely upon the *Duce* and the former German ally; and finally, a glorification of the role of the role played by the Italian people in the struggle against Nazi Germany and its Fascist allies after the armistice (8 September 1943). A cornerstone of this narrative was the image of the *bravo Italiano* (the good Italian), which was often contrasted with the image of the *cattivo Tedesco* (the wicked German). According to such a narrative Italians had taken part in the war reluctantly and without hatred for the enemy; civilians and soldiers had protected Jews from the racial laws; national troops had fought alongside the *Wehrmacht* in Africa or in Russia, yet avoiding brutality

139

against the local populations and protecting individuals from the abuse of the Germans (Focardi 1996).

While the Germans had shown themselves to be fanatical soldiers, disciplined and cruel, the Italians by contrast had taken part in the war without conviction, capable of silent personal sacrifice but not of cruelty and violence. At the popular level, the perhaps best known depiction of Italian WWII soldiers as innocent, peace-loving, charming, and well-meaning human beings was the Oscar-winning film *Mediterraneo* (1991). While the German people had remained loyal to the Führer until the decline of the Reich, the Italian people had risen up against Fascism, liberated the country, and executed the *Duce*. This narrative smoothed over or minimized the aggressive character of WWII, dwelling instead on the humanitarian behavior of the good Italian soldiers. Above all, it highlighted the events of the second war fought by Italians between 1943 and 1945 as the real war, in which the Italian people had been able to reveal their true feelings. The war of the cobelligerent Italy and of partisan Resistance was celebrated by a political and intellectual class that had itself taken a leading part in it, and which drew from it the source of its legitimacy as the country's ruling class. The Resistance was portrayed in epic terms as a Second *Risorgimento*. The *Risorgimento* (Rising Again or Resurgence) had been the nineteenth-century cultural and political movement for the national unification and liberation culminating in the establishment of the Kingdom of Italy (1861). The Second *Risorgimento* became, in the anti-Fascist narrative, a new national and patriotic war of liberation, supported by the entire populace rallying around soldiers and partisans; "*un popolo alla macchia*" (a nation underground) was the eloquent expression coined by the Communist leader Luigi Longo (1947).

This memory was put under considerable strain during the first parliamentary term (1948–1953), coinciding with the definitive breakdown of the unity of the anti-Fascist forces and the development of the Cold War. Catholics, Socialists, and Communists were now contrasting each other in parliamentary politics. Due to its geo-political position and the strong presence of Communists, not to mention the unresolved border to Yugoslavia, Italy was at the forefront of the Cold War. Furthermore, the link between Risorgimento and Resistance was contested by right-wing (e.g., neo-Fascist) interpretations of the Resistance. Such interpretations saw the Resistance as divisive of the nation, and interpreted its military deeds as civil war. The Resistance was accused of being animated and dominated by a political ideology

(Communism) that was incompatible with the ideals of the Risorgimento and did not represent the larger populace or national interest. This interpretation was extremely widespread also among many Italian Istrians who had fled Yugoslavia in the aftermath of World War II. Their version of the war events and the role played by the Resistance in North-East Italy would only gain public attention after the end of the Cold War (Thomassen 2003; 2006). Such interpretations, however, gained very little public voice.

In the late 1960s and 1970s, the canonical interpretation of the war and the Resistance came under attack again, this time from the Left via criticism of the student and worker movements that developed the idea of a *Resistenza tradita* (a betrayed Resistance). From their point of view, the betrayal was tied to an experience of the resistance as a popular uprising that was somehow never brought to a conclusion. The political-cum-cultural institutional framework established from 1946 only partially reflected the dreams and social aspirations that had animated the fight against both Fascism and Nazism: a class war rather than a patriotic war. It was very much such an interpretation of the Resistance as having been betrayed by social and political conservatism that led to left-wing radicalism and armed rebellion. The Red Brigades, for example, consciously played on the image of having taken up the Resistance—this time in order to fulfill it. However, despite the continued existence of different interpretations, the anti-Fascist patriotic narrative of the Resistance was never replaced, nor essentially threatened by a dominant alternative memory. On the contrary it was confirmed and relaunched in the mid-1950s, in order to become truly hegemonic before 1960 (Focardi 2003). Thus, in Italy as well, the history of WWII was not surprisingly written by the winners.

There is no doubt that such a narrative, although it grew from legitimate political needs, produced a distorted version of national history. Far from all of the personal WWII experiences, it found a place in the narrative that dwelt on the Resistance as a popular epic and founding moment for the new national identity. Such experiences, and memories based upon them, were subsequently repressed or denied public expression. These repressed memories included the enthusiasm with which many Italians had actually welcomed the prospect of war alongside Germany in the hope of a rapid victory; the fate of the defeated (the Fascists); the civil war character of the Resistance, which could not be reduced simply to a struggle against the foreigner and his isolated Fascist servants; the divisions between the forces of the Resistance; the

141

violence perpetrated by Italians, both soldiers and civilians, in Italy or abroad (Yugoslavia, Greece, and on the Eastern Front); the fact that solidarity with Jews became obvious and common only when it was clear that Germany had lost the war; the political reality of the period 1943 in which three wars were fought simultaneously: a patriotic war, a class war, and a civil war, and where taking sides was far from easy for many people (Pavone 1991). One of the forgotten questions concerned the so-called *resa dei conti* (settling of accounts). These saw thousands of summary executions all over Italy (but in particular in the North and in the Centre, and especially in Emilia Romagna) in the wake of the end of the war. Communists killed Fascists, but also other public figures, including priests. Many of these killings were in revenge for acts carried out during the rise of Fascism and under the regime. Thus, the *resa dei conti* during and after 1945 was not only a reaction to the civil war and the events that took place during the Republic of Salò, but also a long revenge for events that had taken place a generation before as Fascism rose to power, and for the fact that for more than twenty years Fascist violence against civilians went unpunished (Dondi 1999).

Italy at the End of the Cold War: Political Crisis

The end of the Cold War signaled the dissolution of the political arrangements Italians had known since the end of World War II and the start of a new era—that of the present. It also signaled a return to World War II. Discussion over nationhood and reassessment of World War II were European phenomena at this historical juncture. However, next to Germany, the most direct impact of the fall of the Berlin Wall and the end of Communism in the West was no doubt recorded in the structural crisis of the Italian political system (Fogu 2006: 161). Italy was already floundering in a morass of corruption. The two aspects were in reality related. 1989 hastened the corruption scandal that overwhelmed the Christian Democratic Party (DC), the Socialist Party (PSI), and their minor allies in government.

The Italian political system had degenerated over the decades, losing legitimacy within civil society. Depriving the system of its Communist enemy, the end of the Cold War eliminated an important support base. With the sudden disappearance of the Cold War setting that had significantly structured Italian politics, degeneration could no longer be ignored or tolerated. The massive anticorruption offensive of 1992–1993 was a logical outcome of this process, undermining the parties of the majority. The fall of the Berlin Wall thus had a paradoxical outcome: in the abstract, the collapse of the Soviet Union should have marked the triumph of the parties (DC and PSI) that had been historically opposed to the Italian Communist Party (PCI), pushing the latter to a complete reassessment of its history, if not total disappearance (as happened with Communist parties elsewhere in Europe); in real terms, however, almost the opposite happened.

The founding elements of the Italian political system evaporated quickly: Christian Democracy, the fundamental axis of national government from 1944 to 1994 and the quintessential anti-Communist force, quite simply disappeared. The PSI collapsed, seeing its leader, Bettino Craxi, escaping into exile in Tunisia to avoid prison. The Communist Party changed its name, and then divided into several left-wing parties. The economy was a shambles. The party system collapsed, parliament was defunct, and in 1992 a technocrat government took over. Virtually every day saw the public announcement of another corruption scandal. Operation Clean Hands sought to tackle the systemic economic and political corruption and the trials that followed turned into public spectacles. The period from 1992–1994 is rightly referred to as the earthquake years. By 1994, however, things started to settle down. A new electoral law was passed, and the 1994 elections gave life to the new political parties that would come to dominate what was then seen as the third Republic. The anti-Mafia movement lost much of its fervor, and operation Clean Hands faded out. Regionalism in the north was given new political expression with the formation of the Northern League, which posed a radically new threat to the idea of national unity. The former neo-Fascist *Movimento Sociale Italiano* (Italian Social Movement) transformed itself into the *Alleanza Nazionale* (National Alliance), which in 1994 entered a coalition government led by media-tycoon and political newcomer Silvio Berlusconi, leader of *Forza Italia*. The neo-Fascist presence in Berlusconi's government was a watershed in postwar politics, marking the first neo- or post-Fascist movement to participate in Italy's government since the war. In the mid-1990s, the *Alleanza Nazionale* moved to distance itself from its Fascist past; hence the change in the party's name. This official negation of the party's Fascist heritage, once a source of pride for party leaders and grassroots members, was seen as the precondition for the drafting of former neo-Fascists into a center-right coalition capable of occupying the mainstream of Italian political life.

The crisis was not only political-institutional and structural. It involved the symbolic underpinning of Italy as a national, democratic community. In other words, with the end of the Cold War and following the earthquake years of 1992–1994, Italy plunged into a period of political and historical self-assessment. Seen in such a perspective, the Italian setting was in some ways closer to that of former Eastern European countries, where WWII debates took place within the context of a regime change. Italian public debate focused on the country's identity, the notion of nation and how to interpret it, on the country's historical past and how to link it meaningfully to its political present. The time had come to reassess and to question Fascism, the Resistance, and the entire foundation of political legitimacy that had sustained the Italian republic and democracy for forty years. This led to vivid debates over what actually happened during World War II, over who was right and wrong, and judged from which ethical/political principles (Whittam 2001; Miller 1999).

The End of the Anti-Fascist Paradigm: Historical Revisionism the Italian Way

Historical revisionism of World War II and Fascism was not a sudden event. The famous Italian historian Renzo de Felice had embarked upon his revisionist task from the 1970s. During the 1980s the moral and historical fixtures of Fascism/anti-Fascism had started to lose their solidity. In his analysis of an exhibition of Fascist economy and industrial expansion held at the Coliseum in September–November 1984, *The Italian Economy Between the Wars 1919–1939*, Mason concluded that the event signaled

> . . . the general and vital fact that the political struggle over the interpretation of national history in Italy seems to have entered a new and confused stage, a stage in which old fixed points of reference (progressive/reaction; authority/democracy; nationalism/internationalism) are being eroded. (Mason 1986: 20)

It was this opening of the nation's historical archives that would take new and dramatic developments as the Cold War came to an end. This time the debates over the nation's past would become a public affair. 1995 was a pivotal year: it was the fiftieth anniversary of the collapse of Salò, the death of the *Duce*, and the end of WWII. De Felice added to the already febrile atmosphere by launching a brief but devastating critique of the "myth of Resistance" in a book entitled *Rosso e Nero* (Black and Red). The book was clearly written for a mass audience and became a best seller within days of its publication. De Felice attacked the *vulgata resistenziale* (resistential vulgate) that represented the core element of anti-Fascism and the legitimization of the First Republic (De Felice 1995). De Felice argued that since the end of the war, Italy's political and intellectual class had perpetuated the false myth of Italy as the anti-Fascist nation par excellence. It had done so through a particular construction of the memory of the war and the fight against Fascism, propagating the idea of antifascism as a political and moral virtue shared by the whole of the Italian people. This anti-Fascist orthodoxy, he claimed, had dominated Italian historiography and the cultural life of the nation since the end of World War II. In De Felice's view, the net effect of this myth had been to obscure the actual history of Fascism and the war but also to allow many decidedly undemocratic elements (Fascists and Communists) to hide behind the mask of Italy's so-called anti-Fascist republic.

Historical revisionists now started to emphasize Mussolini's role in Italy's modernization, Fascism's advanced package of social policies; its "good and benevolent colonialism," and the *Duce's* hesitancy and reluctance to introduce the racial laws. Historians started to document how Mussolini had relied on a wide-ranging consensus throughout his regime (Thayer 1995; De Luna and Revelli 1996). The Resistance came under scrutiny. It became more common to speak of a Civil War referring to 1943–45, a claim which until then had been argued solely by the neo-Fascist Right. However controversial some of these revisionist theses were, they had the positive effect of producing a more balanced and less hagiographic view of the Resistance amongst historians. Pavone's book (1991) was a turning point in this respect: it legitimized the idea of the Resistance as a Civil War for the Left. It is now widely accepted that Italy was a divided country during the Regime years, as it was divided when faced with its fall and collapse.

Alternative and repressed stories of World War II surfaced, contradicting the images and narratives that for half a century had been the official memory of the Italian Republic. Historical facts emerged from individual and peripheral memories and slowly made their way into mainstream historiography and national collective memory. Such repressed stories included the fate of "the boys of Salò," the young Italians who had fought alongside the Nazi and against the forces of the Resistance in the Salò Republic from September 1943. Laypeople and historians alike began to interrogate the motives, ideals, politics, and reasons that had animated the Fascist fighters. They were human beings after all. And in their own memories, *they* had fought for Italy.

145

The bad ones had not only been bad. And the good ones had not only done good: stories about the violence within and among partisans of different colors and ideology came to the fore. This involved particular focus on the red violence of Communists against other partisans. The role played by the Communist Party and Communist partisans in the Resistance came up for debate. The journalist Giampaolo Pansa (2003) published research on the violence committed by Communists partisans against Fascists in the so-called triangle of death in the Emilia region.

Historical research also started to engage with the behavior of Italian soldiers on the battlefield, not only during the war (on the Eastern Front or in Greece), but also during the colonial period. In Abyssinia, Italians had deployed gas against local populations. The mythology of Italians as *brava gente* was shattered (Del Boca 2005). The role, the actions and deeds of Allies were also called into question. The very fact that for most Italians the war had been nothing like a heroic event slowly emerged. Some people actively took sides, but most had just tried to survive. Caught in cross fires, escaping their hometowns from fear of allied bombing, exposed to Nazi violence and internal strife, the war had been lived by the majority of Italians as a tragedy, a kind of a total war where all markers of certainty (Lefort 1986: 19) evaporated.

The question of the *foibe*, which up until the 1990s had only been debated among exile Istrians (Thomassen 2006) now became a national issue. The *foibe* are deep cracks scattered all around the karst land of the Istria region where, according to some rough calculations, five to seven hundred Italians (all numbers argued by historians have been contested, especially by Istrian Italians who see the *foibe* as core symbol of their escape from Yugoslavia) were killed by Slovene and Croat partisans closely cooperating with the Italian Communists (Valdevit 1997; Franzinetti 2000). Most Italians knew very little about what had happened in North-East Italy, where the war scenario unfolded very differently, due to the presence of Titoist partisans (with territorial claims on Trieste and Istria), and due to the fact that Trieste and Istria were directly annexed by the Third Reich in 1943, as part of the *Adriatische Küstenland* (Adriatic Littoral). It was as a consequence of these public debates that the Italian Parliament in 2004 passed a law that instituted February 10 as national "memory day," to commemorate the victims of the *foibe* and the sufferings of the Istrian and Dalmatian exiles who during and after the war had fled from Titoist Yugoslavia.

Many people who had lost relatives and friends now started to blame the partisans for provoking these massacres, and/or for failing to protect the population. Their personal experiences were not congruent with the official memory politics based upon the fact of the Resistance. For many survivors and their families the principal responsibility for some of these massacres, while obviously perpetrated by German troops and/or Fascists, lay with the partisans. According to these accounts, the Partisans had carried out irresponsible and useless attacks that had left the civilian population defenseless and had provoked German ferocity.

These narratives flew in the face of traditional left-national discourses concerning the Resistance. From 1994, World War II commemorations became contested, and a new geography of divided memory emerged, from the local level, within single towns, all the way to the national level. In the mid-1990s, World War II had again become a war, now fought by every segment of public opinion, in public gatherings, in coffee bar discussions, and increasingly in the mass media—in radio, television, newspapers, and weeklies. The debates included violent public disputes, in some case leading to episodes of public disorder (Storchi 2007).

However controversial some of these revisionist theses were, they had the positive effect of producing a more balanced and less hagiographic view of the Resistance amongst historians. They also had the crucial effect of writing into history subjects and segments of the population that had felt outside legitimate history. There is little doubt that this confrontation over WWII memories was a necessary one. The prolonged effects of WWII divisions had lain dormant. The very fact that they could not be discussed openly during the Cold War period effectively meant that Italians had lived in what was a repressed yet omnipresent, prolonged civil war, breathing under the thin surface of official history. To be able to treat these unhealed wounds in open confrontation, however painful, was a necessary step.

As we have argued elsewhere (Thomassen and Forlenza 2011; Forlenza 2011), it was against the background of these heated public debates that the Italian Presidency took on a new, symbolic role as unifier of the nation. The president of the Republic Carlo Azeglio Ciampi (1999–2006) explicitly formulated a healing version of WWII memories. From the beginning of his presidency, Ciampi self-consciously adopted a strategy that sought to strengthen Italian national identity and a popular feeling of national unity. He did so through the careful formulation of an inclusive narrative that would serve to overcome Italy's divided memory by inventing or reactivating a vast array of new and old rituals and public commemorations. Ciampi's work on memory proposed a narrative that could hold together the complex differences of national experience and heal lacerations that had become unbridgeable during the postwar period. If he was successful on this account (as we argue he was), this was because he could take up the thread of the non-Orthodox debates that had exploded in the 1990s.

Italy and WWII Memories: European Perspectives

Diverging and contrasting memories of WWII are not an Italian peculiarity. It is possible to identify the ways in which the Italian case exemplifies European patterns of memory politics.

First, historical memories of key political events are always *to some extent* divided and antagonistic. Everywhere in Europe WWII was played out within contexts of traditional, geopolitical conflicts intertwined with ideological and political clashes. The European-wide conflict between collaborationists and partisans meant that there was (at least potentially) a civil war in every country caught up in the general conflict.

Second, World War II, in Italy as well as in other European countries, had been experienced differently by the various sectors of the population: soldiers, civilians, Fascists, Nazis, anti-Fascists, anti-Nazi, collaborators, partisans, expellees, POW, refugees; events unfolded very differently in the South, Center, North, and North-East. It had different impacts on men and women. For many European countries the role played by the nation in the war was unclear, complicated and contradictory: Italy was simultaneously loser, occupied, resistor, and victor. But much the same can be argued for neighboring countries like France and Yugoslavia, occupying similar in-between roles.

Third, most European countries had developed strong ties of nationhood through the founding experiences of the losses in World War I. Throughout Italy, memorials and statues were raised in every town and village, commemorating the ultimate sacrifice for the unity of the country's territory and soul. It was this experience that, as Weber (1976) put it, turned peasants into Frenchmen. The memory of the Great War in all corners of Europe stressed the healing language of tradition vested in nationhood, sacrifice and patriotism (Winter 1999). World War II had much less real potential for such unifying national memory and ritualization. This is why the new political élites developed a narrative based on myths (anti-Fascist or anti-Nazi) that legitimately posited the Resistance as cornerstone of the new national identity, but problematically served to cover internal splits, civil wars, and the real complexity of the drama of WWII.

Fourth, the general ways in which European countries dealt with the past included victimization. Victimization, as argued by Girard (1977), is a very powerful symbolization of experience. While victimhood narratives were often results of politicized propaganda, the question goes deeper. A widespread attitude of victimization can be found in testimonies of people who lived under totalitarian regimes, experiencing helplessness in the face of larger powers. Victimization was the response of people and postwar élites in practically every European country—even those countries generally held responsible for the war, such as Germany and Italy. Moreover, while everyone blamed the Germans for the Holocaust, the Germans blamed the Nazis, and the Nazis blamed Hitler. In West Germany the period 1945–1957 was dominated by the victim syndrome that sustained a clear separation between the Nazi regime and the German people, attributing the role of perpetrator to the former, that of the victim to the latter (see Wilds, this volume; Assman and Frevert 1999). Likewise, in France the period between 1944 and 1954 was the mourning phase where Vichy was silenced and the Resistance focused upon (Rousso 1987). Another wave of victimization took place after 1989 with the collapse of Soviet Union and the democratization in Eastern Europe (Judt 2000).

Fifth, social amnesia was another omnipresent reality in postwar Europe. The events of the war and the partial support for Fascism and Nazism, also within countries occupied by Fascist powers, contributed to some degree to the segmentation of national memory in all European countries after the end of the hostilities; it resulted in the development of an official politics of memory nourished by displacement, forgetfulness, and partiality. According to Jeffrey Herf, even West Germany was characterized by social amnesia and weakening of memory, as the Holocaust for long was a source of taboo (Herf 1997: 7–9). Amnesia and selective remembrance also characterized a country like Yugoslavia. The grand official narrative of the socialist era hid the fact that WWII was not only a struggle against a foreign aggressor, but also a civil war that inevitably produced a conflict of memories. This was concealed down to the dissolution of the Yugoslav Federation, then exploded as the crisis erupted (Bet-El 2002). Such tendencies were equally true of Italy. Italian politicians in the immediate postwar decades were quick to define themselves against a defeated enemy, against whom all

Italians could unite. Annual celebrations of the end of the war ritually focused on the German atrocities and the unity of the Italian nation in the struggle leading to postwar democracy. In this respect Italian politicians remained united throughout the postwar period—until the crisis erupted.

Sixth, and in consequence, the seriousness of the dilemma whether to punish or pardon collaborationists was a real issue in most European countries. The amnesty for the Fascist crimes decided in June 1946 by the ministry of Justice, Communist leader Palmiro Togliatti, in the name of national concord and with the intention of integrating the Fascist rank and file into the democratic and Republican Italy, must be placed in this wider context. Although amnesia and amnesty have the same etymological root, Togliatti's decision was not simply an act of forgetting but rather one of forgiving: trying to put aside the well-remembered and haunting violence of divisive events in order to ensure national cohesion and reinforce group solidarity. This cannot be reduced, as suggested by Poggiolini (2002), to a bifurcated political system dominated by DC and by the amnesia it stood for, and countered by a civil society penetrated by Communists who operated the counter-cultural form of remembrance of the Resistance. Remembrance—Poggiolini argues—inspired the Constitution, whereas amnesia made prosperity and military security in NATO possible at the cost of fifty years of Christian Democrat hegemony. Things were far more complex and much less symmetrical. As everywhere in Europe, amnesia and remembrance were tightly intertwined within parties, institutions, and within society as such—and often even within single individuals.

If divergent memories should be considered a general characteristic of postwar Europe, the Italian case also has its own set of defining features. This is simply because the situation that took place in Italy between 1943–1945 was, at the same time, quite unique. With the movement against Fascism, two occupying armies, the king's flight from Rome, and the coexistence of different Italian governments, there was from September a liminal situation of essentially contested sovereignties, where individuals were faced with moral, political, and existential choices.

Another uniqueness of Italy was the strength of the Communist Party. Upon the end of the war, the Communists stood strong in various West European countries, including Greece and France. America feared Communist electoral triumphs in various countries. However, in

Italy the strength of the Communist Party remained intact throughout the entire postwar period. As late as 1976, the PCI gained 34.4 percent of the votes, against 38.7 percent gained by the Christian Democrats (Ginsborg, 1990: 442). Moreover, at the level of local and regional politics, a so-called red belt emerged in Central/North Italy; large sections of the most productive parts of the country were effectively governed by Communists.

In a way, the elaboration of WWII was therefore more complicated in Italy than in Germany, for example. The division of Germany in two helped to foster two different national identities for West and East. In Italy such narratives flowing from anti-Fascism and anti-Communism coexisted; in Italy the political-territorial border that divided Germany in two instead established itself as an internal moral-political boundary. The Communists had been protagonists of the Resistance and also played a key role in the rebirth of democratic Italy, collaborating in the writing of the Constitution. Constitutional legitimacy was based on anti-Fascism. But with the onset of the Cold War, political legitimacy at the same time became based on anti-Communism. From the 1950s, the Italian Socialists (PSI) openly defended their alliance with DC as a necessary choice to keep Communism at bay and Italy on the right side of the Cold War boundary (and this despite the fact that the party kept making use of the hammer and sickle symbol up until 1985). This anti-Communist narrative became so deeply engrained that Italian right-wing politicians still today, twenty-four years after the fall of the Berlin Wall, use the term communist to delegitimize their left-wing opponents. The coexistence of anti-Communism (political legitimacy) and anti-Fascism (constitutional legitimacy) established deep roots within society, influenced political discourse, and imploded as an underlying antagonism shaping popular imagination and the cultural and symbolic universes of groups and individuals.

Conclusion

In an open society, memories always differ, and this had better be so. A closed, fixed memory of events locked in one officially authorized version of history can hinder cooperation between groups that may or may not agree with the authorized collective memory. Collective memory that is used to close boundaries of ethnic, national, or other identities and that selectively accepts particular versions of the past as true can aggravate conflict, whereas collective memory that is open-ended can be a lubricant for social cooperation (see also Misztal 2005: 1332). Attempts to reach a unanimous memory of WWII events seem implausible and counter-productive. If this is so at the level of national debates, the same point must be made with respect to Europe.

Yet, the very simple, overarching point might very well be the recognition that WWII was, first and foremost, a European war—with global consequences. The war pitted nations against nations, peoples against peoples, classes against classes, collaborators against partisans. The war pitted Europe's powers against each other, created alliances, friends, and enemies, instituted and strengthened a repertoire of national stereotypes with lasting effects. At the same time, the disaster was one that affected everyone and at all levels, from family stories to parliamentary politics to the drawing of political and territorial boundaries. It was, after all, from the ashes of the WWII horrors that the European idea took shape. As living memory of WWII is slowly disappearing, this should be remembered.

When historical revisionism entails ideological denial of documented horrors, it can and should be rejected—or just ignored. However, if revisionism serves to open up new space for recognizing the multifaceted and highly complicated nature of WWII and its endless horrors, it can and should serve as a welcome contribution toward national and European-wide reflexivity. After 1945, European countries built their national identities around highly selective narratives of the war. These narratives created often oversimplified dichotomies of winners/losers and perpetrators/victims. And in the current historical moment of an acutely sensed European crisis, we once again see strong tendencies toward returning to simplified positions that depict one's nation as a victim of somebody else's wrongdoing—and we once again see how WWII becomes a contested touchstone for articulating ever more radical positions in both domestic and European politics. It is such simplification, rather than historical revisionism as such, that opens a door to ideological if not racial radicalism, in all its most undesirable forms across the continent—from England to Greece, from Hungary to France, from Italy to Norway. An open or balanced memory must be sensitive toward the anthropological recognition of symbols and rituals as essentially polysemic and open to social interpretation, without plunging into moral relativism. It will remain a fragile balance. But political certainty and self-confidence in the European project will always hinge on that essential precariousness of Europe's historical existence.

References

Arnason, Johann, S.N. Eisenstadt, and Bjorn Wittrock, eds. 2005. *Axial Civilizations and World History*. Leiden: Brill.

Assman, Aleida and Ute Frevert. 1999. *Geschichtsvergessenheit- Geschichtsversessenheit. Vom Umgang mit deutschen Vergangenheiten nach 1945*. Stuttgart: Deutsche Verlags-Anstalt.

Bet-El, Ilana. 2002. "Unimagined Communities: The Power of Memory and the Conflict in the Former Yugoslavia." In *Memory and Power in Postwar Europe: Studies in the Presence of the* Past, ed. Jan-Werner Müller. Cambridge: Cambridge University Press.

De Felice, Renzo. 1995. *Rosso e Nero*, ed. Pasquale Chessa. Milan: Baldini&Castoldi.

Del Boca, Angelo. 2005. *Italiani, brava gente?* Vicenza: Nezi Pozza.

De Luna, Giovanni and Marco Revelli. 1995. *Fascismo/Antifascismo. Le idee, le identità*, Florence: La Nuova Italia.

Dondi, Mirco. 1999. *La lunga liberazione. Giustizia e violenza nel dopoguerra italiano*. Rome: Editori Riuniti.

Eisenstadt, Shmul Noah. 1995. *Power, Trust, and Meaning*. Chicago: University of Chicago Press.

Focardi, Filippo. 1996. "'Bravo Italiano' e 'cattivo tedesco': riflessioni sulla genesi di due immagini incrociate." *Storia e memoria* 5 (1): 55–83.

Focardi, Filippo. 2003. "Reshaping the Past: Collective Memory and the Second World War in Italy, 1945–1955." In *The Postwar Challenge: Cultural, Social, and Political Change in Western Europe, 1945–58*, ed. Dominik Geppert. Oxford: Oxford University Press.

Fogu, Claudio. 2006. "*Italiani brava gente*: the Legacy of Fascist Historical Culture on Italian Politics of Memory." In *The Politics of Memory in Postwar Europe*, eds. Richard Lebov, Wulf Kansteiner, and Claudio Fogu. Durham and London: Duke University Press.

Forlenza, Rosario. 2011. *La Repubblica del Presidente. Gli anni di Carlo Azeglio Ciampi, 1999–2006*. Reggio Emilia: Diabasis.

Franzinetti, Guido. 2006. "The rediscovery of the Istrian Foibe." *JGKS, History and Culture of South Eastern Europe* 8: 85–98.

Ginsborg, Paul. 1990. *A History of Contemporary Italy. Society and Politics, 1943–1988*. London: Penguin Books.

Girard, Rene. 1977. *Violence and the Sacred*. Baltimore: Johns Hopkins University Press, Herf, Jeffrey. 1997. *Divided Memory: The Nazi Past in the Two Germanys*. Cambridge, MA: Harvard University Press.

Judt, Tony. 2000. "The Past is Another Country: Myth and Memory in Postwar Europe." In *The Politics of Retribution in Europe*, eds. István Deák, Jan T. Gross, Tony Judt. Princeton: Princeton University Press.

Knudsen, Anne. 1989. *En Ø i Historien, Korsika. Historisk Antropologi, 1730–1914*. København: Basilisk.

Lefort, Claude. 1986. *The Political Forms of Modern Society*. Cambridge, MA: The MIT Press.

Longo, Luigi. 1947. *Un popolo alla macchia*. Milan: Mondadori.

Mason, Tim. 1986. "The great economic history show." *History Workshop Journal* 21: 3–35.

Miller, James. 1999. "Who chopped down the cherry tree? The Italian Resistance in history and politics, 1945–1998." *Journal of Modern Italian Studies* 4 (1): 37–54.

Pansa, Giampaolo. 2003. *Il sangue dei vinti*. Milan: Sperling & Kupfer.

Pavone, Claudio. 1991. *Una guerra civile. Saggio storico sulla moralità della Resistenza*. Turin: Bollati Boringhieri.

Poggiolini, Ilaria. 2002. "Translating Memories of War and Co-belligerency into Politics: the Italian Post-war experiences." In *Memory and Power in Postwar Europe*, ed. Jan-Werner Müller. Cambridge: Cambridge University Press.

Rousso, Henry. 1987. *Le syndrome de Vichy*. Paris: Seuil.

Storchi, Massimo. 2007. "Post-war violence in Italy: A Struggle for Memory." *Modern Italy* 12 (2): 237–50.

Szakolczai, Arpad. 2009. "Liminality and Experience: Structuring Transitory Situations and Transformative Events." *International Political Anthropology* 2 (1): 141–72.

Taylor, Charles. 1989. *Sources of the Self*. Cambridge, MA: Harvard University Press.

Thayer, John. 1999. "Renzo De Felice, Rosso e Nero 1995." *Journal of Modern Italian History* 4 (1): 97–116.

Thomassen, Bjørn. 2003. "'The Italian state has betrayed me!' Political borders as cultural defence." In *Focaal, European Journal of Anthropology* 41: 107–18.

Thomassen, Bjørn. 2006. "Italy from below and from the outside-in: an Istrian life story across the Italo-Yugoslav border." In *Acta Histrae* 14 (1): 155–78.

Thomassen, Bjørn. 2009. "The Uses and Meaning of Liminality." *International Political Anthropology* 2 (1): 5–27.

Thomassen, Bjørn and Rosario Forlenza. 2011. "Re-narrating Italy, Reinventing the Nation: Assessing the Presidency of Ciampi." *Journal of Modern Italian Studies*, 16 (5): 705–25.

Turner, Victor. 1967. "Betwixt and Between: the Liminal Period in *Rites de Passage*." In *The Forest of Symbols: Aspect of the Ndembu ritual*. Ithaca, NY: Cornell University Press.

Turner, Victor. 1969. *The Ritual Process: Structure and Anti-Structure*. Chicago: Adline.

Valdevit, Giampaolo, ed. 1997. *Foibe. Il peso del passato. Venezia Giulia 1943–1945*. Venezia: Marsilio.

Van Gennep, Arnold. 1981. *Les rites de passage*. Paris: Picard.

Whittam, John. 2001. "Fascism and anti-Fascism in Italy: History, Memory and Culture." *Journal of Contemporary History* 36 (1): 163–71.

Weber, Eugene. 1976. *Peasants into Frenchmen: The Modernization of Rural France, 1870– 1914*. Stanford: Stanford University Press.

Winter, Jay. 1999. "Forms of Kinship and Remembrance in the Aftermath of the Great War." In *War and Remembrance in the Twentieth Century*, eds. Jay Winter and Emmanuel Sivan. Cambridge: Cambridge University Press.

8

"The Nazis Strike Again": The Concept of "The German Enemy," Party Strategies, and Mass Perceptions through the Prism of the Greek Economic Crisis

Zinovia Lialiouti and Giorgos Bithymitris

Introduction

This chapter discusses the concept of the German enemy in Greek public debate by building on journalistic articles, political discourse, and party documents during the period between May 2010 and June 2012 and by applying Critical Discourse Analysis (CDA). Discourse analysis has been particularly fruitful as an approach to understanding the construction and reproduction of national identities (Wodak et al. 2009; Dolón and Tobolí 2008; de Fina, Schiffrin, and Bamberg 2006; Howarth and Torfing 2005). More particularly, CDA—following conceptualizations of the nation as an "imagined" and symbolic community by Benedict Anderson (1983) and Stuart Hall (1996: 612–613) respectively—examines national identities as products of discourse, taking into consideration its historic, social, political, and linguistic implications as well as the structure of the implicated power relations (Wodak et al. 2009: 7–48). Our goal here is to illustrate how the notion of an external enemy supplants that of an inner enemy in current Greek crisis discourse, and how this became possible due to the strong and emotionally charged memory of German occupation. Our

155

discussion also highlights the ways in which the discourse on otherness is employed in order to delegitimize policies and actors in the context of a severe crisis (Mole and Ciută 2007: 209–210).

The revival of nationalist, anti-German feelings during the Greek economic crisis illustrates the interaction between two distinct levels of analysis: the level of the actual crisis and the level of everyday life, where "unreflexive" perceptions of "the (national) enemy" are negotiated (Edensor 2002: 1–30) and particular "structures of actions and structures of feelings are provided" (Karner 2007: 165). While these two levels influence one another, it is the persistence of anti-German stereotypes and occupation memory in everyday Greek culture, a sort of "banal" (Billig 1995: 1–9) anti-German predisposition, that has created the conditions of possibility for anti-German outbursts and their diffusion in the public sphere. Their most visible symptom was the recent mobilization of Nazi and occupation symbols in public spaces on the basis of "culturally shared meaning" (Karner 2007: 48).

The discourse on the German occupation can also be examined as one of two competing metaphors circulating in Greek public discourse since the country's agreement with the IMF. One of these metaphors, sustained by political and journalistic élites, is a war-and-threat-to-life metaphor that represents the economic crisis as seriously jeopardizing the country's future and even its very survival. This has been used to legitimize extreme austerity measures and foreign guidelines, no matter how unpopular, while delegitimizing reactions against the implemented policies. Following Ringmar's analysis (2007: 120; 135), it can be argued that dissenters articulate their opposition through an alternative war metaphor that proposes a different interpretation by equating the austerity measures and Greece's international agreements with the IMF and the EU as foreign (German) occupation. By using the occupation metaphor, resistance to the above policies is presented as a patriotic duty.

Scholars have discussed the role of crises in their various manifestations in the expression of nationalism, and particularly in the "transformation of 'cold' or everyday national identities into 'hot' nationalism," through the prism of the dynamic relationship between globalization and the enduring symbolic and ideological power of nation-states (Karner 2011: 58; see also Castells 2010; Castles 2000: 163–186). These processes have acquired a new tension in the EU in the context of the current economic crisis, highlighting the interactions and contradictions between the role of supranational institutions, the function of globalized and deregulated market economies, the role of nation-states, and the influence of nationalisms (Karner 2011: 89).

The Memory of the German Occupation: Continuities and Discontinuities

The German occupation of Greece (1941–1944) was experienced as an extremely painful historical period, supplanting the memory of both the Italian and the Bulgarian occupations during the same period. The main features of the German occupation were oppression and terror, sometimes leading to brutal massacres of civilians and exhaustive exploitation of Greece's resources (Mazower 1993; Fleischer 1986). A special chapter in the history (and the memory) of occupation is the famine suffered by the Greeks, the "last 'significant' European famine in terms of mortality," which cost the lives of approximately 5 percent of the population (Hionidou 2006: 1–2).

In the postwar period, however, the establishment of the post-Civil War authoritarian regime with its strong anti-Communist orientation resulted in the elimination of both the German enemy concept and of memories of the popular, pro-Communist resistance in public discourse (Papadimitriou 2006: 178–207). This development is inscribed in the context of the "voluntary amnesia" that characterized Cold War European politics and its relationship to the Second World War (Judt 2004: 167). The pro-Atlanticism of the Greek élites led to the repression of public memory of the issues above and the consolidation of a gap between official and popular memory. It also influenced the attitude of successive Greek governments on the issue of German war reparations—an open question to this day—leading to accusations of compliance and to a controversial stance on the prosecution of German war criminals (see Fleischer 2009: 508–538; Apostolopoulos 2003: 223–243).

Nevertheless, the concept of the German enemy remained a powerful symbol in Greek popular culture, particularly on the left, from the post-Civil War period to the dictatorship (1949–1967). Those defeated in the Civil War (1944–1949) constructed a counter-narrative, which also employed the concept of the German enemy, and in which the appeal to the memory of occupation functioned like a "flag of combat" (Price 2003: 137), a manifestation of memory as a form of resistance (Liakos 2008/2009: 57–74). The German occupation thus became a metaphor for the postwar American hegemony over Greece and served to construct the concept of the "American conqueror" to delegitimize the anti-communist political establishment and the country's international (Western) alliances (Lialiouti 2010).

On the level of popular culture, films referring to the German occupation, numbering around sixty-three between 1945 and 1966 (Andritsos 2005: 21; 35; 44; 56), are indicative of the persistence of these historical memories, juxtaposing the harshness of the Germans to the heroism of the Greeks, despite seemingly neutral references to the resistance. A manifestation of the anti-German stereotype can be detected in two commonly used Greek expressions that both originated from popular film productions and became part of everyday discourse. The first was the title of a 1948 film, *He Germanoi Xanarhontai* (Alekos Sakellarios 1948), which was translated into English as *The Nazis Strike Again*, although the Greek original translates as *The Germans Strike Again*. This phrase is now used sarcastically, to describe an ultimate threat that provokes great fear. The element worth emphasizing here is that the enemy is defined in ethnic terms (the Germans), and not in ideological terms (the Nazis). Both in official and everyday Greek discourse, it is the German nation that Greece faced in World War Two. The second phrase is "the Germans are our friends," which is used sarcastically to stigmatize traitorous or self-serving behavior. It was first uttered in a 1971 film on the Occupation, *He Haravgi tis Nikis* (*The Dawn of Victory*), by a character depicted as a caricature of a German collaborator. The full quotation, "The Germans are our friends, they want what's good for us, they are more powerful, they will prevail," became legendary.

During the first years after the dictatorship from 1974 to 1980, Karamanlis's pro-European strategy discouraged the development of an official anti-German discourse. During Andreas Papandreou's administrations in the 1980s, moments of tension in Greek-German relations in the context of the European Community were recorded. The Greek prime minister and the majority of the press denounced the Germans as anti-Greek and as US servants (Lialiouti 2010: 467–468). Previously, the PASOK government had officially recognized the National Resistance to German occupation and granted honorary pensions to its members. The widespread anti-Americanism of the post-authoritarian period also incorporated the symbolic identification of US imperialism with Nazism, a tendency manifested in the youth protest cultures of the 1960s and the 1970s in the Western world, including in Germany itself (Diner 1996: 118–130). Moreover, in the dominant leftist narrative of the period from the Civil War to the dictatorship, American domination and the German occupation were presented as a continuity, as two links in a historical chain of foreign intervention (Lialiouti 2010).

The end of the Cold War signaled the revitalization of Greek nationalism and anti-Americanism (Georgiadou 1995: 295–315; Voulgaris 2006: 141–153; Madianou 2007: 95–115). Greek public opinion responded with apprehension to Germany's role in the Balkan region, particularly its support for Croatia and its unfriendly attitude toward Serbia. NATO's intervention in Kosovo (1999) led to an outburst of anti-NATO and anti-American feeling in Greece. The conceptual legacy of the totalitarian paradigm and of Nazi atrocities was applied to denounce American foreign policy, especially toward Serbia (Lialiouti 2011: 127–156). Overall, the discourse on Nazism and the German occupation has had a lasting legacy in Greek political culture—regardless of the absence of significant tensions in bilateral relations in recent decades.

The Concept of "The German Enemy" in Greek Public Discourse in the Context of the Economic Crisis

As with all constructions of otherness, the current discursive reification of the German enemy cannot be studied separately from changes in the national self-image. The economic crisis came after a period of relative prosperity combined with a rise of consumerism. In public discourse, the legacy of the "modernization movement" of the Costas Simitis governments (1996–2004) had established a sense of optimism concerning Greece's international status after the country's accession to the European Monetary Union in 2001 and the hosting of the Olympic Games. The euro was taken as tangible proof of the success of the path the nation had taken. This mood was the product of a moderate, bourgeois nationalism that prioritized economic development and was summed up in the Simitis slogan "strong Greece." With the economic crisis high on the public agenda by the end of 2009, the erstwhile consensus was brutally shattered. Among the interpretative schemes proposed in public discourse, the narrative concept of an external enemy became particularly popular in the context of widespread disillusionment.

Memories of World War II now had a negative influence on the perception of German attitudes toward Greece in dealing with the crisis. The mass media and public opinion interpreted the German instructions for the recovery of the Greek economy as a direct challenge to national sovereignty. The image of the German conqueror who brutally offends national pride became a popular interpretive scheme. According to recent surveys, 67 percent of Greeks reported a negative opinion of Germany in contrast to 62 percent positive opinions of France; it is interesting to note that there is no significant differentiation between the Center-Right and the Center-Left in their opinions on Germany (Public Issue Opinion Poll 2011).

The revival of memories of the German occupation has become a common theme and strategy in both left-leaning and right-leaning populist publications seeking to delegitimize government policies and foreign instructions. However, even columnists who have generally confronted populist outbursts and tried to repudiate nationalist discourse now appear unable to avoid invoking elements of the Germany enemy discourse, especially at a time of popular indignation at the austerity measures, which are widely perceived as cruel. Certain liberal and anti-nationalist voices have thus come to share the perception that there is a distinct German essence, which is held responsible for Germany's purported aggressiveness throughout history. From this perspective, Germany's attitude toward Greece in the current economic crisis, but also toward the problems of the Eurozone as a whole, is seen as a continuity, as a link in a chain that is perceived to stretch back to the Franco-Prussian War of 1871. One columnist who, according to his own claims, used to denounce national stereotypes and essentialist approaches, was tempted to produce the following anti-German outburst:

> I am writing something that I am going to regret. I wish that an article like this with my signature on it didn't exist; that it could somehow be read and then burnt, like instructions to a spy. When my classmates at school blamed the Germans for both world wars—and especially the second one—I used to correct them: "Not the Germans, guys, the Nazis. They are not identical . . ." I am sorry that I am about to forget this for a while . . . Germans. For the third time in less than one hundred years you practice the sport of humiliating and crushing people. The corpses and the skins of their citizens (become) prey to your barbaric instincts for entertainment . . . With a euro that is actually a disguised mark, you nullify any notion of a meaningful life, unless the life you propose for us is to work twenty hours a day for 800 Euros in order to be productive . . . You exist only to humiliate, to blackmail, when you get the chance at the historical crossroads. And then, when . . . your cities are burned you whimper apologies to mankind . . . You are dead and you don't know it. . . . (Ioannou 2011)

What underlies such discourse on victims and enemies is the concept of war, which in many cases is explicitly mentioned as such:

> I've been wondering the past few days why I couldn't write – not even think . . . I was following the news about Portugal, about Spain and once again my antipathy for Germany that I have struggled so hard to bury rose from the depths of my subconscious where I had hidden it. I don't think there is anyone on the international scene at the moment who provokes such negative emotions in me as Mrs. Merkel and the Germany she represents . . . in her look and her deeper aspirations, in her "vision" I see once again the paradoxical and unexplored psyche of a "Great Germany," cruel and determined to be the one to dictate whatever goes on in Europe even if that leads to blood baths, as she has proven in the past – and not just once . . . Great Germany is moving to a new "world war" for the third time in recent history. (Davarakis 2010)

However, the perception of victims and enemies does not always follow the WWII pattern. Greece is presented as a member in a group of fellow victims (and hence potential allies), the so-called P.I.I.G.S., none of whom were her allies in the War. Socioeconomic realities in this case substitute for historical memories and identifications:

> A Europe with a "boss" is not an appealing development for any people, any free citizen, either Greek, or Irish, or Spanish or Portuguese – or, surely, Italian. (Davarakis 2010)

On other occasions, the memory of WWII and the identities of victims and enemies crystallized at that time are extended beyond the evaluation of the German role to the involvement of other European players as well. A good example for this was the outcry in the Greek media over Slovakia's unwillingness to support the European rescue plan for Greece, despite pressure from the EU, which ultimately led to the fall of the Slovakian government. Greek commentators pointedly referred to Slovakia's lack of resistance to the Germans during the war, while presenting a derogatory outline of Slovakian national history:

> In 1939 you became a puppet state whose strings were pulled by Nazi Germany, you managed to get at least 80,000 Jews murdered . . . after the War you chased 80,000 Hungarians from your land, over 100,000 Germans from the Carpathians, while you are still blamed today for your behavior towards the Roma. Lately you chose the Greeks as the next target for your hatred . . . At times you were united

> with the Czechs; you were enslaved by the Hungarians from 1000 to 1918 (!); after the Second World War you were under the yoke of the Soviets until 1989 . . . a people that lived almost a thousand years as a slave, and therefore even when they are free they are always used to looking for someone to hate. (Galdadas 2011)

The concept of the German occupation is also linked to perceptions of a German hegemony in the EU. The fear of German domination has a socioeconomic dimension (Germany as an agent of neoliberalism) and a cultural dimension (Germany as an agent of Protestantism). It is a widespread perception that Germany will impose a strict model of labor relations and low wages. This element of cultural and religious otherness, based on a particularly negative perception of German Protestantism, has been persistent in interpretations of the German attitude. The belief that the Germans will punish the Greeks for their sins motivated by a Protestant zeal has found expression in stereotypes used by politicians, journalists, and ordinary people alike, constructing the image of a vengeful German God. It is not accidental that in the above reference to the unfortunate fate awaiting other Europeans (i.e., Irish, Spanish, Portuguese, and Italian), the people listed are Catholics also considered to be facing the enmity of Protestants.

In parts of the press there have also been references to the physical appearance of German officials as an expression of a supposed German essence, stereotypically identified with cruelty, arrogance, or aggressiveness, or to the perceived harshness of the sound of German names, which is interpreted as a sign of animosity. Horst Reichenbach, the name of the officer in charge of the so-called Task Force for Greece, for example, has been presented as an alien sound expressing a potentially dangerous quality (Vayanni 2011). There have also been negative, stereotypical comments on what is deemed to be a typically German physical appearance. Described as strict, unappealing, and somehow aggressive, Chancellor Merkel has been portrayed as the current incarnation of the German enemy. Cartoonists have merged the image of her face with Hitler's. More generally, clichés of allegedly German physical characteristics (i.e., blond, tall, and especially the blue, supposedly cold and threatening eyes) have been powerful stereotypes concerning the image of the enemy in Greek postwar culture.

The incorporation of anti-German feelings into popular culture, their display through performance, in Edensor's terms (Edensor 2002: 69–78), can be illustrated with recourse to two events that took place in October 2011. The first involved a popular ritual, namely a football (soccer) game between Olympiakos and Borussia Dortmund, in which Olympiakos won a surprise 3–1 victory. This was celebrated as a national victory, as a kind of vengeance against the perceived cruelty of the measures imposed on Greece by the Germans. The chairman of Olympiakos claimed that his team gave "joy to all Greeks," while a Greek sports newspaper argued that Dortmund "went bankrupt in Piraeus." The reversal of roles between Greece and Germany in the previous phrase is obvious. The slogans emphasized the humiliation and submission of the Germans and the manliness and superiority of the Greek team, expressed in sexual metaphors (*Protathlitis* 2011).

The second event involved a formal ritual, namely the official celebrations and the student parades organized on the national holiday of 28 October, the day of remembrance for Greece's contribution to WWII, a national holiday of which 94 percent of Greeks say they are proud (Public Issue Opinion Poll 2007). The ultimate symbol of this holiday is the word *NO*, referring to the rejection of the Italian ultimatum by the Greek prime minister (and dictator) Ioannis Metaxas on 28 October 1940, and to the Greek resistance to the German invasion later on. NO is supposedly a symbol for the Greek heroic spirit and the commitment to safeguarding national independence despite the military superiority of the enemy. The 2011 celebration was different from previous years: anti-German feeling was revived and pervasive, while various groups urged citizens to say NO to the EU decision of 26 October on Greece's debt problem, and to the country's impoverishment they believed it would entail. The articles that were written and the symbols and images used by protesters suggested a country under attack (e.g., *Demokratia* 2011). Banners with the word NO and Nazi symbols were hung on balconies, while rioters in some cities burnt German flags. Militant outbursts against government policies led to the cancellation of the parade in Thessaloniki and the President of the Republic himself was booed.

The discursive merging of internal and external enemies manifested in these behaviors was expressed in the following statement by Manolis Glezos, a leftist politician and emblematic figure of the Greek Resistance, who inspired the Greeks by tearing down the German war flag from the Acropolis on 30 May 1941:

> 71 years ago our people said NO to the abolition of their freedom and today the say NO to the transformation of our country into a protectorate. . . . Who should we pay respect to? To the

> current state and the governments or to those who sacrificed for our freedom? The meaning of the parade had been distorted and the Greek people have restored it today in Thessaloniki. (Glezos 2011)

A particular dimension of the anti-German discourse concerned the issue of German war reparations, most commonly linked to the German occupation loan and to the massacres of civilians in Kalavryta and Distomo. The emergence of this issue has a twin content: the restoration of national pride by equating Greece's current debt with Germany's historical debt on the one hand, and the revival of a narrative of victimization through German actions on the other. Newspaper columns, TV news reports, and talk shows were filled with emotionally charged narratives and powerful photos of the events. Kalavryta and Distomo returned as sites of martyrdom in the media, functioning as symbols of Greece's war fate and presented as proof of the historical cruelty of Greece's lenders in the current situation. Part of the national "mythscape" (Bell 2003), memories of Kalavryta and Distomo were used to reify Greek victimhood.

These various aspects were condensed in the publication in a newspaper of the story of Vassiliki Katsini, a sixty-eight-year-old woman who was born in Kalavryta on the day of the massacre (13 December 1943). Her father had been among the eight hundred victims. The first interesting element in the story is the paper's comment on the character of the narration, which is framed as a personal memory, even though Vassiliki had only just been born that day:

> In places such as Kalavryta and Distomo, men and history become one. They are fermented with stories. . . . Therefore, when Vassiliki Katsini describes the German invasion on 13 December 1943, it's as if she narrates her own personal memories. (Theodorakopoulos 2011: 29)

Vassiliki herself says about German guilt: "Germany has not paid for her atrocities. If she had paid for what she owed, our country wouldn't have the debt she now has" (ibid.). In her adolescence, Vassiliki—and other victims' children—was offered the chance by the German government to study in Germany. However, she returned home after two months: "I just could stand it there. . . . I couldn't bear the thought of being in the country that deprived me of my parent, the country that set fire on to my land" (ibid.).

Anti-German Discourse and the Greek Party System

The EU memoranda (1 and 2) were the frameworks for the painful austerity measures and other reforms, which the Greek government committed to implementing in order to receive the bailout package. The memoranda have been presented by some leftist and far-right parties as evidence of Germany's "dark plan" to conquer the Greek economy.

The Pro-Memorandum Camp

Anti-German feelings were not only a result of the spontaneous resurgence of historical memory, anti-German discourse was also integrated into the political communication strategies of Greek political parties. In the context of this strategy, the economic crisis was interpreted as an ethnic crisis and the focus on an internal enemy (those responsible for the country's economic failure) was replaced by an external enemy. The Greek parties' discourse cannot be fully understood outside the framework shaped both by the socioeconomic consequences of the crisis and the political-institutional implications of the loan agreements between Greece and Troika (the European Commission, the European Central Bank, and the International Monetary Fund).

In socioeconomic terms, mass unemployment (recorded at unprecedented levels of 19 percent in 2012), a rapid decrease in wages, and the deterioration of an already residual welfare system have led to popular discontent with the traditional dominant parties: the Socialist Party collapsed in the elections and the conservative center-right party suffered severe losses. The traditional bi-partisan system currently appears to be substituted by a fragmented, centrifugal party system with strong extremes on both the left and the right. The traditional cleavages within the Greek party system have undergone a dramatic change, the most obvious manifestation being the substitution of left-versus-right politics with a new dichotomy between "pro-memorandum" and "anti-memorandum" political powers.

The first coalition government involving socialists (PASOK), conservatives (New Democracy or ND) and the far right, which tried to implement the austerity measures between December 2011 and May 2012, endorsed a largely unpopular pro-memorandum line. One would have expected that these parties, which governed in the name of "responsibility" and "common sense," would have had no reason to cultivate their electorate's anti-German sentiment. But was this actually the case?

PASOK won an impressive 44 percent share of the vote in 2009 by promising a "new social contract" with profound redistributive features. Two years later, it was the main proponent of an aggressive neoliberal policy. Even though a pro-European orientation was a cornerstone of their program, many top executives in the socialist party tried to attribute the austerity policies to the "lenders who want their money back" and, more interestingly, to Germany. The latter, dominated by the conservatives under Merkel, was accused of challenging the European social model by promoting a nationalist, German-centered plan.

In January 2011, the then socialist Prime Minister Giorgos Papandreou, who had previously argued that the economic crisis represented a loss of national sovereignty, decided to intervene in a case before the International Court of Justice between Germany and Italy involving compensation claims for the 1944 Distomo massacre. With this "highly symbolic" gesture, as he called it, Papandreou rekindled public debate on German war reparations (Ethnos online 2012). For almost two years, PASOK tried to maintain a balance between a) a defensive political discourse which victimized PASOK and the Greek people, while incriminating lenders, and above all Germany, for the hard austerity measures and b) a pro-European social-liberal discourse. "It's not our fault," seems to be the message that underlies PASOK's communication strategy.

New Democracy's political discourse on Germany was no less contradictory. The Greek conservative party faced two tensions. The first of these concerned the endorsement of an explicit pro-memorandum stance as a precondition for the second bailout package. Second, it was difficult to present Germany as an unscrupulous enemy due to the fact that Merkel's and Samaras's parties are both members of the European People's Party, a center-right European-level political formation. However, in November 2011, Antonis Samaras highlighted his dispute "with Merkel and half of Europe" in the name of Southern Europe (Samaras 2012). ND's stance on German war reparations was also ambiguous: although historically reluctant to support this demand, they appeared as a moderate and efficient claimant in January 2012.

The populist far-right party LAOS had to deal with its own ambiguities and inconsistencies. In particular, LAOS resorted to populism in order to defuse popular discontent while, in essence, supporting the government on the implementation of its austerity policy. LAOS's anti-German stance served a dual strategic purpose, firstly as a feature which distinguished LAOS from its "compliant" governmental partners

(PASOK and ND) and, secondly, as purported evidence of LAOS's patriotic stance, which might be able to halt an observed shift of far-right voters from LAOS to its immediate competitor, Golden Dawn, an extreme right-wing party.

To sum up, PASOK and ND, the two main political parties in Greece, both invested in the German enemy concept until recently, although modestly and not continuously. PASOK needed an external enemy in order to convince its shrinking electorate that the neoliberal agenda had been externally imposed. The opportunistic revival of the Distomo case reflected a strategic answer by PASOK to its frustrated voters. ND also employed an instrumental and contradictory stance toward Germany, by exploiting the memory of Nazi oppression in Greece.

The Anti-Memorandum Camp

The cases of left-wing and right-wing anti-memorandum political parties are more immediately relevant to an examination of the discourse on the German occupation of Greece as a metaphor for the recent German role in Greek politics, revealing some striking dissimilarities and discontinuities in party strategies.

The Communist Party of Greece (KKE), with its strategy of radical rupture with the bourgeois or pro-EU political powers, distances itself from the other anti-memorandum forces and their rhetoric of German-friendly traitors and occupiers. The KKE has not utilized the anti-German discourse, even though the memory of German occupation is very important in the political mythology of the Party and despite the fact that the stereotype of the German enemy is very powerful among its electorate. According to one poll, 92 percent of the party's voters have a negative opinion of Germany (Public Issue Opinion Poll 2011). According to the KKE narrative, the Greek economic crisis is a typical crisis of capital accumulation. It is above all big Greek capital as a whole, and not an external enemy, that is here held responsible for the dramatic wage and welfare cuts. The political struggle should therefore not be oriented toward the cruel lenders, or the compromised bourgeois governments, but against capitalism in its local, national, and European forms. Moreover, according to the KKE, metaphors of traitors and German occupiers serve as a defensive strategy for those factions of capital that encourage a developmental path outside the Eurozone.

In contrast to this class-oriented analysis, the other main competitor within the Greek Left and now the main opposition party, SYRIZA, has employed a rather inconsistent stance toward anti-German ethnocentric sentiments. It should be emphasized that SYRIZA is an alliance of the party representing of Greek euro-communism (Synaspismos) with a host of smaller parties, groups, and networks of the extra-parliamentary left, which has given the party an open, unitary, and more radical profile. Despite the party's explicit pro-EU orientation, and even though it called for a "pan-European message" in the 2012 election campaign against the neoliberal leadership in Germany and France ("Merkozy"), SYRIZA has instrumentalized the occupation and incorporated it subtly in its anti-memorandum discourse. Certain parts of SYRIZA harbor anti-German feelings and patterns of selective use of resistance memories against the Nazis can be traced. It is also difficult to ignore that at the head of SYRIZA's list of election candidates was the ninety-year-old Manolis Glezos, a symbol of anti-Nazi resistance (see above). Notably, there were also party candidates who incorporated slogans against the "4th Reich" in their election campaign. Even the party's leader seemed to adopt a conceptual dichotomy between patriotic vs. traitorous élites. Finally among the party's programmatic declarations, one can find demands for German war reparations (Syriza 2012).

The right-wing anti-memorandum camp consisted of a populist right party, the so-called Independent Greeks, and an extreme right-wing party, Golden Dawn. The Independent Greeks were created by conservative MPs who disapproved of ND's pro-memorandum turn at the end of 2011. The party focused on national sovereignty and social issues and in its political program, German reparations represented a significant expected resource for the country's economic recovery. The party's president, Panos Kammenos, invested symbolically in the memory of the German enemy, as reflected in his founding of the party in Distomo (Independent Greeks 2012). Furthermore, in March 2012 Kammenos raised the issue of German war loans and reparations. The party leader repeatedly accused the coalition government of treason, swore "to chase the Nazis away again," and made references to the "Troika's occupation" (Kammenos 2012).

The last major anti-memorandum political force, which saw an impressive increase in its share of the vote at the 2012 elections, was the extreme-right Golden Dawn, a party with a barely disguised neo-Nazi profile. Although the pro-Nazi background of the party stood as an impediment to a consistent anti-German discourse, Golden Dawn exploited the public belief system, according to which the dominant political powers governed as agents of foreign, and primarily German, interests. Its "anti-systemic" polemic was grounded socially and organizationally in its steady presence around the "Indignants' movement," which has centered on Syntagma square in Athens. Prominent slogans during the massive mobilizations of the Indignants in Greece were "Death to the 300 MPs," "Let Parliament burn," and "Out with the Parties and the Trade Unions." Not accidentally, this dominant discourse during the Indignants movement called for an uprising against "traitorous" and "corrupted" politicians. This resonated among people who attributed their downward social mobility to the party system as a whole and helped Golden Dawn attach such rhetoric to an ethno-populist discourse. According to Laclau (2005), populism functions as a unifying action around symbols that mobilize heterogeneous groups against an actual or a constructed enemy. Golden Dawn's ethno-populism allowed the coexistence of a militarist, racist, neo-Nazi profile, with a strongly patriotic, self-governing, anti-German discourse.

Concluding Remarks

Summarizing our analysis of the Greek parties' response to a general anti-German feeling, there are four points to be noted: (a) the instrumental usage of the German enemy concept, however uneven, has served party strategies horizontally; (b) the socialists and the conservatives have employed the German enemy concept in order to shift the blame for unpopular austerity policies away from themselves and onto Germany's role as a lender; (c) with the notable exception of the Greek Communist Party, the radical left and especially some leftist constituents of SYRIZA have endorsed the German enemy concept as a means of resonating with public beliefs about contemporary Germany; (d) the populist and the extreme Right exploit anti-German sentiments in two ways: both populist parties, LAOS and the Independent Greeks, have tried to present themselves as the genuine patriotic forces, while instrumentalizing metaphors of occupation and treason. Golden Dawn, the extreme right-wing party, has attempted to divert attention from its neo-Nazi profile by opposing the "traitorous" stance of the political system benefiting the German enemy. Finally, anti-German discourse has two aspects: one that is disseminated strategically by members of the political and media élites; and a second one rooted in popular culture and memory. It is the severe economic and social crisis that has enabled them to merge.

References

Anderson, Benedict. 1983. *Imagined Communities: Reflections on the Origin and Spread of Nationalism*. London: Verso.

Andritsos, Giorgos. 2005. *He Katoche ke he Antistasi ston Elliniko Kinimatographo 1945–1966*. Athens: Aegocerus.

Apostolopoulos, Dimitrios. 2003. "Greece and Germany in Post-War Europe: The way towards reconciliation." *Journal of Modern Greek Studies* 21(2): 223–243.

Bell, Duncan. 2003. "Mythscapes: memory, mythology, and national identity." *The British Journal of Sociology* 54(1): 63–81.

Billig, Michael. 1995. *Banal Nationalism*. London: Sage.

Castells, Manuel. 2010. *The Power of Identity. The Information Age: Economy, Society and Culture*. Vol. II. Chichester, West Sussex: Wiley-Blackwell.

Castles, Stephen. 2000. *Ethnicity and Globalization: from Migration Worker to Transnational Citizen*. London: Sage.

Davarakis, Aris. 2010. "Is it 'Great Germany' once again?" *Protagon.gr*, 23 November. http://www.protagon.gr/?i= protagon.el.article&id=4135. Accessed 20 February 2012.

De Fina, Anna, Deborah Schiffrin and Michael Bamberg, eds. 2006. *Discourse and Identity*. Cambridge, UK: Cambridge University Press.

Demokratia. 2011. Editorial: "The New NO," 29 October: 1.

Diner, Dan. 1996. *America in the Eyes of the Germans. An Essay on Anti-Americanism*. Princeton: Markus Wiener Publishers.

Dolón, Rosana and Júlia Tobolí. 2008. *Analysing Identities in Discourse*. Amsterdam and Philadelphia: John Benjamins.

Edensor, Tim. 2002. *National Identity, Popular Culture and Everyday Life*. Oxford/ New York: Berg.Ethnos online. 2012. http://www.ethnos.gr/article.asp?catid=22767 &subid=2&pubid=50314948

Ethnos online. 2012. http://www.ethnos.gr/article.asp?catid=22767 &subid=2&pubid=50314948

Fleischer, Hagen. 2009. *He Polemi tis Mnimis. Ho B' Pagkosmios Polemos sti Demosia Historia*. Athens: Nefeli.

Fleischer, Hagen. 1986. *Stemma ke Svastika: He Ellada tis Katochis ke tis Antistasis*. Athens: Papazisis.

Galdadas, Alkis. 2011. "Dear Slovakians." *Protagon.gr*. 13 October. http://www .protagon.gr/?i=protagon.el.article&id=9412. Accessed 10 March 2012.

Georgiadou, Vassiliki. 1995. "Greek Orthodoxy and the politics of nationalism." *International Journal of Politics, Culture and Society* 9 (2): 295–315.

Glezos, Manolis. 2011. http://www.youtube.com/watch?v=0Jjvq38j84oHall, Stuart. 1996. "The Question of Cultural Identity." In *Modernity: An Introduction to Modern Societies*, eds. Hall, Stuart, David Held, Don Hubert and Kenneth Thompson. Cambridge, Massachussetts and Oxford: Blackwell.

Hionidou, Violetta. 2006. *Famine and Death in Occupied Greece, 1941–1944*. New York: Cambridge University Press.

Howarth, David and Jacob Torfing, eds. 2005. *Discourse Theory in European Politics: Identity, Policy and Governance*. Basingstoke: Palgrave Macmillan.

Judt, Tony. 2004. "The past is another country: myth and memory in post-war Europe." In *Memory and Power in Post-War Europe. Studies in the Present of the Past*, ed. Jan-Werner Müller. Cambridge: Cambridge University Press.

Independent Greeks. 2012. www.http://anexartitoiellines.gr/diak.php

Ioannou, Odysseas. 2011. "Quiet, don't weak up the Germans!" *Protagon.gr*. 30 May. http://www.protagon.gr/?i=protagon.el.article&id=7087. Accessed 20 February 2012.

Kammenos, Panos. 2012. http://anexartitoiellines.gr/post.php?post_id=71.

Karner, Christian. 2011. *Negotiating National Identities*. Farnham: Ashgate.

Karner, Christian. 2007. *Ethnicity and Everyday Life*. London/ New York: Routledge.

Laclau, Ernesto. 2005. *On Populist Reason*. London/ New York: Verso.

Liakos, Antonis. 2008/9. "History Wars: Notes from the Field." *Yearbook of the International Society for the Didactics of History*: 57–74.

Lialiouti, Zinovia. 2010. *O Ellinikos Antiamerikanismos 1947–1989*. Unpublished Doctoral Thesis. Athens: Panteion University.

Lialiouti, Zinovia. 2011. "Greek anti-Americanism and the war in Kosovo." *National Identities* 13 (2): 127–156.

Madianou, Mirca. 2007. "Shifting Discourses: Banal Nationalism and Cultural Intimacy in Greek Television News and Everyday Life." In *Discursive Constructions of Identity in European Politics*, ed. Richard Mole. Basingstoke/ New York: Palgrave Macmillan.

Mazower, Mark. 1993. *Inside Hitler's Greece: the Experience of Occupation, 1941–1944*. New Haven: Yale University Press.

Mole, Richard and Felix Ciută. 2007. "Conclusion: Revisiting Discourse, Identity and 'Europe.'" In *Discursive Constructions of Identity in European Politics*, ed. Richard Mole. Basingstoke/ New York: Palgrave Macmillan. Papadimitriou, Despina. 2006. *Apo ton lao ton nomimofronon sto ethnos ton ethnikofronon. He syntiritiki skepsi stin Ellada, 1922–1967*. Athens: Savvalas.

Papadimitriou, Despina. 2006. *Apo ton lao ton nomimofronon sto ethnos ton ethnikofronon. He syntiritiki skepsi stin Ellada, 1922–1967*. Athens: Savvalas.

Price, Monroe. 2004. "Memory, the media and NATO: Information intervention in Bosnia-Hercegovina." In *Memory and Power in Post-War Europe*. ed. Jan-Werner Müller. Cambridge: Cambridge University Press.

Protathlitis. 2011. Editorial: "The troika of . . . Piraeus." 20 November: 1.

Public Issue Opinion Poll. 2007. "Greek Public Opinion and the National Holiday of October 28th." 24 October. http://www.publicissue.gr/158/28oct/. Accessed on 10 April 2012.

Public Issue Opinion Poll. 2011. "Memorandum and Debt." 18 May. http://www.publicissue.gr/1747/debt-afieroma/. Accessed on 20 May 2011.

Ringmar, Erik. 2007. "The Power of Metaphor: Consent, Dissent and Revolution." In *Discursive Constructions of Identity in European Politics*. ed. Richard Mole. Basingstoke/ New York: Palgrave Macmillan.

Samaras, Antonis. 2012. TV interview. 24 April. http://www.star.gr/Pages/Politiki_Oikonomia.aspx? art=92922&artTitle=parathyro_gia_sygkyvernisi_apo_ton_antoni_samara. Accessed 10 June 2012.

Syriza. 2012. www.syriza.gr/theseis

Theodorakopoulos, Panos. 2011. "Born in the Ashes," *Ta Nea*, 10–11 December: 29.

Vagianni, Rika. 2011. "Occupation? What Occupation?" 26 October. *Protagon.gr*. http://www.protagon.gr/?i=protagon.el.article&id=9731. Accessed 10 March 2012.

Voulgaris, Yannis. 2006. "Globalization and national identity: Monitoring Greek culture today." *Portuguese Journal of Political Science* 5 (2): 141–153.

Wodak, Ruth, Rudolf de Cillia, Martin Reisigl and Karin Liebhart. 2009. *The Discursive Construction of National Identity*. Edinburg: Edinburg University Press.

9

Who Were the Anti-Fascists? Divergent Interpretations of WWII in Contemporary Post-Yugoslav History Textbooks

Jovana Mihajlović Trbovc and Tamara Pavasović Trošt

Even if one might not agree with the statement that there is a common European collective memory of the Second World War, there seems to be an imagined consensus on which political and military organizations stood against Fascism. However, when one shifts from a pan-European to a regional and national layer of historical memory, this seemingly clear-cut division becomes more nuanced. The Manichean narrative of socialist Yugoslavia, in which there was only one anti-Fascist movement, has been challenged and distorted by memory-makers of successor states to various extents. The dispute over who opposed Fascism, who fought against the occupation, to what extent the anti-Fascist liberators were legitimate, and who defended national interests is still vigorous and ongoing (Brunnbauer 2004; Pavlaković 2008; Ramet and Listhaug 2011). The aim of this chapter is to deconstruct how the main political groups and military formations, active in Yugoslavia during WWII, are presented in *contemporary* history textbooks written in the language that used to be dominant in Yugoslavia[1]—that is the textbooks from Bosnia and Herzegovina, Croatia, Montenegro, and Serbia. Our goal is to answer these questions by utilizing history textbooks as a lens through which to examine the ongoing contestations of WWII memories in the post-Yugoslav states.

Due to the open textbook market in the last decade, most of the post-Yugoslav states currently offer multiple interpretations of history to pupils. Thus, studying textbooks allows us to capture the critical junctures—and points of contention—within each country as well as between the countries. As Karner and Mertens point out in their introduction, national mythscapes are internally contested domains, and examining the variations in the interpretations of the same historical events in textbooks allows us to ascertain the main sites of memory contestation in the present. Additionally, textbooks can play an important role in reproducing social structures and transmitting ideology and frequently participate in "creating what a society has recognized as legitimate and truthful" (Apple and Christian-Smith 1991: 4); they do not only define events in the past, but also aim to forge "continuity in national memory, upon which a collective identity is founded and the future is predicated" (Soysal and Schissler 2005: 14).

Because of their apparent role in advancing a particular representation of history, textbooks in the Balkans have been a hot topic for research over the past two decades. Many conferences have been organized, edited volumes composed, and workshops held, all focusing on how history is being taught in the post-Yugoslav states (see Hopken 1996; Kolouri 2002; Dimou 2009). The innovation of this paper in this prolific field of research is three-fold: it is methodologically systematic, examining the entirety of textbooks used during the past school year; it examines the narratives of the post-Yugoslav countries side-by-side, allowing us to ascertain what is written as well as what is kept silent; and it approaches the text as a discursive whole by examining quotations in the context of the entirety of the text, paying equal attention to accompanying material including images, maps, sidebars, and points for discussion.

We reviewed history textbooks currently in use for the final year of primary education (age of fourteen),[2] on the basis that it is compulsory for all citizens and that, for many students, the knowledge acquired in primary school represents the entirety of their history education, unless they decide to go to university-preparatory or social science–geared high schools. We examined textbooks in use during the 2011–2012 school year: in Serbia and Croatia, this included four publishers,[3] while Montenegro still uses only one official version. Bosnia's education system is more complex, since it is practically divided into three separate ethnic clusters, each for one of the official languages/ethnicities:[4] one Serbian language textbook, five[5] Croatian, and four[6] Bosnian. Students generally attend separate, mono-ethnic classes. The Bosnian language textbooks are predominantly chosen by the Bosniak (Slavic Muslim) population. History syllabi for Croatian and Serbian classes in Bosnia generally follow those of their respective kin states; where their narrative overlaps, we refer to the Serbian and the Croatian one, where it does not, we refer to Bosnian-Serbian and Bosnian-Croatian, respectively.

Background

World War II represented a particularly contentious era in the former Yugoslavia. In 1941, the Kingdom of Yugoslavia was divided by German, Italian, Hungarian, Bulgarian, and Albanian occupation forces, while the Independent State of Croatia (Nezavisna Država Hrvatska—NDH), an Axis puppet state, was created on the territory of Croatia and Bosnia and Herzegovina. A pan-Yugoslav anti-occupation movement emerged, organized by the Communist Party of Yugoslavia (KPJ) and its leader Josip Broz Tito, called the Partisans. Apart from the ongoing resistance, the Chetnik movement, led by Dragoljub "Draža" Mihailović, was closely connected to the royal government-in-exile under the Serbian Dynasty and was initially supported as the official resistance movement by the Allied Powers. In the NDH the official military was known as *domobrani* (the Home Guard), while the Fascist movement in charge of mass terror, deportation, and concentration camps are known as the Ustasha.[7] In Bosnia, some local voluntary Muslim militias acted mostly autonomously. By intensifying their attacks against the occupation forces, the Partisans acquired the support of the Allied Powers in 1943 and were eventually successful in defeating their internal competitors. After the war, the Partisans and the Communist Party took control of power and established the Socialist Federal Republic of Yugoslavia, comprising six republics (Serbia, Croatia, Bosnia and Herzegovina, Slovenia, Macedonia, and Montenegro). They dealt harshly with wartime opponents and at the same time imposed strict controls on the public discussion of contentious WWII events, attempting to keep a tight rein on animosities. However, when Yugoslavia began unraveling in the late 1980s, the events, actors, and symbols of WWII were again brought into the mainstream and were heavily utilized for political purposes. The debate over these events—who was guilty, to what extent, who collaborated with the occupier, which side suffered more victims, and similar—continues in most of the post-Yugoslav countries to this day.

In the first section of the paper, we describe the WWII stakeholders in the countries, examining the way these groups are defined and evaluated; in the second, we comparatively assess the portrayal of the Partisans during the war activities and their takeover of power immediately after the war.

The Stakeholders: Political and Military Groups
Active during WWII in Yugoslavia

Partisans

The most positive and often quite romanticized picture of Partisans is portrayed in the Montenegrin textbook and those written in the Bosnian language. These textbooks adopt phraseology used by Partisans themselves (as well as later Yugoslav socialist historiographers) naming the war as "struggle for national liberation" (*narodnooslobodilačka borba*). Here, military successes of the Partisans as a "national liberation movement" are discussed almost as enthusiastically and in as much detail as in Tito-era textbooks (Pavasović 2006). In Bosnian-language textbooks the Partisans are described as the only genuine anti-Fascist military formation: "the largest antifascist movement in enslaved Europe" (Valenta 2007a: 135). These textbooks praise its pan-national character embodied in the slogan "brotherhood and unity." In the light of the emerging "fratricidal war" among Yugoslav ethnic and social groups (Hadžiabdić et al. 2007: 105), the Communist party plea to fight the occupation forces was the only "rational voice" (Šehić et al. 2007: 177). Thus the Partisan movement halted the nationalism that dominated before the war and during the occupation (ibid: 178).

Although generally providing a similarly positive picture of Partisans as brave, patriotic, and devoted to freedom-fighting, the narrative by Montenegrin authors is much more nuanced. It is the only otherwise pro-Partisan textbook to mention crimes conducted by Communist Partisans themselves against those they saw as "class enemies" (in quotation marks), suspected opponents of the national liberation and Chetniks—the practice referred to as "left errors" (*lijeve greške*, in quotation marks) (Burzanović and Djordjević 2009: 99). However, the narrative continues by stating that the Partisan headquarters ordered mass liquidations to be stopped in April 1941, which gives the impression that such practices did not continue afterward.

While Partisans are also explicitly defined as anti-Fascist in Serbian textbooks, it cannot be said that there is one uniform interpretation. Instead, the narrative varies: the most critical textbook describes the movement as full of "dogmatism, exclusivity, and lack of tolerance of dissent" and "rejection of tradition in the name of the future" (Ljušić and Dimić 2010: 182), while others portray the Partisans more neutrally and as a powerful and well-organized resistance movement (Djurić and Pavlović 2010: 141–2, Pavlović and Bosnić 2011:115–6), although emphasizing their Communist, illegal, and Soviet-idealizing nature (Vajagić and Stošić 2010: 146). By the same token, the Bosnian-Serbian textbook puts the Partisan movement in the frame of their revolutionary Communist ideology, as a political force that envisioned the new Yugoslav state designed according to the Soviet model. It condemns the Communists for "planning to divide Serbian ethnic space" (Pejić et al. 2009: 131) and juxtaposes it to the Chetniks' presumably honorable aim of "enveloping Serbian lands" (*omeđiti srpski prostor*) within a reestablished Yugoslav kingdom (ibid: 136).

In Croatian textbooks, the Partisans are similarly unequivocally defined as the principal and only genuine anti-Fascist movement: "one of the best organized and most successful [resistance movements] in Europe" (Erdelja and Stojaković 2009: 131), it was quickly clear that in Yugoslavia, "*only the Partisans* were battling against the Axis powers" (Koren 2009: 132, emphasis added). However, they are criticized for their "hidden agenda" (ibid.) and desire to "take over all power after the war" and create a Soviet-like state (Djurić 2009: 96). Bosnian-Croatian textbooks provide the most negative image among the textbooks analyzed. Although the textbooks state that the Partisans fought against the occupation, they are portrayed as political opportunists whose prime aim was to seize the power in a restored Yugoslavia, thus their main target was the NDH and the Croats (Matković et al. 2009: 90). One of the authors never places "anti-fascism" and "Partisans" in the same sentence (Miloš 2008).

Chetniks

In the Serbian narrative, Chetniks are described as one of the two main resistance forces, which, for a host of reasons—ranging from the interests of the Great powers, lack of internal organization, indiscipline, passivity, a mistaken decision to wait it out—eventually lost the support of the British and succumbed to the Partisans. Their military actions against the occupying forces are described in as much detail as those of the Partisans. They are frequently described as "traditional" (Chetnik being "a term that aroused historical association to the . . . fighters for freedom against the Turks in the 19th century," Djurić and Pavlović 2010: 140) and it is mentioned that the movement "stood against the dismemberment of the country and protected the interests of the Serb people" (Vajagić and Stošić 2010: 148). However, the narrative differs in the degree to which the various textbooks offer a sympathetic view of Draža Mihailović and justify the collaboration. While Mihailović's collaboration with the occupation forces is openly included in all of the narratives, one of the textbooks explicitly defends him by listing his military background and heroism, providing justification for the collaboration and portraying him as a "victim of the exclusivity of the two movements and the lack of understanding of international affairs" (Ljušić and Dimić: 157). On the other hand there is the more balanced narrative that openly criticizes the Chetnik movement, including the "collaboration of particular commanders," their "lawlessness and indiscipline," and "the reprisals and atrocities committed against [the] Serb people" (Vajagić and Stošić 2010: 181). The only Serbian textbook that does mention Chetnik atrocities notes only those committed against fellow Serbs, while the main narrative of all other textbooks, the mass killings of Muslims and Croats, is completely silenced. The Bosnian-Serbian textbook does state that Partisans accused Chetniks of collaboration, without however confirming whether or not this is true (Pejić et al. 2009: 141). The political aim of the Chetniks, to unite Serbian lands within Yugoslavia, is regarded as a legitimate goal in Serbian textbooks, whereas in all other textbooks it is characterized as criminal and racist, legitimizing and leading to the ethnic cleansing of non-Serbs.

Conversely, the textbooks in Montenegro, Croatia, and Bosnia all openly mark Chetniks as a quisling organization, grouping them together with Ustashas. The Montenegrin textbook, for instance, critically presents the Montenegrin branch of the Chetnik movement that terrorized the local population, providing five photographs clearly showing Chetnik collaboration. Although Chetniks sporadically cooperated with the liberation movement "in order not to lose influence and trust of the people" in the first months of the war (Burzanović and Djordjević 2009: 92), they invariably sided with the occupation forces in their fight against Partisans by the end of 1941. A similar narrative is given by the most moderate Bosnian-language author (Valenta 2007a: 137), while the rest of the Croatian and Bosnian-language textbooks focus on the fact that the Chetnik movement was embedded in Serbian nationalism. The Croatian narrative emphasizes its roots in the nineteenth-century movement with the goal of Serb predominance (Erdelja and Stojaković 2009: 131): the Chetniks are described as harboring a "plan for the creation of a 'great Serbia' which would . . . include the whole of Bosnia and large parts of Croatia" (ibid: 132), a point that resonates with political claims by the Serb radical nationalists of the 1990s. The plan deemed it necessary to exterminate all non-Serbs in this area in order to create what the two Bosnian authors term a "homogeneous Serbia." The atrocities of Chetniks are listed in detail in both cases: they broke into Croat and Muslim villages, robbed and brutally killed people, and destroyed Catholic churches and mosques (Bekavac and Jareb 2009: 121), especially in Muslim-populated areas (Hadžiabdić et al. 2007: 104). This narrative similarly draws parallels with the conflict of the 1990s by giving the example of Momčilo Djujić, a priest and a Chetnik who "committed grave crimes" in WWII, later in the 1990s enthusiastically supported the Serb rebellion in Croatia and praised its leaders as his worthy successors (Bekavac and Jareb 2009:122). Finally, one Bosnian author calls Chetnik acts "a genocide against Muslims" (Šehić et al. 2007: 176). Interestingly enough, the author mentions Ustasha crimes against Serbs in the same sentence, but does not call it genocide, which is the main argument in Serbian textbooks.

Chetnik-Partisan Parallel

As mentioned previously, the Serbian narrative portrays the Chetniks and Partisans as two resistance movements, literally giving them equal physical and visual space in the textbooks. The reasons given for their eventual falling out range from "misunderstandings and minor skirmishes" (Djurić and Pavlović 2010: 142), a "different military strategy and vision of a future Yugoslav state and the Serbs within it" (Pejić et al. 2009: 130), and "conflicts over the capture of individual settlements, mobilization methods, and the division of war booty" (Vajagić and Stošić 2010: 149). Serbian textbooks describe the Chetnik as the first grassroots anti-occupation movement, while the open conflict between the movements is attributed to the Partisans. The Bosnian-Serbian textbook in particular insists on the initial cooperation of the two movements, providing photos of them fighting together against the Germans or even being one and the same movement until the spring of 1942 (Pejić et al. 2009: 136). One of the Serbian textbooks concludes that the Serbian people joined both movements because of their fear of the Ustasha, but were largely undecided between the two, and were instead mostly concerned with staying alive (Pavlović and Bosnić 2011: 124).

The Croatian narrative discusses the Partisan and Chetnik movement as having the common goal of destroying the NDH and restoring Yugoslavia, which led to their initial cooperation (Djurić 2009: 98). However, the Chetniks "quickly realized that the Partisans were dangerous contenders for government after the war, so they turned against them [and] collaborated with Germans and Italians, and sometimes even with Ustasha" (Koren 2009: 133). Bosnian-Croatian textbooks agree on the point of the common Partisan-Chetnik agenda, but they present Chetniks as the prime villains, never mentioning their cooperation with Ustashas. One Croatian textbook explicitly refers to the Serbian narrative, stating, "in our neighboring Serbia, *Chethnikism* and Draža Mihailović were recently officially declared as anti-fascism fighters, despite the entirely different historical truth" (Bekavac and Jareb 2009: 122).

Ustashas

In Serbian textbooks, the Ustasha movement and the whole narrative of the Independent State of Croatia (NDH) is described in unambiguously negative terms. Atrocities of the NDH are accentuated, the role of the Catholic Church in the atrocities is explicitly emphasized, and the killing and suffering of the Serb people under the NDH is discussed at great length. The textbooks emphasize the intent of the Croatian state to "forever exterminate the Serb population" (Ljušić and Dimić 2010: 197) and outline its presumed plans: to exterminate one-third of the Serb population, to convert another third to Catholicism, and to deport the rest (Pavlović and Bosnić 2011: 114). The atrocities in the concentration camps are described in particularly gory detail and accompanied by many pictures and sidebars: "The methods of killings were exceedingly brutal: shootings, throwing into deep pits, hangings and torture" (Vajagić and Stošić 2010: 159), "all sorts of torture that were unknown to the world until then" (Pejić et al. 2009: 128). It is emphasized that the terror was committed by Croats themselves, not by the German occupation forces (Djurić and Pavlović 2010: 152). The Montenegrin narrative also presents Ustashas in a negative light, but makes a distinction between the Ustasha and the Home Guard, who were mostly forcefully mobilized by Ustashas from the population in the NDH, and many of whom deserted to the Partisans by the end of the war (Burzanović and Djordjević 2009: 97).

Textbooks in the Bosnian language also paint a very negative picture of Ustashas, condemning them for racist terror and crimes against Serbs, Jews, and Roma, but also for taking over part of the territory of Bosnia and Herzegovina, "breaking down [its] territorial unity" (Hadžiabdić et al. 2007: 103) and destroying Bosnian "historical borders" (Valenta 2007a: 138). The policy of the NDH to claim that

Muslims were actually Croats in origin, not a separate ethnic group, is seen by two Bosnian-language textbooks as insulting (Hadžiabdić et al. 2007: 103; Šehić et al. 2007: 174–5), while the Bosnian-Serbian textbook presents it as a proof of Muslim collaboration (Pejić et al. 2009: 127). Additionally, Bosnian-language textbooks emphasize that part of the Muslim community issued resolutions condemning the Ustasha's crimes and distanced themselves from the Muslim militias that participated in the atrocities.

While the Ustasha regime is also portrayed unambiguously negatively in Croatian textbooks, the Croatian narrative nonetheless emphasizes that the majority of Croats at first welcomed the creation of the Ustasha NDH state because of its independence: "they considered it to have ended greater-Serbian hegemony, violence and economic exploitation of Croatia" (Djurić 2009: 89), after twenty years of "unequal position" in the common Yugoslav state (Erdelja and Stojaković 2009: 128). Bosnian-Croatian textbooks similarly frame the creation of the NDH as a reaction to the "Greater-Serbian regime" (*velikosrpski režim*) of the Yugoslav kingdom and its failure as a state, rather than as a result of the occupation (Miloš 2008: 129). The creation of the NDH "returned statehood to Croats" because the Yugoslav Kingdom broke "the centennial thread of Croatian statehood" (ibid: 117). The Croatian narrative continues by arguing that despite this initial exhilaration, Ustasha terror quickly changed people's minds, since it became obvious that the new Croatian state was "neither independent nor autonomous" (Koren 2009: 125). The textbooks discuss Ustasha crimes at varying length, with the more liberal textbooks mentioning the crimes and concentration camps in detail, while the more right-wing narrative offsets it with a section on "cultural life and media in the NDH," listing various cultural achievements (Bekavac and Jareb 2009: 100).

The magnitude of the difference between the Serbian and Croatian narrative on the Ustasha period is best exemplified by their diametrically opposed presentations of Alojzije Stepinac, the archbishop of the Catholic Church in Croatia. Three of the Serbian textbooks explicitly highlight his involvement in Ustasha crimes, for giving "the committed genocide a spiritual blessing" and organizing "Serbs' mass conversions to Catholicism under the excuse that this was done for their rescue" (Vajagić and Stošić 2010: 159). Conversely, the Croatian narrative explicitly emphasizes Stepinac's involvement *against* Ustasha activities: he is described as "one of the greatest opponents of the Ustasha terror" (Bekavac and Jareb 2009: 102) who "condemned those priests who stood on the side of the Ustasha rule or joined the persecutions" (Koren 2009: 127).

The Official Anti-Fascists: Qualitative Assessment of the Partisans

The Partisans as Guerilla Fighters during the War and their Heroism

The Montenegrin textbook and those in the Bosnian language devote proportionally the most space to describing the "national liberation war" and important battles, providing plenty of anecdotes and often highlighting Partisan heroism and dedication. They are depicted as fearless guerilla fighters, talented at deceiving the enemy, capable of enduring superhuman suffering and sacrificing their life for the cause. One of the Bosnian authors even falls into the trap of idolatry to such an extent that he uncritically relies on (and suggests students should watch) Yugoslav socialist state-produced films as a historical source (Hadžiabdić et al. 2007: 107–8). In the Bosnian narrative, the Partisans are also the most individualized group of all (for instance, only some of their biographies are provided, Šehić et al. 2007: 171–173). Josip Broz Tito is presented as a hero of the people, resembling the way he was portrayed in the textbooks during Yugoslav socialist times (Najbar-Agičić 2006). The underlying assumption of the pro-Partisan narrative is that the movement had pan-Yugoslav popular support.

Despite the frequently critical tone of the Serbian narrative on Partisans, the discussion of the Partisan wartime involvement is described in great military detail: including precise movements and positions of particular units and number of people killed and wounded in each battle. Crucially, however, this narrative is interspersed with the same amount of detail on the wartime activities of the Chetniks, so the overall tone is not necessarily one of Partisan superiority. In the Croatian narrative, more attention is given to the gradual state-building conducted by the Partisans than to their actual wartime activities. The textbooks occasionally emphasize the acts of sabotage and the guerilla fighting (Djurić 2009: 96–7), and they list the main events in a neutral way. Bosnian-Croatian textbooks avoid any glorification of the Partisan liberation, not even mentioning any concrete activity or battles. Instead they state that the Partisans dealt with their adversaries "ruthlessly and in the most severe manner," while terrorizing those who did not support the Communist ideology (Miloš 2008: 146). It is emphasized that they particularly targeted the Croat population, plundering villages, killing civilians and Catholic clergy, especially "in the regions from where the NDH soldiers were recruited" (Matković et al. 2009: 90).

The Partisans' Reprisals

In discussing postwar Partisan or Communist actions, the Croatian narrative is the most elaborate and openly critical. One particular grievance stands out: the Partisan capture of enemy combatants withdrawing near the Austrian border town of Bleiburg and the subsequent mass murder of thousands of prisoners-of-war, an event also named the Way of the Cross (*Križni put*). The discussion of what is called "the Bleiburg tragedy" is detailed: "contrary to international conventions" (Matković et al. 2009: 91), prisoners "were killed in mass executions," died "exhausted of hunger and thirst" (Erdelja and Stojaković 2009: 154), and were "exposed to torture along the way" of their forced return (Koren 2009: 152). Among the victims were members of the Ustasha, but also Chetniks and Slovenes, as well as "numerous civilians who feared Communist violence" (Bekavac and Jareb 2009: 130), "residents of villages who did not give the Partisans material help," "Catholic priests, nuns, and prominent and wealthy people" (Djurić 2009: 112). The narrative typically mentions tens of thousands of people, while the most radical author gives an estimate of around three hundred thousand *Croats* (Miloš 2008: 150), putting an ethnic label on all the opponents of the Communist regime who were killed. Notably, one of the Croatian textbook points out the contemporary relevance of the Bleiburg question: "Even though it was only in recent times . . . that Bleiburg and the Way of the Cross have begun to be spoken and written about, there is still resistance to the clarification of the circumstances and punishment of the perpetrators" (Bekavac and Jareb 2009: 130).

Interestingly, the same number of three hundred thousand is also mentioned in the Bosnian-Serbian textbook, only here it refers to the total number of captured "German and quisling soldiers from the NDH and Slovenia, together with . . . parts of the Chetnik army," thus no civilians are mentioned (Pejić et al. 2009: 153). However, there is silence about what happened to these men. Similarly, the Montenegrin textbook mentions three hundred thousand German soldiers and quislings captured by the Partisans: "Some of [them] were shot in Slovenia, the others were subjected to a trial, while some of the younger ones were recruited into the Yugoslav army" (Burzanović and Djordjević 2009: 96), which is a point no other textbook makes. The Serbian narrative about the activities of Partisans and Communists in the immediate postwar period is often vague and the postwar reprisals against the prisoners-of-war are mentioned only in passing: in one case, this information is completely absent, while elsewhere only a brief paragraph explains that Partisans "prosecuted collaborators together with the occupier," "national enemies," and war profiteers as well as "a large number of innocent people" (Ljušić and Dimić 2010: 194). One textbook mentions that Partisan forces committed liquidations of political opponents in Slovenia and Bleiburg, totaling "between tens of thousands and 100,000 people" (Djurić and Pavlović 2010: 150). However, even when the Serbian textbooks mention these events, they do not denote it specifically as a crime. In Bosnian-language textbooks, not a single atrocity, crime, or fault of any kind is attributed to the Partisans. The only exception is the Bosnian textbook for Catholic Schools, which discusses their crimes within an otherwise pro-Partisan account (Valenta 2007b: 105), in effect bridging the Croatian and Bosniak narratives.

The Partisans as Communist Leadership

In representing the Partisans and the KPJ as political actors, the Croatian narrative blames them for repressing political freedoms after the war. The KPJ is said to have eliminated civic liberties, limited private ownership, subjected religious communities and their members to great pressures, eliminated freedom of press (Bekavac and Jareb 2009: 168), and forged elections (Miloš 2008: 171). It is also blamed for the mass purges after the war, of "all people who were opposed to the new leadership and those who fought in the war on the other side. . . Many people were taken to court and convicted to long jail sentences, forced labor or death as 'national enemies,'" including members of the Ustasha movement, members of the Croatian Peasant Party, and German and Italian minorities (Koren 2009: 198). The subjugation of the Catholic Church immediately after the war receives particular emphasis. Catholic monasteries had land confiscated, many priests were convicted without evidence, while religious people in general were considered insubordinate (Bekavac and Jareb 2009: 169). These postwar sections, however, attribute blame explicitly to "Communists"; the word "Partisan" is no longer used.

The Serbian narrative criticizes the postwar Communist forces for their actions toward political opponents and the nature of their regime, although such accounts range from an apologetic tone (i.e., forced labor was sometimes used in rebuilding the country, Pejić et al.

2009: 183), relatively moderate criticisms (e.g., "elections were followed by pressure on voters," Vajagić and Stošić 2010: 182), and more vocal ones (e.g., the "revolutionary radicalism of the KPJ" included "open pressure and terror over political opponents," Ljušić and Dimić 2010: 224,6), to an explicit list of grievances: detentions, executions without due process, confiscation of property: "The number of people killed without judicial process in Serbia has not been determined, nor have the graves been discovered and marked" (Djurić and Pavlović 2010: 173). However, the persecution of religious and particular national groups is not mentioned, in contrast to the Croatian narrative. The Montenegrin narrative also describes Communist manipulations in the process of taking over power, but without a harsh tone: the Communists "simply declared as national enemies and traitors" members of opposition parties, but violent persecution is not explicitly mentioned (Burzanović and Djordjević 2009: 114).

Political oppression and persecution of opponents by the Communist regime in the aftermath of the war is completely absent from the Bosnian-language textbooks. They praise the Communist state-building project for the same reason as they praised the pan-national character of Partisan movement under the slogan "brotherhood and unity," since they see it as creating a balanced representation "guaranteeing equality to all nations" (Hadžiabdić et al. 2007: 110), and "a solution to national question in Yugoslavia" (Šehić et al. 2007: 182). The authors emphasize as most significant the creation of the federal unit of Bosnia and Herzegovina as "not Serbian, not Croatian, not Muslim, but also Serbian, also Muslim, also Croatian" (Šehić et al. 2007: 182). This, it is argued, ended nationalist strife, which is perceived as imported (Valenta 2007a: 146), and protected Bosnia from the hegemonic aspirations of Serbian and Croatian nationalisms (Šehić et al. 2007: 179). Additionally, this political arrangement recognized Muslims (later to be named Bosniaks) as an equal Yugoslav nation (ibid: 226) and was the foundation for the contemporary Bosnian state, which is probably the best explanation of the positive picture of the Partisans and Communist leadership in the textbooks used predominantly by Bosniak students. Nowadays, the heritage of Partisan state-building in Bosnia is nurtured by Bosniak political representatives and supporters of a civic concept of the state, who advocate a more unitary state and see the contemporary state organization—comprising two entities—as a temporary, unsustainable, and unjust solution (Bieber 2006: 147).

While the slogan "brotherhood and unity" is generally depicted in a neutral or a positive light in Croatian textbooks, one of the authors presents it as a way of suppressing Croatian national identity (Djurić 209: 144). The Bosnian-Croatian textbooks go one step further, criticizing the new state in which Serbs held key public posts (while Croat party members were mistrusted, Matković et al. 2009: 108) as "carrying out greater-Serbian politics" (Miloš 2008: 173). The Bosnian-Serbian textbook expresses a similar grievance over the withholding of national rights, but in the opposite direction: it disputes the legitimacy of the KPJ leadership's arbitrary decision on borders between federal units, making the point that "many territories with a majority Serbian population . . . were given to Croatia" (Pejić et al. 2009: 141). The idea that federal borders were "unjust" because they divided the Serb people was the leading argument in the revival of the Chetnik movement in the late 1980s, and the prime legitimation of the Serbian war effort in Croatia and Bosnia in the eyes of Serb nationalists (Thomas 1999: 429). Overall, it seems that, more often than not, Partisan war conduct and Communist rule are evaluated depending on the perceived victim-perpetrator ideology of the nation for which the textbook is written.

The Issue of the Partisans' Ethnic Composition

Even though the Partisan movement bore the name of National Liberation Army of Yugoslavia and was declared pan-Yugoslav, fraternally uniting all of its nations, the issue of the ethnic composition of the Partisan troops permeates the textbooks. Reading the Serbian narrative, one would get the impression that this was in fact a Serbian movement, since the entire discussion of the war is centered on the Partisan activities toward freeing what is considered to be Serbian territory. One author mentions in passing that after the capitulation of Italy, the national liberation movement was joined by Croats and Muslims in greater numbers (Ljušić and Dimić 2010: 191), but otherwise it is assumed that the Serbs were its driving force. According to the Bosnian-Serbian textbook, the Serbian people constituted an "absolute majority, which means that [they] gave the largest contribution to the victory over fascism" (Pejić et al. 2009: 153). Similarly, the Croatian narrative emphasizes Croatian contributions to the Partisan struggles, mentioning that the first Partisan activities occurred in Croatia (Erdelja and Stojaković 2009: 131) and that, by 1943, Croats were "among the most numerous participants in the anti-fascist movement" (Koren 2009: 132). It is stressed that the contribution of Croat Partisans "to European and world anti-fascism was great" (Bekavac and Jareb 2009: 106). By focusing only on the Partisan movement in Croatia, the Bosnian-Croatian textbook similarly gives the impression that it was an endeavor only of the Croat people (Miloš 2008: 131).

The Bosnian-language textbooks do not go into the question of the ethnic identity of the Partisans, since it is assumed to be an all-encompassing Yugoslav movement. Only one author states that a greater number of Muslims and Croats joined the Partisans after September 1941. The majority of Partisan forces were Serbs, while some of the leaders were also Muslims, Croats and Jews (Šehić et al. 2007: 177). The Montenegrin textbook specifically states that the Partisan units were comprised of "all Yugoslav and national minorities," but Montenegrins staffed half of the special units ("proletarian brigades") (Burzanović and Djordjević 2009: 94), and the "overall contribution of Montenegro to the fight against fascism surpassed its proportion of the total population" (ibid: 107). It seems that each textbook seeks to present members of its nation as a significant part of the anti-Fascist movement.

Conclusion

In summary, our comparative analysis has revealed several important patterns. We have found great variation between the narratives of the four countries—in some cases including diametrically opposed information—as well as significant variation within each country. First, even the basic question as to who was anti-Fascist differs widely across the narratives. The greatest differences concern the interpretation of the Chetniks, who in the Serbian textbooks are considered to be one of the two main anti-occupation forces, while they are unambiguously defined as collaborators and perpetrators of war crimes everywhere else. Second, the Partisans are personalized in a manner appropriate to the coherence of the national narrative. While they are praised for their anti-Fascist activities throughout all of the textbooks analyzed, the level of criticism against them seems to be proportional to the need to justify the political cause of their opponents. The level to which authors praise the independence of the Croatian state, or the unification of presumed Serbian lands, dictates the degree of the apologetic tone in describing the NDH and the Chetniks respectively. In a similar way, the pro-Partisan narrative in the Bosnian and Montenegrin case seems to reflect the fact that these two countries achieved proto-statehood (as Yugoslav federal units) in the process of Communist Partisan state-building. In all cases, the imagined national interest is the yard-stick by which the stakeholders are evaluated. Finally, our analysis of the textbooks points to ongoing debates *within* the countries: the varying levels of sympathy for Chetniks and Ustasha in Serbian and Croatian textbooks respectively reflect unsettled historical revisions in both countries. This is also true in Bosnia and Herzegovina: the most nationalist lines of Croatian and Serbian discourses contrasts with the most idealistic portrayal of the Partisans and silence about their culpability in Bosnian-language textbooks.[8] In many ways, these three contradictory narratives reflect ongoing political divisions in this country.

The differences that we have shown in the interpretations of which military and political groups were anti-Fascist, and which were not, are embedded in the European memory legacy of World War II, which establishes anti-Fascism as its common denominator and as the basis of European integration. They are also deeply rooted in the notion, pronounced in the countries of the former Yugoslavia, that history curricula have the goal of building national identity and pupils' patriotism, and so they narrate history from an ethnocentric point of view. The need to reconcile the positive connotation of anti-Fascism with a positive image of one's own nation is exemplified by the tendency in all the textbooks to go out of their way to attribute Partisan successes in the anti-Fascist struggle to their own ethnic group. On the other hand, the pretensions to be part of a European and anti-Fascist tradition, seen in these textbooks, are belied by their nationalist inclinations.

However, in these textbooks, the contemporary understanding of *anti-Fascism* as being against all Fascist ideologies is conflated with a more particular understanding imported from the context of WWII, in which an anti-Fascist opposed the occupation or the quisling regimes. As the Yugoslav example (and some others) demonstrates, some of those who fought Fascism employed similar methods of exclusion and persecution to the Fascists themselves; the fact that a given group opposed the occupation, and was thus "anti-Fascist" in the historical context, does not mean that it did not adhere to a genuinely Fascist ideology itself. To tackle the issue of the ideo-logical background of the military and political groups active during WWII *without* associating it with questions of national belonging and identity is still a task awaiting the writers of history textbooks in post-Yugoslav countries.

Notes

1. The language spoken by the majority of the Yugoslav population, at that time named Serbo-Croatian, was a polycentric language with several national centers; after the dissolution of Yugoslavia it has been standardized by each successor country into a Bosnian, a Croatian, a Montenegrin, and a Serbian language.
2. Eighth or ninth grade, depending on the school system of the particular state/region.
3. In Serbia, the Rajić et al. (2008) textbook in use from 2005 was also approved for the 2011–2012 school year, but since it has been withdrawn in the meantime, it is not included in the analysis.
4. Bosnia and Herzegovina as a state is comprised of federal units (entities): Republika Srpska (with a Serb majority) and the Federation of BH, which is further divided into ten regions (cantons). (In the whole of the Federation, Bosniaks are in the majority, while Croats dominate in four cantons.) The Republika Srpska approves one history textbook for the Serbian language. The BH Federation approves the textbooks in the Bosnian language, which is in practice taught in the areas with Bosniak dominance. However, cantons with a Croatian majority maintain the prerogative to approve textbooks in the Croatian language.
5. Two Bosnian-Croatian textbooks, Bekavac et al. 2010 and Erdelja et al. 2010, are virtually identical copies of the textbooks published in the Republic of Croatia regarding the WWII chapter, therefore we refer to the original from Croatia throughout the article. The Bekavac et al. textbook from 2007, which is in use in a few schools, is currently off the market and therefore not included in the analysis.
6. Valenta published two versions of the same textbook: one for Bosnian language public schools (2007a) and one for the Catholic School Centers (2007b), attended predominantly by Croats. The latter has a few additions, which are marked in this chapter.
7. In addition to the movements reviewed here, there were several smaller movements operating in Yugoslav lands. In Serbia, particularly, the pro-Fascist movement led by Dimitrije Ljotić and the followers of Milan Nedić's collaborationist government, similarly to Mihailović's Chetniks, have been a topic of considerable revisionism in the past years (see Ramet and Listhaug 2011).
8. The only exception is the textbook for Bosnian Catholic Schools (Valenta 2007b). However, these schools attract a very small proportion of the overall Croat population in Bosnia.

Acknowledgments

The authors would like to thank Milorad Kapetanović, Azra Hromadžić, and Tea Temim for their help in collecting all the textbooks in the dispersed local markets.

References

Apple, Michael and Linda Christian-Smith, eds. 1991. *The Politics of the Textbook*. New York: Routledge.

Bieber, Florian. 2006. *Post-War Bosnia: Ethnicity, Inequality and Public Sector Governance*. New York: Palgrave Macmillan.

Brunnbauer, Ulf, ed. 2004. *(Re)writing History: Historiography in Southeast Europe after Socialism.* Münster: Lit.

Dimou, Augusta, ed. 2009. *"Transition" and the Politics of History Education in Southeast Europe.* Georg Eckert Institute, Gottingen: V&R Unipress.

Hopken, Wolfgang, ed. 1996. *Oil on Fire? Textbooks, Ethnic Stereotypes and Violence in South-Eastern Europe.* Georg Eckert Institute Studies on International Textbook Research 89. Hannover: Hahnsche Buchhandlung.

Kolouri, Christina, ed. 2002. *Clio in the Balkans: The Politics of History Education.* Thessaloniki: Center for Democracy and Reconcilliation in Southeast Europe.

Najbar-Agičić, Magdalena. 2006. "Od kulta ličnosti do detitoizacije: Prikaz Josipa Broza Tita u hrvatskim i srpskim udžbenicima povijesti." In *O Titu kao mitu: Proslava Dana mladosti u Kumrovcu*, ed. Nevena Škrbić Alempijević and Kirsti Mathiesen Hjemdahl. Zagreb: FF Press & Srednja Europa.

Pavasović, Tamara. 2006. "Reconstructing Ethnic Identity in Post-Communist Serbia: Ethno-Nationalist Socialization through Textbooks." Paper presented at the Association for the Study of Nationalities Annual Conference, New York, NY.

Pavlaković, Vjeran. 2008. *Red Stars, Black Shirts: Symbols, Commemorations, and Contested Histories of World War II in Croatia.* Seattle, WA: The National Council for Eurasian and East European Research.

Ramet, Sabrina P. and Ola Listhaug, eds. 2011. *Serbia and the Serbs in World War Two.* Houndmills: New York: Palgrave Macmillan.

Soysal, Yasemin and Hanna Schissler. 2005. "Introduction: Teaching beyond the National Narrative." In *The Nation, Europe, And The World: Textbooks And Curricula In Transition*, eds. Hanna Schissler and Yasemin N. Soysal. Oxford: Berghahn Books

Thomas, Robert. 1999. *Serbia under Milošević: Politics in the 1990s.* London: C. Hurst & Co.

History Textbooks

Bekavac, Stjepan and Mario Jareb. 2009. *Povijest 8: Udžbenik za 8. razred osnovne škole.* Zagreb: Alfa. Second edition.

Bekavac, Stjepan, Mario Jareb and Miroslav Rozić. 2010. *Povijest 8: Udžbenik za osmi razred osnovne škole.* Mostar: Alfa. Second edition.

Burzanović, Slavko and Jasmina Djordjević. 2009. *Istorija: za deveti razred devetogodišnje osnovne škole.* Podgorica: Zavod za udžbenike i nastavna sredstva. Third amended edition.

Djurić, Djordje and Momčilo Pavlović. 2010. *Istorija za osmi razred osnovne škole.* Beograd: Zavod za udžbenike.

Djurić, Vesna. 2009. *Povijest 8: Udžbenik povijesti za osmi razred osnovne škole.* Zagreb: Profil. Third edition.

Erdelja, Krešimir and Igor Stojaković. 2009. *Tragom prošlosti 8: Udžbenik povijesti za osmi razred osnovne škole.* Zagreb: Školska knjiga.

Erdelja, Krešimir, Igor Stojaković, Ivan Madžar and Nikolina Lovrinović. *Tragom prošlosti 8: Udžbenik povijesti za 8. razred osnovne škole* Mostar: Školska naklada.

Hadžiabdić, Hadžija, Edis Dervišagić, Alen Mulić and Vahidin Mehić. 2007. *Historija: udžbenik za osmi razred osnovne škole.* Tuzla: Bosanska knjiga.

Koren, Snježana. 2009. *Povijest 8: Udžbenik za osmi razred osnovne škole.* Zagreb: Profil. Third edition.

Ljušić, Radoš and Ljubodrag Dimić. 2010. *Istorija za osmi razred osnovne škole sa čitankom i radnom sveskom.* Beograd: Freska.

Matković, Hrvoje, Božo Goluža and Ivica Šarac. 2009. *Povijest 8: udžbenik za VIII. razred osnovne škole.* Mostar: Školska naklada.

Miloš, Miljenko. 2008. *Povijest novoga doba: udžbenik povijesti za 8. razred osnovne škole.* Mostar: Znam.

Pavlović, Zoran and Jova Bosnić. 2011. *Mozaik prošlosti 8: udžbenik istorije za osmi razred osnovne škole sa istorijskim kartama i odabranim istorijskim izvorima.* Beograd: BIGZ školstvo.

Pejić, Ranko, Simo Tešić and Stevo Gavrić. 2009. *Istorija: za 9. razred osnovne škole.* Istočno Sarajevo: Zavod za udžbenike i nastavna sredstva. Third edition.

Rajić, Suzana, Kosta Nikolić and Nebojša Jovanović. 2008. *Istorija za 8. razred osnovne škole.* Beograd: Zavod za udžbenike i nastavna sredstva. Fourth edition.

Šehić, Zijad, Zvjezdana Maričić-Matošević and Alma Leka. 2007. *Historija/Istorija/Povijest: udžbenik i čitanka za 8. razred osnovne škole.* Sarajevo: Sarajevo Publishing.

Vajagić, Predrag and Nenad Stošić. 2010. *Istorija za osmi razred osnovne škole, radni udžbenik.* Beograd: Klett.

Valenta, Leonard. 2007a. *Historija – Povijest: za 8. razred osnovne škole.* Sarajevo: Bosanska riječ.

Valenta, Leonard. 2007b. *Povijest: za 8. razred osnovne škole.* Sarajevo: Bosanska riječ.

10

Multiple Dimensions and Discursive Contests in Austria's Mythscape

Christian Karner

Introduction

On 27 January 2012, the international day commemorating the liberation of Auschwitz, the Viennese Ring of Corporations (*Wiener Korporationsring*)—a network of twenty-one (far-) right-wing, pan-Germanic fraternities (Zöchling 2012)—organized its annual and highly controversial prom in Vienna's *Hofburg*, the former Habsburg and now presidential palace. Prior to the event there had been a week of protests "against racism, anti-Semitism and rightwing extremism," involving sixty organizations including NGOs, political parties, religious associations, and churches (http://wien.orf.at/news/stories/2517511/). On the night, to the backdrop of demonstrations and scuffles leading to nine injuries and twenty arrests (http://www.orf.at/stories/2102025/2102021), Heinz-Christian Strache—head of the far-right Freedom Party (FPÖ)—was reported by an undercover journalist as comparing the protests against the prom to the Nazi pogroms in November 1938 and as boldly stating that "we are the new Jews" (http://derstandard.at/1326504047903/). While the prom's critics were shouting *"Nazis raus!"* ("Nazis leave!") outside the venue (Eisenreich and Narodoslawsky 2012), the head of Austria's largest opposition party whose ideological and organizational roots reach deep into Austria's history of direct involvement in national socialism (e.g., Adunka 2002: 15–18) thus compared today's far right to the victims of the Holocaust.

This mind-boggling analogy juxtaposed to the inverse historical links made by the prom's opponents reflected opposite ends of Austria's political spectrum and threw the significance of World War II to competing discourses of Austrian identity, their different historical understandings, and uses of those understandings into sharp relief. This discussion builds on Duncan Bell's (2003) notion of the "national mythscape" to illuminate diverse Austrian invocations of this past. Such invocations are ideologically varied in motivation and intent, they are inherently contestable and frequently contested, and get articulated in a range of social and political realms. My analysis of Austria's mythscape, and of the rhetorical centrality of World War II within it, proceeds through a qualitative discussion of select, recent snapshots of historical comparisons made by diverse social actors and across a range of media. My intention, then, is not to offer a quantitative assessment of the relative salience of competing forms of historical consciousness but to capture the discursive contours of their manifestations and of the political positions they inform.

Following a brief theoretical outline and contextualization in Austria's postwar history, this discussion reveals several dimensions that structure, or divide, the country's mythscape: top-down and bottom-up historical analogies; invocations—for very different purposes—of World War II by far-right extremists and some on or near the political left respectively; transnational debates with Austrian contributors or audiences. Returning to the prom controversy, I then formulate analytical key-questions to be put to contemporary, analogical invocations of the history of World War II.

Theoretical Context

Conceptualizations of social memory subdivide into three broad categories: first, continuing the Halbwachs-ian tradition, the "collective memory approach" focused on a group's shared narratives and "ritualized re-enactments" of the past; second, the "official memory approach" that concentrates on dominant versions of the past and their top-down dissemination through "mass media, the education system, mainstream art, public commemorations . . . official chronologists"; finally, the "popular memory approach" with its emphasis on "popular resistance" through counter-memories contesting "official representations" (Jing 1996: 16).

Duncan Bell illuminates the embedded-ness of memories in power relations further. Starting with an insistence on the "centrality of nationalist story-telling" that links past, present, and future, Bell concurs that some memories provide "counter-hegemonic sites of resistance." This leads to Bell's central formulation of the national *mythscape*, which he defines as follows:

> [T]he temporally and spatially extended discursive realm wherein the struggle for control of people's memories and the formation of nationalist myths is debated, contested and subverted incessantly . . . the page upon which the multiple and often conflicting nationalist narratives are (re)written; it is the perpetually mutating repository for the representation of the past for the purposes of the present. (Bell 2003: 66)

Bell's conclusion (2003: 73)—that there can be "no singular national narrative" (also see Wodak and de Cillia 2007: 317) and that myths-capes are constituted by mutually contesting "governing" and "subaltern myths"—is developed further in the following analysis of recent Austrian materials. Such conceptual refinement is achieved through a dual focus: first, on the questions as to who formulates competing narratives, from which position, and for which purposes; second, on frequently evoked historical points of reference (i.e., World War II and the Holocaust) that are widely (mis)used as "analogies" (see Müller 2002: 27) or "anchors" to interpretations of the present or claims about the future.

From Dominant Amnesia to Interpretative Contests

As is now well established (e.g., Thaler 2001: 75–90; Hanisch 1994: 403; Karner 2005: 419), postwar Austria developed a "governing myth" pertaining to World War II premised on a selective mis-reading of the Moscow Declaration of 1943: portraying the country as "Hitler's first victim," this enabled widespread amnesia of many Austrians' ideological and organizational commitment to national socialism before and after 1938, of their rapturous response to the *Anschluss*, as well as of Austrian contributions to—and perpetrators of—the Holocaust (e.g., see Heer and Wodak 2008: 8–10). Against the backdrop of postwar reconstruction, the "victim thesis" became the "foundational narrative" of the Second Republic in its early decades, sitting alongside continuing anti-Semitism and widespread uncritical reifications of former "dutiful" Wehrmacht soldiers (Uhl 2006: 40–54; Wodak and de Cillia 2007).

As in other parts of Europe, the generational changes of the 1960s brought some attempts to confront the past more critically and moments of polarization (e.g., Uhl 2006: 54–61). The latter were epitomized in the tragic events precipitated by the infamous anti-Semitic tirades of Taras Borodajkewycz, a professor of economic history, in 1965: in clashes between his supporters and opponents, a neo-Nazi student killed concentration camp survivor Ernst Kirchweger, whose funeral included a "march of silence" organized by the "Anti-fascist student committee" and the "Austrian resistance movement" and was attended by twenty-five thousand people (Adunka 2002: 33). Moments and pockets of attempted *Vergangenheitsbewältigung* notwithstanding, disinterest in confronting Austria's World War II history persisted amongst large parts of the population until the 1980s. This also emerges from the biography of the late Leon Zelman, Holocaust survivor, founder of the annual publication *Jewish Echo* (*Jüdisches Echo*), and initiator of the Jewish Welcome Service that hosts Austrian Jews visiting Vienna decades after escaping the genocidal machinery of Nazism: Zelman's reflections on postwar Austria testify to the "official repression" of the country's darkest historical chapter, to a "silent anti-Semitism" pervading the large majority (also see Wassermann 2002; John and Marschik 2002: 198–199), but also to "another Austria" of individual politicians and organizations committed to honest and self-critical historical consciousness (Zelman 2005: 171; 189–192).

The presidential election of former UN General Secretary Kurt Waldheim in 1986 arguably ruptured Austria's dominant postwar self-understanding (e.g., Uhl 2006). The international controversy over Waldheim wartime past was met with anti-Semitism in and beyond parts of the country's press (e.g., Mitten 1992; Reisigl and Wodak 2001; Gottschlich 2012) but also led to a belated critical interrogation of Austria's self-construction as Hitler's first victim by other sections of the public. The most official versions of a new, self-critical historical consciousness acknowledging Austrian "perpetrators and victims" were articulated by SPÖ-Chancellor Franz Vranitzky (e.g., Rathkolb 2005: 205). Since the 1990s this more honest historical consciousness has manifested amongst "political and church leaders," in new educational emphases and public discussions of anti-Semitism, the establishment of a "national fund" for Holocaust survivors, the finally "expeditious" handling of restitution claims, and in a law granting dual nationality to Austrian refugees (Pick 2000: 201; for more critical readings see Wodak and de Cillia 2007, Gottschlich 2012). These developments notwithstanding, Austria's mythscape has—as the concept predicts—remained internally contested. This is reflected in parts of the far right's at best "sloppy" relationship to the Nazi past and their more than occasional reluctance to unambiguously condemn it (e.g., Gärtner 2009: 58; 160).

Moreover, recent years have seen a series of anti-Semitic scandals, variously involving a regional FPÖ politician, a Tyrolean hotelier, a group of teenagers' violent interruption of a commemorative event at a former concentration camp, and racist graffiti smeared onto the outer walls of another (Karner 2011: 64–65).

The country-specific relevance of World War II to national debates and self-understandings is also invoked in a recent collection of reflections by Germans living in Austria. Its editor postulates a continuing contrast between Germany and Austria in terms of their respective responses to the past: the difference between an alleged German maturity and an assumed Austrian reluctance to face their darkest memories (Steffen 2009: 9). While this captures real discursive and institutional differences between (West) Germany's and Austria's postwar cultures of *Vergangenheitsbewältigung* or lack thereof, it also overlooks the internal contestations and historical shifts that have defined both contexts. In contemporary Germany, for instance, recent revelations of neo-Nazi murders and the emergence of a discourse of German "victimhood" since the 1990s (Niven 2006) problematize the idea of a nationwide, singular response to World War II and the Holocaust. Avoiding (potentially self-serving) reifications, the notion of a *national mythscape* provides analytical advantages here: locating memories in their national contexts and particularities, it alerts us to competing claims about and uses of the past made from different social positions and for different ideological purposes. A closer look at contemporary Austria's mythscape reveals several internal rifts and competing positions.

Top-Down, Bottom-Up

Reflecting the earlier-mentioned distinction between official and popular memory, Austria's mythscape is internally divided along axes of (relative) power and status. Competing memories are articulated both in a top-down fashion (e.g., by members of the political, scientific or media establishment) and bottom-up (i.e., by so-called ordinary citizens in the course of everyday life). While this happens constantly, over diverse issues and in reference to different pasts (e.g., Özkan 2011), space permits discussion only of some specific recent instances of competing invocations of the same historical anchor for diametrically opposed argumentative purposes by social actors positioned very differently along the spectrum of power.

The context to such recent top-down and bottom-up invocations of the same historical reference, albeit for mutually opposed purposes, was the Euro-debt-crisis. The social actors engaged in such diverging analogizing were Austria's President Heinz Fischer and the authors of readers' letters to the country's most widely read paper, the tabloid *Kronen Zeitung* (or *Krone*), respectively. The historical reference each of them utilized, in order to formulate very different conclusions and prognoses, was a famous speech delivered in a radio broadcast by Leopold Figl, first chancellor of the Second Republic and previous concentration camp inmate in Dachau and Mauthausen, at Christmas 1945.

In an interview with the daily regional *Kleine Zeitung* sixty-six years later, President Fischer was reminded of Figl's speech and asked about its contemporary relevance:

> ...at Christmas 1945 Leopold Figl said: "I can only ask you to believe in this Austria." Today, many people have lost faith in Europe. What's your response?

> Fischer: Christmas 1945 the cities were in ruins and people were hungry, this cannot be compared to our affluence. But it is still vital to believe in Austria and Europe. 2012 will demand tough measures.... I can therefore also say today, under entirely different circumstances: "Believe in this Austria!" ... and also "Believe in this Europe!" Europe must become stronger ... especially now that insufficiently regulated financial markets are causing problems. (Jungwirth, Weissenberger 2011, my translation)

While rejecting facile, decontextualized analogies, Fischer here confirms the continuing symbolic resonance or Figl's words; in the "entirely different circumstances" of an affluence now potentially threatened by "insufficiently regulated" financial markets, Fischer argues for closer European integration, for a European Union not content with being at the mercy of financial actors and forces.

Very different responses to the Greek (and other) debt-crises are regularly encountered in readers' letters in the daily *Kronen Zeitung*. Read by some 40 percent of Austrians, the paper is sometimes called the "world-champion in circulation" relative to population-size. Critics have highlighted the paper's increasingly xenophobic tone particularly since the 1980s (Rittberger 2009); its political influence and strong EU-skepticism over recent years (Karner 2010) are well-known. Even before the subsequent escalation of the Greek debt-crisis, numerous *Krone* readers opposed European financial solidarity, portraying it as a bottomless pit. This is exemplified by the following letters that, with altogether different intentions, also made rhetorical reference to Figl's 1945 speech:

> The late Hans Dichand, *Krone*-founder and editor . . . once supported European integration but, confronted with the facts, . . . became one of the most outspoken critics of this EU. Today, Hans Dichand would say: "Believe in this Austria, but not in the European Union in its present form" . . . Like Austria's patriotic forces . . . he would demand . . . a Europe of homelands [*Europa der Vaterländer*]. (*Krone* reader's letter, 18 June 2011, p. 29)

> The EU-parliament is a risk for the Austrian and other nations. . . . Austria's former success during post-war reconstruction was based on a shared will uniting the state and the people, [on] freedom and sovereignty. . . . This is how the young should understand Figl's historic Christmas-speech: "Believe in this Austria!" . . . [and not in] the cross-border sale of Austrian assets and speculation on the guarantees for debts amassed by others. (*Krone* reader's letter, 17 June 2011, p. 33, my translations)

As in many Krone readers' letters and everyday sentiments expressed elsewhere, we here encounter a nation-focused discourse of nostalgia that opposes European integration through a central *topos* of right-wing populism—the notion that the EU should be, at most, a decentralized network of distinctive "fatherlands" (e.g., Fillitz 2006: 152). Crucially for our purposes, these EU-skeptical arguments derive parts of their momentum from the same historical reference that Heinz Fischer, in the earlier example, invokes as an argument *for* EU-integration: Figl's famous words uttered in the aftermath of World War II. The very same historical context is thus invoked for diametrically opposed rhetorical purposes.

Far-Right Extremism, Right-Wing Populism, Left-Leaning Pluralism

The context-bound uses of selective historical narratives that constitute mythscapes emerge with clarity from "today's neo-nationalist groups . . . instrumentalis[ing] the past . . . for purposes . . . rooted in the present" (Banks and Gingrich 2006: 17). Ines Aftenberger broadens and elaborates on this by observing, first, an ideologically wider range of appropriations of particular memories and, second, what is distinctive about the (far-) right's accounts of World War II in Austria and Germany. She argues that while contemporary interests infuse memory politics across the political spectrum, the new far right's narratives are premised on particular *topoi*: the idea that Austria and Germany have been "prevented" from developing "normal," positively connoted national identities by the alleged outside "imposition" of "collective guilt" for the Holocaust, the singularity (or even reality) of which far-right extremists contest (Aftenberger 2007: 83). This alerts us to another major source of disagreement within Austria's mythscape: the history of World War II and its contemporary relevance are told very differently from different ideological vantage points. Without being able to capture the full range of positions, this section sketches particular appropriations and claims variously formulated by advocates of far-right extremism, right-wing populism, and left-leaning pluralism.

The possible depths of discursive, analogical depravity could be gleaned from a far-right extremist statement smeared onto the walls of the former concentration camp—and now site of commemoration—in Mauthausen, Upper Austria, in February 2009. Translating the hatred and violence of the original German into English is no easy task; it came close to this: "The breed of Muslims is to us what the Jew was to our fathers, beware!" As stressed by Bunzl and Hafez (2009: 7), this was so shocking a symbolic attack for several reasons: its location; its "positive historical reference" to the Holocaust; and its derived outline of a "future program" of genocide. On the level of social scientific discussion, Christoph Hofinger has commented on increasingly widespread comparisons of contemporary Islamophobia with the anti-Semitism of the 1930s and beyond. "Measured" by the Shoah, he concludes, Muslims are certainly not "the new Jews." Yet, current Islamophobia across Europe, with its "grotesque inflation" of the differences between Muslims and the "majority population," entertains "deportation phantasies" that have reached the levels of central European anti-Semitism of the early twentieth century (Hofinger 2012).

In the Austrian context, examples such as the above return us to definitional and taxonomical debates concerning the boundaries separating far-right extremism from right-wing populism and the FPÖ's position in relation to it. According to Heribert Schiedel, differing attitudes toward the history of Fascism/Nazism mark this boundary: while far-right extremists display an "ambivalent" and neo-Nazis an "affirmative" relationship to this past, right-wing populism generally distances itself from it (2011: 9). In this respect, commentators have shown, parts of the FPÖ differ from otherwise comparable right-wing populisms elsewhere in Europe: in their "sloppy relationship" to the past, a lack of clear distance from—or actual "belittling" of—national socialism (e.g., Gärtner 2009: 58; 160). Such reluctance to categorically condemn the crimes of the Nazi regime has indeed been a recurring feature of some FPÖ rhetoric, at times cutting across its internal organizational hierarchies. One infamous manifestation was Jörg Haider's 1991 description of the Third Reich's employment policies as "orderly," which he contrasted to the government's employment legislation at the time (Wodak 2000: 187).

Analytical rigor demands broader contextualization: Haider's growing appeal in the 1990s reflected his ability to speak to different constituencies and fulfill partly "contradictory roles"; while sections of the FPÖ tended toward historical revisionism and favored pan-Germanic self-understandings, maximizing the party's electoral success necessitated an ideological shift toward "Austrian patriotism" (Sickinger 2008: 116). The remainder of Haider's political biography is well-known, from the FPÖ's inclusion in a coalition by Austria's People's Party (ÖVP) and the ensuing temporary "sanctions" by her then fourteen EU partners in 2000, Haider's split from the FPÖ and foundation of a new Alliance Future Austria (BZÖ) in 2005, to his fatal car accident in 2008. Some rhetorical-ideological readjustments undertaken by the FPÖ under Heinz-Christian Strache since are worth noting here: the party's 2011 program reaffirmed its commitment to "protecting our homeland Austria" and the romanticist, pan-Germanic construction of the "majority of Austrians as part of the German people and linguistic and cultural community"; further, it stressed that Austria was "not a country of immigration"; and, most relevant to this discussion, the new party program failed to explicitly condemn Nazism, opting instead for a general—arguably leveling—rejection of "fanaticism and extremism" (http://www.orf.at/stories/2064288/2064293).

While many contributions to the mythscape emanating from the far right offer "uncritical, affirmative memories constructing [external] pariahs" (Stiegnitz 2011: 110), there are prominent counter-narratives we may broadly characterize as left-leaning and inclusivist and that, notably, engage (with) similar historical points of reference, including World War II. Crucially, however, they do so in very different ways: Austria's co-responsibility for the crimes committed under national socialism is emphasized, the events of 1938–1945 are remembered as warnings of potential future recurrences, Austria's present responsibilities are stressed, and shortcomings criticized. Constraints of space only allow a sketch of two illustrative examples of such critical counter-memories and the analogies and arguments they propose.

The first snapshot is provided by song-lyrics by the Styrian band STS, prominent and politically engaged (Karner 2002) exemplars of the musical genre Austro-Pop:

"It's starting just as it did then," says old Franz,
"it's the same old song and dance,
it's starting just as it did sixty years ago,
and at the time it began with only a few of them, too." (STS 1998, my translation)

Memories of the rise of Nazism here serve as a stark warning. Against the backdrop of xenophobic attacks against asylum-seekers and refugees across Central Europe in the 1990s, the song likens the past to the present, analogically linking the 1930s to contemporary neo-nationalism and racist violence.

A recent example of critical engagement with Austria's memory politics emerged from a speech by Christian Rainer, editor of the weekly news magazine *Profil*, at the commemoration of the liberation of the Upper Austrian concentration camp in Ebensee. Rainer (2011) argued that Austria's moral (as opposed to economic) postwar reconstruction had failed, that agreements concerning restitution of surviving victims of Nazism reached under the ÖVP-FPÖ coalition were but a "fig-leaf" hiding a renewed forgetting of—and end to the public engagement with—the horrors of the Holocaust. While Rainer's speech was met with much agreement by *Profil* readers (16 May 2011: 6–9), one should not assume complete interpretative agreement among people with a shared commitment to critically confronting Austria's World War II past: Ariel Muzicant, former president of Vienna's Jewish community, thus recently credited Wolfgang Schüssel's controversial post-2000 government with at last achieving what successive previous governments had not—the aforementioned restitution agreement (http://oe1.orf.at/artikel/298514; for a more ambivalent assessment, see *Salzburger Nachrichten*, 6 August 2012).

Transnational Debates

Mythscapes are not exclusively national. More accurately, some of their constitutive narratives and disagreements cross the institutional and symbolic boundaries of the nation, implicating transnational actors and audiences.

In the Austrian context, the clearest recent illustration of this was provided by the debates surrounding the temporary sanctions by

Austria's then fourteen EU partners in the aftermath of the formation of the controversial ÖVP-FPÖ coalition government in 2000. The transnational dimensions of the underlying disagreements manifested in supporters and opponents of the sanctions—inside and outside of Austria—utilizing similar arguments, to which the history of World War II and contemporary responses to it were central: supporters of the sanctions saw in Haider's FPÖ a historically revisionist affront to a European value-consensus concerning human rights; opponents, conversely, saw the sanctions as illegitimate and hypocritical interventions in Austria's internal, democratic decisions; further, opponents argued that Austria's reputation had been tarnished by the unjustifiable accusation of an imminent "revival of national socialism" (Wieland 2001: 12). Seen as mutually opposed narratives in a mythscape of transnational reach, these clashing interpretations emphasized altogether different dimensions: the symbolic (i.e., supporters of the sanctions reading the FPÖ as a contradiction to defining European values) and the structural (i.e., opponents of the sanctions stressing that the controversial coalition did certainly not mark an institutional return of Nazism) respectively. Such an analysis helps make sense of the strength of emotions on both sides and of the fact that as an interpretative disagreement it remained unresolved—the opposing sides were ultimately talking about different things. This further complements the following suggestion that the sanctions reflected *both* political self-interests elsewhere *and* a European commitment to core values:

> [W]ithout the particular concerns about domestic politics of certain politicians, it is unlikely that the sanctions against Austria would have been adopted. . . . On the other hand, without the recent establishment of concerns about human rights and democratic principles as an EU norm, it is unlikely that these particular sanctions would have been adopted collectively. . . . Thus, while norms might have been used instrumentally, such instrumental use only works . . . if the norms have acquired a certain degree of taken-for-grantedness within the relevant . . . actors or institutions. (Merlingen, Mudde, Sedelmeier 2001: 59)

More recently, the ongoing Euro-debt-crisis has seen numerous transnational debates, some of which reference and employ World War II for different rhetorical purposes. Austrian media reflect and participate in such transnational debates over the past and its (ir)relevance to the present.

Instances of Austrian (broadsheet) journalists commenting on sub-sections of other national mythscapes and their instrumentalization for present purposes have included the following: an argument against offensive, utterly decontextualized analogies suggested by images of Angela Merkel with a "Hitler moustache" in Greek and Polish papers that fail to acknowledge that "Germans have learned their lesson from the past" (Lackner 2011); admiration for former German Chancellor Helmut Schmidt's plea to regulate the financial markets and for Germany to recognize her historical obligation to provide European solidarity (Hoffmann-Ostenhof 2011); conversely, criticism of the German "hegemony of austerity" for having allegedly misrecognized that Hitler's rise to power was less due to spiraling inflation than to Brüning's politics of austerity in the early 1930s (Thurnher 2012a). At the same time, there are also prominent external voices commenting—from the outside in—on some contemporary analogies drawn within Austria's mythscape. In an interview with the Viennese weekly *Falter*, Ian Kershaw thus recently refuted commonly made comparisons of the current crises with those faced by the Weimar Republic: despite widespread political disenchantment then and now, Kershaw argued that deeper structural dissimilarities made such analogies problematically inaccurate (Zwander 2011a). Interviewed by the same paper, political scientist Ivan Krastev argued that while the 1930s saw a crisis of legitimacy affecting the economy and the 1970s a loss of faith in politics, today's crisis was premised on a "double loss of trust"—in *both* politics and the economy (Zwander 2011b).

Approaching Analogies Analytically

Having sketched some fault lines structuring and dividing Austria's mythscape internally as well as some transnational debates and historical analogies featuring in it, we return to the prom-controversy mentioned earlier. In light of this discussion, what else should be said about an event the FPÖ defined as a "sign of freedom and democracy," while to its opponents it constituted—particularly given its timing and venue—an "insult to the dignity of the victims of Nazism" (http://wien.orf.at/news/stories/2518125)? In particular, how should one respond to Heinz-Christian Strache's staggering description of the far right as "the new Jews" or indeed to similar analogies encountered elsewhere? As argued in the remainder of this chapter, these are key-questions—both analytically and ethically—for anyone interested in the enduring presence and employment of memories and narratives of World War II in the here and now.

Strache's comparison was strongly condemned across most other parties: for instance, a Green politician described it as a "belittling of Nazi crimes and criminals"; an SPÖ politician similarly saw in it a rhetorical strategy typical of the FPÖ, in which "the inciters [of hatred] portray themselves as victims"; and to the ÖVP's general secretary it showed that Strache was willing to "employ any historical comparison, no matter how tasteless, to appeal to his core audience and portray himself as a victim" (http://www.orf.at/stories/ 2102605/2102606, my translations). Further, Austria's president Heinz Fischer decided, in light of the comparison, not to present Strache with a political medal, for which the latter had been earmarked (http://www.orf.at/stories/2102525/2102518). Strache himself responded by arguing that he had been misquoted, that he felt "deep compassion with all victims of the terrible Nazi regime," that he had not made the comparison as attributed to him but had merely wanted to illustrate—following "insults and attacks suffered by prom guests"—how "such mass-psychoses" can come about; further, Strache insisted that he had nothing to do with Nazism and anti-Semitism but stood for "reconciliation." The FPÖ's general secretary Harald Vilimsky, meanwhile, described the controversy as "artificial and ridiculous" and Strache as the "victim of a witch-hunt by left-wing extremists": Strache had not, Vilimsky added in seemingly inadvertent self-contradiction, wanted to "relativize the suffering inflicted on Jews" but had "merely related the demagoguery [*sic!*, *Hetze*] of the Nazi-regime against people of other faiths to the violent demagoguery of left-wing extremists against people of other opinions" (http://www.orf.at/stories/2102605/2102606, my translations).

Vilimsky's account is remarkable for several reasons: seemingly intended to diffuse the situation, it achieved precisely what it purported not to intend—a relativizing belittling of the Shoah; the systematic Nazi murder of six million Jews is reduced to—in a truly mind-boggling euphemism—"demagoguery" against now unspecified "people of other faiths." Conversely, the protests against the prom, which—as mentioned earlier—involved sixty diverse organizations in a week of activism against racism, anti-Semitism and right-wing extremism (http://wien.orf.at/news/stories/2517511), are discursively re- and mis-constructed as "violent demagoguery" (as opposed to, it seems, the Nazis' mere demagoguery) by "left-wing extremists." Finally, the state persecution and attempted annihilation of European Jewry is likened to contemporary civil society activism and demonstrations against far-right fraternities, whose "opinions"—Vilimsky suggests—now need protecting. All of this raises questions about how to analytically, and ethically, respond to such and similar historical analogies that are distorting and clearly self-interested (see Müller 2002).

Similar questions were addressed by *Falter*-editor Armin Thurnher: he suggested that some reactions to Strache's comparison, while entirely justified, had been counter-productively emotional, which had in turn inadvertently helped Strache's "obscene perpetrator-victim reversal"; Thurnher argued that sober and dry responses would have been more effective at pointing to the FPÖ's historical roots and at naming what the description of far-right prom guests as "the new Jews" was— "a scandal" (Thurnher 2012b).

However formulated, in detached analytical fashion or with emotional outrage, responses to the kinds of historical analogies encountered in Austria's and other mythscapes should be informed by the following key-questions (also see Gottschlich 2012: 181–182): *who is comparing whom or what with whom or what? For which rhetorical purposes and with which ideological intentions?* This acknowledges that the positions, from which people speak and compare, are crucial in judging the relevance and justifiability—or their frequent lack—of their analogies. It is from this analytical starting point that we can begin to gauge possible structural or discursive (dis)similarities between historical contexts, as well as the motivations of those asserting them.

An argument that the questions as to *who speaks, about whom and how* are crucial in judging political rhetoric was also recently made by journalist and human rights activist Susanne Scholl. In a commentary on the Austrian minister of interior's distrust of (some) unaccompanied, teenaged asylum-seekers, Scholl argued that this is particularly worrying in a national setting that should remember the fate of Austrian Jewish children who only survived the Holocaust thanks to their unaccompanied escape and exile in England during World War II:

> Especially an Austrian minister of interior accusing parents sending their children off, so that they survive, of fraudulent intentions is utterly tasteless. (Scholl 2012, my translation)

Not only are contemporary exclusions endured by asylum-seekers being criticized here, but Scholl also invokes key questions similar to those outlined above: who postulates which historical comparisons and with which intentions? Or, and more relevant to the particular instance Scholl criticizes, which historical echoes are or are not, but should be, recognized in particular statements?

Immediately after the prom-controversy surveys revealed a decline in the FPÖ's and Strache's popularity (http://www.orf.at/stories/2103269). However, commentators agreed that this would be a short-term effect only (Lackner, Lahodynsky, Zöchling 2012). If this turns out to be the case and the FPÖ's renewed appeal to Austrian voters continues to grow, then the above questions—to be put to all historical analogies drawn in Austria's mythscape—need to be communicated widely. The urgency of this was also shown by a 2011 survey, in which a staggering 42 percent of Austrian respondents endorsed the view that "Israel's treatment of Palestinians is as inhuman as the Nazi treatment of the Jews" (Gottschlich 2012: 180; Lackner 2012).

Concluding Remarks

Nations do not just *possess* internally contested mythscapes. Nations are, aside from their institutional structures, partly constituted by such mythscapes (also see Wodak and de Cillia 2007: 317). The latter are in turn, as this analysis has corroborated, negotiated by social and political actors located very differently along the ideological spectrum. What is more, such a contested mythscape is continually added to, in top-down and bottom-up fashions, by political élites and ordinary citizens alike. Further, such mythscapes have porous external boundaries, not only but especially in our globalizing era: there are discourses that circulate transnationally and in both directions, looking and "flowing" into as much as out of Austria (or any other nation-state), and that are also part of the "perpetually mutating repository for the representation of the past for the purposes of the present" (Bell 2003: 66). Finally, this analysis has drawn attention to historical analogies, particularly those involving the history of World War II, within Austria's mythscape. As not the only but arguably the most prominent anchors for such analogies, different dimensions of World War II and the Shoah are invoked by diverse social actors, for a variety of rhetorical purposes, and with contrasting motivations. The latter range from "dehistoricizing" constructions of an "all-encompassing 'community of victims'" premised on the self-serving "deletion of agents" and thus of the difference between perpetrators and victims (Wodak and de Cillia 2007: 334), to an ethical commitment to mourning the millions murdered in the Holocaust.

This resonates with scholarship warning us against "over-extending" conceptual categories and thereby losing "historical specificity," without which "the political and ethical connotations of acts of remembrance

[are] overlooked" (Crownshaw and Leydesdorff 2008: ix). More concretely, there is a moral imperative to remember—in and beyond Austria—that "there was—and is—no analogy" for the Holocaust (Stern 2008: 25). "What is our relationship," asks Renate Siebert (2008: 165), "with our recent Fascist and National Socialíst past? . . . Who are we . . . in relation to [it]? Do we have choices in the face of what the past forces upon us?" The concept of a (national) mythscape applied and extended above reveals diverse relationships to this past, with individuals and groups positioning themselves very differently in relation to it, and employing it for varied contemporary purposes. It is fitting to conclude with an example of an ethical relationship to this past, one that mourns the victims of Nazism and stays alert to the possibility of future recurrences without denying historical specificity. Former inmates of the Mauthausen concentration camp Hans Maršálek and Kurt Hacker (n.d.: 31, my translation) summarize its contemporary significance as follows:

> Now a site of remembrance and warning, it maintains a tie to all those murdered there, whatever their nationalities, religious backgrounds and gender. It also enables consciousness-raising among the young, who—we sincerely hope—will never experience a comparable historical period, neither at home nor elsewhere.

References

Adunka, Evelyn. 2002. "Antisemitismus in der Zweiten Republik." In *Antisemitismus in Österreich nach 1945*, ed. Heinz Wassermann. Innsbruck: Studienverlag.

Aftenberger, Ines. 2007. *Die neue Rechte und der Neorassismus*. Graz: Leykam.

Banks, Marcus and Andre Gingrich. 2006. "Introduction." In *Neo-Nationalism in Europe and Beyond*, eds. Andre Gingrich and Marcus Banks. New York: Berghahn.

Bell, Duncan. 2003. "Mythscapes: memory, mythology, and national identity." *British Journal of Sociology* 54 (1): 63–81.

Bunzl, John and Farid Hafez. 2009. "Vorwort." In *Islamophobie in Österreich*, eds. John Bunzl and Farid Hafez. Innsbruck: Studienverlag.

Crownshaw, Richard and Selma Leydesdorff. 2008. "Introduction." In *Memory & Totalitarianism*, ed. Luisa Passerini. New Brunswick: Transaction Publishers.

Eisenreich, Ruth and Benedikt Narodoslawsky. 2012. "Eine Nacht unter aufrechten Demokraten." *Falter* 5: 13

Fillitz, Thomas. 2006. "Neo-nationalism, the Freedom Party and Jörg Haider in Austria." In *Neo-Nationalism in Europe and Beyond*, eds. Andre Gingrich and Marcus Banks. New York: Berghahn.

Gärtner, Reinhold. 2009. *Politik der Feindbilder*. Wien: Kremayr & Scheriau.

Gottschlich, Maximilian. 2012. *Die große Abneigung*. Wien: Czernin.

Hanisch, Ernst. 1994. *Der lange Schatten des Staates*. Wien: Ueberreuter.

Heer, Hannes and Ruth Wodak. 2008. "Introduction." In *The Discursive Construction of History: Remembering the Wehrmacht's War of Annihilation*, eds. Hannes Heer et al. Basingstoke: Palgrave Macmillan.

Hoffmann-Ostenhof, Georg. 2011. "Drei Tröstungen." *Profil* 50: 73.

Hofinger, Christoph. 2012. "Das Mobbing der Moslems." *Falter* 12:14–15.

http://derstandard.at/1326504047903/ "Strache auf WKR-Ball: 'Wir sind die neuen Juden." Accessed 30 January 2012.

http://oe1.orf.at/artikel/298514 "Muzicant zieht positive Bilanz." Accessed 21 February 2012.

http://wien.orf.at/news/stories/2517511/ "Viele Zeichen gegen Rechts." Accessed 26 January 2012.

http://wien.orf.at/news/stories/2518125 "WKR-Ball: Schlagabtausch FPÖ-Grüne." Accessed 26 January 2012

http://www.orf.at/stories/2064288/2064293/ "Die 'zehn freiheitlichen Gebote." Accessed 20 June 2011.

http://www.orf.at/stories/2102025/2102021 "WKR-Ball: Kritik an Polizeinsatz." Accessed 30 January 2012.

http://www.orf.at/stories/2102525/2102518 "Fischer verweigert Strache Orden." Accessed 1 February 2012.

http://www.orf.at/stories/2102605/2102606 "Strache sieht sich missinterpretiert." Accessed 1 February 2012.

http://www.orf.at/stories/2103269 "FPÖ fällt in Umfragen zurück." Accessed 6 February 2012.

Jing, Jun. 1996. *The Temple of Memories*. Stanford: Stanford University Press.

John, Michael and Matthias Marschik. 2002. "Ortswechsel: Antisemitismus im österreichischen Sport nach 1945." In *Antisemitismus in Österreich nach 1945*, ed. Heinz Wassermann. Innsbruck: Studienverlag.

Jungwirth, Michael and Eva Weissenberger. 2011. "Interview: 'Glaubt an dieses Europa!'" *Kleine Zeitung*, 25 December: 8–9.

Karner, Christian. 2002. "Austro-pop since the 1980s: two case studies of cultural critique and counter-hegemonic resistance." *Sociological Research Online* 6 (4): http://www.socresonline.org/6/4/karner.html.

——— 2005. "The 'Habsburg dilemma' today: competing discourses of national identity in contemporary Austria." *National Identities* 7 (4): 411–434.

——— 2010. "The uses of the past and European integration: Austria between Lisbon, Ireland and EURO 08." *Identities: Global Studies in Culture and Power* 17 (4): 387–410.

——— 2011. *Negotiating National Identities*. Farnham: Ashgate.

Kronen Zeitung. Various dates and page numbers as in text.

Lackner, Herbert. 2011. "Die guten Deutschen." *Profil* 50: 15.

——— 2012. "Auf schmalem Pfad." *Profil* 16: 22–27.

Lackner, Herbert, OtmarLahodynsky and Christa Zöchling. 2012. "Rechtswalzer." *Profil* 6: 18–24.

Maršálek, Hans and Kurt Hacker. n.d. *Das Konzentrationslager Mauthausen*. Wien: Österreichische Lagergemeinschaft Mauthausen.

Merlingen, Michael, Cas Mudde and Ulrich Sedelmeier. 2001. "The right and the righteous? European norms, domestic politics and the sanctions against Austria." *Journal of Common Market Studies* 39 (1): 59–77.

Mitten, Richard. 1992. *The Politics of Antisemitic Prejudice*. Oxford: Westview.

Müller, Jan-Werner. 2002. "Introduction." In *Memory & Power in Post-War Europe*, ed. Jan- Werner Müller. Cambridge: Cambridge University Press.

Niven, Bill, ed. 2006. *Germans as Victims*. Basingstoke: Palgrave Macmillan.

Özkan, Duygu. 2011. *Türkenbelagerung*. Wien: Metroverlag.

Pick, Hella. 2000. *Guilty Victim*. London: I.B. Tauris.

Profil. Dates and page numbers as in text.

Rainer, Christian. 2011. "Gescheitert am moralischen Wiederaufbau." *Profil* 19: 38–39.

Rathkolb, Oliver. 2005. *Die paradoxe Republik: Österreich 1945–2005*. Wien: Zsolnay.

Reisigl, Martin and Ruth Wodak. 2001. *Discourse and Discrimination*. London: Routledge.

Rittberger, Michael. 2009. "Wie kommt die Ausländerfeindlichkeit in die Kronen Zeitung?" In *Dazugehören oder nicht?*, eds. Sevgi Bardakçi et al. Innsbruck: Studienverlag.*Salzburger Nachrichten*. 2012. "18,000 NS-Opfer entschädigt." 6 August: 2.

Schiedel, Heribert. 2011. *Extreme Rechte in Europa*. Wien: Steinbauer.

Scholl, Susanne. 2012. "Von Ankerkindern und anderen Neujahrsungeheuerlichkeiten." *Megaphon* 195: 5.

Sickinger, Hubert. 2008. "Jörg Haider." In *Kreisky-Haider: Bruchlinien österreichischer Identitäten*, eds. Anton Pelinka, Hubert Sickinger, Karin Stögner. Wien: Braumüller.

Siebert, Renate. 2008. "Don't forget." In *Memory & Totalitarianism*, ed. Luisa Passerini. New Brunswick: Transaction Publishers.

Steffen, Eva. 2009. "Vorwort." In *Wir sind gekommen, um zu bleiben*, ed. Eva Steffen. Wien: Czernin.

Stern, Frank. 2008. "Antagonistic memories." In *Memory & Totalitarianism*, ed. Luisa Passerini. New Brunswick: Transaction Publishers.

Stiegnitz, Peter. 2011. *Politik der Gewalt*. Wien: Löcker.

STS. 1998. "Es fangt genauso an." *Auf a Wort*. Polygram [CD].

Thaler, Peter. 2001. *The Ambivalence of Identity*. West Lafayette: Purdue University Press.

Thurnher, Armin. 2012a. "Die Ratingagenturen und die Sparstrumpfmaskenpolitik." *Falter* 3: 5.

——— 2012b. "Elf Antworten auf die Frage: Wird Hazeh Strache ungerecht behandelt?" *Falter* 6: 5.

Uhl, Heidemarie. 2006. "From victim myth to co-responsibility thesis: Nazi rule, World War II, and the Holocaust in Austrian memory." In *The Politics of Memory in Postwar Europe*, eds. Richard Ned Lebow et al. Durham: Duke University Press.

Wassermann, Heinz, ed. 2002. *Antisemitismus in Österreich nach 1945*. Innsbruck: Studienverlag.

Wieland, Carl, ed. 2001. *Österreich in Europa*. Wien: Amalthea.

Wodak, Ruth. 2000. "Echt, anständig und ordentlich." In *Haider: Österreich und die rechte Versuchung*, ed. Hans-Henning Scharsach. Reinbek: Rowohlt.

Wodak, Ruth and Rudolf de Cillia. 2007. "Commemorating the past: the discursive construction of official narratives about the "Rebirth of the Second Austrian Republic." *Discourse & Communication* 1 (3): 315–341.

Zelman, Leon. 2005. *Ein Leben nach dem Überleben*. Wien: Kremayr & Scheriau.

Zöchling, Christa. 2012. "Ein letztes Hurra." *Profil* 3: 26–27.

Zwander, Wolfgang. 2011a. "Der Historiker Ian Kershaw über die Begeisterung für die Nazis und die Lehren aus Weimar für die Eurokrise." *Falter* 51–52: 22–23.

——— 2011b. "Das Volk hat ausgevolkt." *Falter* 49: 14–15.

11

World War II in Discourses of National Identification in Poland: An Intergenerational Perspective

Anna Duszak

Introduction

This chapter draws on a framework known as Critical Discourse Studies (CDS), a family of interdisciplinary approaches to communication that combine discursive *and* social analyses (e.g., Fairclough 2003; Wodak 2001). The discursive part covers language (verbalizations, texts, and genres), yet it also accommodates social practices that do not centrally involve language. In our case this applies for instance to visual exhibits and war reconstructions, which largely do without language unless, or until, they are brought meta-textually into the realm of speech. The social dimension, in turn, is informed by nonlinguistic expertise from sociology, social psychology, history, or political sciences.

There are some consequences of a critical discursive view on social practice that need to be spelled out. It is the tenet of any discourse analysis, and critical discourse analysis in particular, that research topics can hardly be treated as isolates. With our focus on WWII narratives we need to remember that any discursive construal of the War is part of an unending process of its recontextualization, rereading, and rewriting, as well as re-semiotization into various modalities and (sub)codes. In linguistic nomenclature, all discourses are *polyphonic* or *multi-voiced* (the terms adopted from Bakhtin 1981), so that any single text resounds in voices of other texts, while also lending itself to such insemination. The porous nature of communication, sometimes described as *interdiscursivity* (Fairclough 2003), explains why texts and genres invite the metaphor of *dialogization* (also after Bakhtin): texture is essentially an interactive process of meaning negotiation between social actors, positions, ideologies, motivations, and goals.

This discursive regime also applies to WWII discourses and their counter-discourses, all of them caught up in a spin of cooperative, competitive, and conflictual values. In other words, an interdiscursive approach undermines strict divisions into text types, genres, and fields of social practice, let alone human competencies and identities. The result is a search for interactions across domains: politics, the media, education, art, entertainment, and others. One way of conceptualizing such flows is to identify ideologies, i.e., dominant systems of values that interface rather than segregate the human worlds in focus: political speeches, textbooks, museum exhibits, and personal narratives. Thus, the political relevance of WWII is not limited to any core political discourse, but can be viewed instead as a gradient in social practices, social thinking, and talking.

Next to such horizontal flows there are vertical (historical) connections between genres and domains. In this view WWII serves as an interface between the past and the present. It can be integrative as well as disintegrative, depending on how national values and interests are (re)defined: What is to be remembered, how, why, and to what current purpose? WWII legacy engages politicians and political commentators, historians, journalists, teachers, clergy, and artists, as well as parents. In an intergenerational perspective, it becomes an important aspect in the formation of national identification, historical knowledge, and cultural values among the young in particular.

If, as some sociologists argue (e.g., Szacka 2010: 119), the scope of human memory rarely goes beyond the lifespan of three generations, WWII today has reached the stage when individuals' living memory is giving way to the cultural memory of a nation. With the eyewitness generations passing away, the War is losing its tangible format. Personal narratives of what was once a lived experience are being replaced by symbolic representations of the past. Yet, chronology always goes hand in hand with contextual change. New frames of reference are created for how the past can be seen in its capacity to influence the present and the future condition of individuals, social groups, and entire nations. In some countries, of which Poland is an example, radical sociopolitical transformations at the end of the last century have led to substantial rereadings and reevaluations of the War and its heritage. In addition, the ongoing cultural changes impact on the readability and acceptability of traditional semiotic codes for historical narration. Consequently, we are dealing today with a growing cognitive and communicative distance between generations when it comes to what is remembered, imaginable, appealing, or useful.

In this, the medium of historical narration constitutes an important frame of reference. It also construes the pivotal point for the present discussion. I start with the traditional polarization into private (family) and public (official) communication, and go on to recent controversies over pop cultural tendencies in how WWII-knowledge is mediated as part of patriotic formation of the young. Here I focus on intergenerational differences in addressing such issues. In keeping with CDS, I examine various sources and data. My main frame of reference are the results of a project on *The dynamics of inter-generational discourses: values and styles of communication*, which I designed and coordinated in 2010. These were semi-structured interviews (approximately sixty minutes each) on memories (/images) of WWII and its current legacy. I report on some findings from two groups of respondents: "the Old" (sixteen people in their eighties) and "the Young" (twenty-two people in their twenties).

A Historical Model of Polish Patriotism

A socio-discursive approach needs a historical frame of reference in order to locate currently observable phenomena against culturally entrenched patterns of social conduct. It is important therefore to anchor WWII in a historical model of Polish patriotism, especially as many scholars recognize that the orientation toward the nation's past is a characteristic marker of national thinking among generations of Poles (Niewiara 2010: 17–18). Some facts and cultural emphases need to be mentioned here.

Poland lost her independence at the end of the eighteenth century to regain it only in 1918. For over 130 years, Poles were a nation without a state. Not surprisingly, this condition impacted on Poles' national consciousness, on how patriotic and national values were conceptualized and verbalized. The *we-nation* sense of community became most salient as well as vulnerable. Polish national identity was construed around grand words like *God, Honor, Homeland*, building a national *mythology* on *martyrdom, sacrifice* and *nostalgia*. We need to recognize here the role of literature and art. Gilejko (2005: 67–68) describes, for instance, the omnipresent figure of an ideal Pole, a Romantic hero and a martyr, ready to sacrifice his life in the name of faith, Homeland, or a cause. The cultural specificity of Polish *ojczyzna* (homeland) has been discussed by ethnolinguists including Wierzbicka (1997), who underscores the word's emotional and nostalgic overtones, demonstrating also how *ojczyzna* differs from its near equivalents in other languages, homeland in English, *rodina* in Russian, or *Vaterland* in German. Among the historical components of Polish national identity Łastawski (2004: 78) includes gentry and Catholic traditions, coupled with the vision of Poland as an outpost of Europe and a protector of European (Western!) values. The formative role of the Catholic Church, and the cult of Virgin Mary (Mother Poland), was and is important in this context. Under such conditions the family assumed the leading role in mediating the past, and thus safeguarding the nation's continuity.

After WWII the family ethos survived as a form of resistance to Communist indoctrination. Until the democratic turn in 1980s, it was first of all the family that generated national memory, preserved what was silenced or barred from public circulation, and filtered the official truths. In important way the family created a discourse space for debating public matters among intimates, relatives, and friends. For generations now it has played a major role in Poles' national and political socialization (Dubisz 2011).

The Dynamics of WWII Memory in Poland

As much as WWII was, and remains, a human trauma, it also left idiosyncratic imprints in the countries affected. These are often linked to dates, names, and events, and treated as symbolic of national collective memory. For Poles WWII began on 1 September 1939 with the Nazi invasion of Westerplatte in Gdańsk. This was followed by the Soviet Invasion on 17 September 1939, opening the second front under the Hitler-Stalin agreement; the Katyn massacre in April 1940, the extermination of over ten thousand Polish officers and intellectuals upon Stalin's order. There was the Ghetto Uprising and, above all, the Warsaw Uprising in 1944, an icon of an ideological struggle during and after the War. For many Poles the War did not end in May 1945, with a new form of oppression being introduced by the postwar Soviet-based Communist regime. For a long time under Communism, Poles were divided into heirs of the Home Army, operating on the Western front, and the People's Army, fighting the Nazis under the Soviet military command.

For nearly forty-five years under the Communist rule, the War was construed under what was commonly described as *a red victory over Nazism*, and used for fueling anti-German sentiments in Polish society.

The removal of Communism heralded a new stage in remembering and commemorating the War. Here, 1989 marks an important caesura. On 4 June, the first democratic elections took place in the aftermath of transformations sparked by the social movement of *Solidarity*. Poles stopped talking about the Germans as the only perpetrators of the War, and turned their attention to the East, speaking openly of the Hitler-Stalin pact, the Katyń massacre, and the brutal killings on the Ukrainian border. Under the democratic transformations the accents were relocated, blame and merit were redefined. New voices were added, many of which had been muted or distorted under the Communist regime. This concerned first of all taboo topics previously banned from official circulation, such as the Katyń massacre or Warsaw Uprising. Revisited at home, they also entered the sphere of international historical discussion (for Katyń see, e.g., Allen 2009; Kadell 2011; Bosiacki 2012; for the Warsaw Uprising see, e.g., Ensink and Sauer 2003; Davies 2004; Sawicki 2004).

In post-Communist realities, the traditional split between *public* and *private* (family) talk assumed a new dimension. The relation between grand politics and common knowledge has featured in much recent research, particularly by sociologists and historians (esp. Kwiatkowski et al. 2010). Various countrywide studies emerged, drawing mainly on interviews, surveys, and focus group discussions (Kwiatkowski 2010; Szacka 2010; Szpociński 2009; Kaźmierska 2002; Czyżewski et al. 1997). The outcomes of this research are noteworthy here: the comparison of Poles' collective *and* autobiographical memory, whether eyewitnesses or recipients of family narratives, revealed—among other things—regional emphases in how the War was experienced and memorized. Nijakowski (2010), for instance, shows that in the eastern parts of the country it was not the Germans but the Russians and the Ukrainians who were portrayed as Poles' major enemies and perpetrators of the worst atrocities. Analyzing comprehensive data from 2003 and 2009, Szacka (2010: 116) claims that the question "who was worse" remains a source of dispute across, and even within, Polish families, which she links to stereotypes of a *cultural* German, a *primitive* Russian, and a *cruel* Ukrainian. By and large, it was now the Russians, and not the Germans, who were more negatively assessed. One of Szacka's quotes is particularly revealing: telling her family story, a young woman (age bracket eighteen to thirty-five) thus claimed that "the Germans were humanitarian enough to kill right away" (Szacka 2010: 116; my translation). However, Szacka adds, there is parallel quantitative evidence that the respondents believed that their families suffered more as a result of Nazi repressions than because of Soviet wrongdoing (Szacka 2010: 123–4). She is probably right in explaining this contradiction by the fact that the image of the German has already been *worked on* in public talk and individual contacts, while the relationship to the Russians was never properly taken issue with, and still incites emotions in private and political talk.

Linking politics and memory became particularly evident in the first decade of the twenty-first century, largely as a result of an increased popularity of rightist political parties. "Wars over memory" (Machcewicz 2012) led to recontextualizations and reassessments of various aspects of Poland's history and the country's current politics, including the Communist past and post-Communist transformations, as well as Poland's relations with Germany and Russia (Kochanowski 2011; Nijakowski 2008; Nowinowski et al. 2008). This also led to discussions among élites about the social consequences of manipulating memory by some politicians (e.g., Samsonowicz 2008: 24).

In the above-mentioned research, my respondents from both age groups argued that they were interested in passing on (or learning) the truth about the War. Yet, what that truth was turned out more difficult to establish, and that it actually might be relative was suggested by some of the interviewees. A statement by an eighty-year-old woman is perhaps symptomatic of such doubts (in each case the number of the interview in its sub-corpus is given, followed by the age and gender of the respondent; for reasons of space truncated utterances are sometimes provided; translations by Danuta Przepiórkowska; emphases mine):

> 43; 80, F
> I mean, well, many people distort history depending on when it's written. It was a different truth when it was written in Communist Poland and it's different now so there is one truth and another truth. And if you dig deep and talk to people who actually do know the truth from their personal experience, the truth would still be different, it would be the third truth, so anyone who writes will write in a completely different way, depending on who writes and when they write.

Revisiting (the Language of) Polish Patriotism

As already suggested, traditional Polish patriotism was linked to emotionality and a language marked by pathos, on the one hand, and intimacy, on the other. Now attempts are being made to redefine it in terms of more rational beliefs and expectations, as well as concrete social duties following from one's participation in a community. Such postulates are in part at least to be linked to Poland's accession to the European Union. They also meet the needs of the young generation, born and living in conditions radically different from those known to their parents and grandparents. As a result, historically sanctioned values in Polish national culture are now being reread and redefined. This applies to the founding category of Polish patriotism, the Romantic model of heroism. Yet, it also involves its connotative meanings, such as "turning failures into moral victories, poverty into virtue, or popular religious routines into spirituality" (Krzysztofek 2005: 289).

Academic discussions over the past and future of Polish patriotism, national continuity, dignity, and power have been heavily mediatized. Some internationalization of this debate took place with the Polish condition compared to the situation in other countries (see Polish in *National Identity Study* 1995 overviewed by Skarżyńska 2008; also Skarżyńska and Golec de Zavala 2006). Distinctions have been drawn between *blind* patriotism, correlating with uncritical nationalist attitudes, and *critical* patriotism, when next to having pride in their nation, people are also able (and willing) to recognize its bad sides, whether in the past or at present. According to Skarżyńska (2008: 64) only 9 percent of Poles agree today that there are "some things in Poland they are ashamed of," while some 71 percent answer the question in the negative. In turn, addressing the young only (ages seventeen to twenty-nine), Przecławska (2008: 83–4) argues that in 1993 very few events were seen as shameful (e.g., Poland's partitions, Polish anti-Semitism), while in 2003 the young also declared they were ashamed of politicians and Poland's defeat in soccer world cup. In Poles' national disposition some social psychologists see symptoms of "collective narcissism" (esp. Golec de Zavala 2010; also Bilewicz 2012; Kofta and Bilewicz 2011), which could mean that—as with individuals—a group's narcissistic preoccupation with its own image may be a sign of instability and insecurity.

Relevant here is an ongoing debate over a proposed reform of history teaching in schools, which turned into an emotional controversy, a "hysteria over history" (Podgórska 2012). It is an open issue today whether Polish schools remain strongholds of the traditional, if not archaic, models of history teaching, whether they cultivate a kind of romantic-martyrological patriotism that easily leads to "self-centeredness and distrust towards others," and fosters "national-patriotic" rather than "critical-patriotic" attitudes, which are believed to be more desirable today (e.g., Bilewicz 2012: 36). Some evidence in support of Bilewicz's concerns comes from Przecławska's data (2008: 79), which document that young Poles today still subscribe to this traditional meaning of patriotism, centered around historical key words like *God* and *honor*: the cultivation of traditions and customs is thus highly valued (61 percent), as is knowledge of the country's history (40 percent), and one's readiness to defend the country in case of war (61 percent), while only a small percentage includes among patriotic duties paying tax (7.7 percent), participating in elections (5.8 percent) or observing the law (15.3 percent). It may well be the case that an emotional attitude to the country's history still dominates among the young, and that national pride is seen first of all in Poles' victorious battles, national insurrections, and heroism during WWII. One of the reasons why the martyrological key should endure is that it stays in tune with "fear and suffering," the dominant motifs in WWII family narratives (Szacka 2010: 113).

Despite conservative tendencies in how many of the young still think (or talk) about their national identity, and how they are educated in matters involving it, calls to update the Polish model of (the language of) patriotism become increasingly prominent. A number of my young respondents made that point quite emphatically:

> 51; 22, F
> Sixty years ago, when one talked about the war, one would talk to people who had known it, the war had just ended . . . it's just that everyone lived in those times, they knew what it looked like, they knew what it involved, they saw it with their very own eyes, all the cruelty, and now, sort of, ourselves, those seventy years later, we take a completely different approach because we haven't had that kind of experience in our lives, we can't imagine those things. So . . . that kind of dry information, that official language we hear, that's something which we'll just hear and get on with our lives . . . 'cos we've got, we are already a different generation. Someone who really didn't have a clue of what things were like in the past, that's why this just must change, the language which is employed to talk about the war. . . .

Today many politicians and educators realize that they cannot ignore the needs and expectations of the generation that is far too young to accept the old patterns of thinking and talking. As regards the mediation of WWII, there is growing popularity of media (and genres) including comic books, murals, posters, and billboards, as well as reconstructions of combats and online war-games. This means the entry of visualization, informality, and interactive performance in how historical knowledge is conveyed. Seeing, touching, and playing are key words for what is described sometimes as a "pop cultural" model of patriotic expression (see Ziębińska-Witek 2012). Some Polish politicians endorse, if not encourage, the new patterns of communication. The late President Kaczyński scored extra points initiating the building of the Museum of Warsaw Uprising, opened in 2004. In 2008, his former rival and now the prime minister, Donald Tusk, commissioned a project for a Museum of WWII in Gdańsk. Yet, no matter how technologically innovative, "pop museums" may still tell "heroic, romantic stories with a messianic touch" (Ziębińska-Witek 2012: 12; my translation). For instance, the Museum of Warsaw Uprising communicates traditional Romantic war mythology (Janion 2009). On the other hand, the traditional focus on military actions and military heroes, typical of official War narratives, is being relocated to the vicissitudes of ordinary people, their struggle with the atrocities of the war, as well as their attempts to lead a normal life.

War Reconstructions: Toward a "Pop Cultural" Model of Patriotism?

Such new modes of patriotic ideation are a source of ambivalent evaluations. Is pop culture an appropriate format for WWII narration? In "Pornography of the war," Olszewski (2009) writes:

> Poland is changing into a huge training ground for historical reconstructions, with World War II scenes being replayed with a particular penchant. In Warsaw, viewers could see . . . a soldier pouring petrol on insurgents' dead bodies or enemy soldiers selecting women to be raped. . . . There is something pornographic in those games . . . a transgression, powerful yet not conscious. How must our sensitivity have changed if we need to see violence in order to imagine the tragedy of violence? This is no longer a game of getting through the canals in the Warsaw Uprising Museum, this is a gesture of much more significance than a comic strip about Auschwitz. The viewer takes part in a rape and a mass execution. I ask: what is the purpose? . . . Even if it *is* the case that in order to build historical awareness among new generations we need more than a faded map of army movements . . . the price does look high indeed. What is supposed to foster imagination and knowledge might as well be seen as a theatre of cruelty pursued under the pretence of a good cause. (translation by Danuta Przepiórkowska)

This sounds like a radical opinion, tinged with helplessness ("something must be done, but what?") and emotional protest ("we must not tamper with war atrocities"). One would be inclined to associate such views with the older generation, as some media suggest, yet this need not be the case. The respondents in my project were asked to voice their opinions on war reconstructions and the text excerpted above. The differences between the two age groups—those in their eighties and those in their twenties—were negligible, with all respondents tending to opt for a midrange position. They were cautious in legitimating staged violence ("this is the true nature of the war"), yet they also believed that "the line should not be crossed"; scenes of rapes or drastic cruelties should have no place in an open-air theater of war.

Interestingly, both age groups defended war reconstructions in similar terms: they are needed for "the young" to learn about the War. However, it was the young respondents who were more elaborate on why they endorsed such forms of patriotic education.

> 37; 22, F
> I think that such reconstructions in a sense reinforce patriotic feelings among young people who, well, in times of the European Union integration eternal emigration, seeking money or higher education, they are more of cosmopolitans than patriots, and that patriotism is a bit dusty, I mean that traditional Polish patriotism 'I'm going to die for my nation' and: I will defend my homeland forever' ((laughter)) in a sense it's already out of date, so you would need just to develop a new definition of patriotism, a new one. . . .

> 51; 22, F
> Well . . . those staging events, like the direct ones it's mostly young people who take part in it, and for them it is a way of meeting history and feeling unity with the previous generations and: this is a token of patriotism, they learn the living history so it's not just dry facts from schoolbooks, the date when the war broke out and the date when the war ended, instead they can feel how heavy the rifle was, they can see what the military uniform looked like so the staging is actually something that can just have an effect sort of getting closer to history, this is no longer a fact which is far away in books and you read about it with a peace of mind, it becomes an immediate thing instead.

On closer examination, there are differences in how the categories of respondents conceptualized "the young," to whom they first of all dedicated such new genres as sources of historical knowledge and patriotic inspiration. Significantly, "the old" tended to limit themselves to an accommodative, however presumptive position: if this is what the young want, let them have it. Rare criticisms concerned "historical truth"—an alleged inaccuracy in how particular reconstructions were staged. For instance, one respondent (eighty-one, male), a former participant in the battle at Mława, accused the organizers of falsifying the historical truth because "there were no tanks or motorcycles" in that battle. More importantly, however, the respondents varied in their opinions about (potential) performers or viewers of war reconstructions. Elaborations to this effect were common among the young, but practically absent with the old. In terms of a critical discursive approach, the replies of the young construed a more elaborate model of social reality than those of the old, especially as regards participants' features, goals, and motivations. They were also more argumentative, and persuasive, in how they accounted for their own positioning on the issues concerned. Some findings to this effect are briefly discussed below.

War Reconstructions: Social Self-Diversification of the Young

In contrast to older respondents, the young produced more complex and diversified responses in their discussions of WWII reconstructions. They pointed to various dimensions of such practices and, in principle, were quite specific about how to evaluate them. For instance, they saw in such events a means of historical education, an occasion to enhance patriotic feelings, a form of entertainment, but also a source of income and promotion for the local community. What seems a recurring pattern is that war reconstructions were not seen as alternatives to traditional forms of mediation of historical knowledge, written sources in particular. It was emphasized that one needs to go beyond the observational and the performative in order to get a true image of the War and to be able to empathize with its victims. That is, some preparation is needed for a proper consumption of such spectacles. The examples below illustrate such positions:

> 7; 20, F
> I mean, I think that if someone is supposed to take part in those . . . types of events, in a reconstruction then to make sure they get the right picture, they have to have some knowledge of history. . . . I think it must be somehow it must be logically arranged so that they should first read those books, so that-so-that they really know, so that they just know what those people felt back then and only then would I just perhaps recommend such reconstructions so that they just know what this is all about.

221

> 12; 22, M
>
> [Y]ou first need to equip people with knowledge, and the emotional attitude will depend on the person and everyone will easily build their emotional attitude but it's harder to build knowledge. That's why you first need to equip them with that knowledge.

> 41; 24, M
>
> [T]he whole thing must be done earlier . . . with a bit of a commentary . . . to make sure they don't become mindless spectators who can watch and get excited about gunshots and military uniforms without knowing the essential aspects of the event.

At the same time young respondents construe a core category of war-reconstruction participants and enthusiasts. Although in their early twenties, with the young they themselves refer to an out-group, some younger-than-young, the younger youth. The distance is made still more apparent with the use of the pronoun *they*, as in the following answers to the question for whom such reconstructions might be a source of historical knowledge:

> 7; 20, F
>
> I think that . . . it's the young but, as I say, I'm not sure it's a good way to communicate. Because then they will not have such . . . deep reflections on the war, only superficial because of those reconstructions. . . .

> 48; 22, M
>
> [I]n particular it is the young participants, the young audience who are interested in that kind of narrating history . . . this is the idea of such staging, I think, to attract the younger viewers.

Yet, it is not only the younger youth, for whom such staged events are deemed most attractive or dedicated by the organizers. The chronological age may not be the main indicator of preference at all. This is suggested by socially evaluative clues, as illustrated below:

> 12; 22, M
>
> [T]his is mainly to give fun to the mob so that they could have their chops and look at fireworks, all that not being quite in place. . . .

> 39; 23, M
>
> I think that most of the people go there for entertainment; . . . well, this is not an ideal [form of education—AD], but a minor . . . I think that for 100 people 2 may recall what they read or learnt and 98 will just enjoy the show.

The next quote illustrates an elitist attitude on the part of the speaker:

> 40; 24, M
> I think it is a very interesting way of popularizing history. If I were to choose a man who does not know anything about the war, and a man who knows something because when sitting in a trench over a bowl of beans soup he got a flyer and learnt some basic things, I would choose this other guy. . . . Let's be honest, there are some things for twenty percent of society and there are some for the remaining eighty. One cannot expect everybody to get knowledge about the War from very clever books, documentaries and staff, because simply people differ and you have to get at each and every one in a different way.

Concluding Remarks

In conclusion, I would argue for a general continuity in how young Poles orient themselves to the traditional model of Polish patriotism and national identification. Even though the martyrological pathos in public remembrance of WWII is often rejected, the respondents in this project still seemed to appreciate patriotic values based on solid historical knowledge and respect for national symbols. In view of frequent references to home narratives and teaching, the family maintains its role in national and political formation of the young. For both age groups it was important—and often obligatory—to pass on (or listen to) what were their family truths about the War:

> 18; 83, F
> [I]f we don't [tell our stories—AD], if people who are still alive and can say something, if they don't pass it on to the young ones, well, unfortunately, after a few years this will be literally erased from the memory of that young generation. It has to be done, it's a duty. . . . It's a duty . . . for every Pole. If that person who can still speak, who can still remember, it's their duty to share it, share those memories from that period, it's a duty. . . . It's actually very lucky that I can, being 83 years old . . . I can still say something.

A number of limitations of, and concerns about, such family stories were mentioned, though, on both sides. For instance, the following participant reflected self-critically:

> 29; 82, M
> There were all kinds of situations. I've got, I sometimes think, perhaps I'll have enough time to do it when, when I get the chance, sometimes I think that . . . I've got a cousin in Cracow and she is always telling me

to write something, says I should write something about that period, 'cos I was in Cracow twice, during the Nazi occupation, never for pleasure. So perhaps one day I'll get round to do it. Yeah. If I had, if I had a computer right now, I might get down to writing things. 'Cos that's different then. It's a different story when you write by hand. You would first need to write a draft, then review it, then rewrite it and so on.

In the following instances, both the storyteller and the listener are skeptical about the real (or documentary) value of what such narratives can convey:

1; 81, F
[M]emories, memories of eye witnesses those are transient things. Firstly, quite a few of the people from those years have already passed away, perhaps even most of them . . . and the only thing left is their memories handed over to the future generations, to children and grandchildren. . . . But also human memory can be fallible and things that used to seem obvious do change after many, many years . . . the sense of those events does.

39; 23, M
I had the opportunity because both of my grandmas, who are still alive, were participants but they were 9 years old then so their accounts are very hazy and they are, so to speak, from a child's perspective. . . . those stories, told by my grandmas who experienced that at the age of 9, they are very hard to listen to. They are really hazy and they usually make no sense whatsoever. . . . this is more of an abstract thing, it's more about emotions experienced by a child who doesn't understand the events around her.

In turn, the following respondent complains about not being able to learn much at home, even though at the same time he accepts, however not unconditionally, the reasons for why such narratives may not be easy to tell to others.

40; 24, M
[W]ell, it's good that many [eyewitnesses] are still alive, but it seems to me that they talk too little, that is my impression, especially in my family, in my home, you need to "pull" things out, some information about the war, which is understandable to some extent, because I understand that: those events are not, often not pleasant for the people who lived through the war, the Holocaust, lived through Warsaw Uprising, these are awful pictures I am aware that they are trying to forget them, or somehow suppress them, but this is history, and that is treasure, that knowledge they have.

Psychological barriers in recalling the War were also noted by Szacka (2010), who explained them by the ambivalent status of many of such experiences, when suffering and everyday heroism mixed with shame or guilt. In reporting their family War talks, both the old and the young in my data tried to accommodate to the perspective of the other. This could be interpreted in terms of politeness, yet concern and empathy are probably the best explanations. How can narrating (or hearing) War stories affect the other? Could such memories hurt, shock, or otherwise influence the other? In itself, intergenerational empathy constitutes an important area of exploration and further research.

I have argued that the family still plays a major role in generating the collective memory of WWII among Poles. On the whole, my data support Szacka's (2010) and Przecławska's findings (2008: 91) that the family provides "the main frame for national identification" among the young. This is not contradicted by another observation, namely that the family is losing today its capacity to mediate the real experience of the War, and that other sources and media of information become more relevant and popular. Not only the imminent passing away of the last witnesses to the War but a host of other factors matter here too. The family model is changing, and the distance between generations is growing as a result of social and cultural transformations, with values and priorities being redefined. And yet, we may still assume that the *we*-family and the *we*-nation models remain central categories for social identification of Poles. I do not have sufficient data to assess whether, as Przecławska argues, ties with people other than intimates remain weak. There is some evidence to the contrary, however. Going by what some members of war-reconstruction groups said in this project, such involvements have a growing potential to start new forms of social identification. Some sociologists may be right in arguing that member-ship in such groups goes beyond interest in folk or pop culture, and that it turns into a style of living and a site of new social connectivity (Pęczak 2012: 92–94).

Finally, while addressing the pop cultural turn in historical narration, the young—in comparison to the old—produced more *interdiscursive traces* engaging domains of meaning other than those directly relevant to WWII memories for national identification. At least two topics of dense *interdiscursivity* lend themselves to attention. The first relates to social diversification among the young, which was briefly discussed in the previous section with reference to elitist attitudes on the part of some of the respondents. The second concerns the emergence of non-martyrological visions of WWII and critical-patriotic attitudes to how the past and the present need to be interfaced. The gist of such a new perspective is illustrated in an extended example below:

> 17; 24, M
>
> [T]his shouldn't be [a] martyrisation of the Polish nation, how we got beaten up and destroyed and: everyone got murdered, that's not how things should be shown, it should be shown in many different aspects: people died 'cos they died but also people got born because they did, right? Of course, you need to maintain the right balance to make sure it all makes sense, right? Describing just military actions or how people died, it means that all of the war, which is a horrible thing, right, everyone knows that all-too-well but we don't need to stress it all that much, we should be looking for positive things, even in those worst moments of history, shouldn't we? . . . and we also need to remember that during those hard times we managed to achieve things such as illegal education, secret schooling, underground state, mm, which had its judiciary which had its social welfare, political parties—the prewar political parties actually did exist during the World War II. They were operating clandestinely, as far as possible. . . . [Society] would understand its past better, and the past would also enable it to embrace opportunities in a better way, social, economic or private opportunities, if we understood that in such a difficult moment, right, we managed to achieve this and this and that, so it might be easier for us now to mobilize ourselves and achieve some other successes. And those don't have to be really huge successes, do they? Those could be small, ordinary successes, not like passing an exam, don't know, building a house, right? It's not only about getting those huge events from history, such events that everyone knows, it's about taking those, those tiny little things, right? That's, that's the basic thing, that's my opinion.

Such inverse interpretations of WWII memory and heritage are worth noting—to paraphrase Szacka (2010:128)—no matter whether statistically significant or not. Szacka makes this point commenting on responses to the question in a recent questionnaire: "Did anyone from your family acquire—as a result of the War—any practical knowledge or wisdom that helped him/her in the future?" (my translation). Those who responded in the affirmative (16.7 percent) listed such features as resourcefulness, endurance, early maturation, or psychological resistance. Recently, in a local weekly, Celiński (2012) makes an appeal: "Let us create Museum of Success at last! Isn't it time to end the national cult of defeats, harms, and failures?" Coming from a politician, this can be taken in good or bad faith. Still, it remains a voice in the polyphony of voices, genres, and ideologies that Poles can follow or ignore.

In order to build up an integrative framework of analysis, critical discourse studies need access to a plurality of contexts and texts. They need interdisciplinary contact (Chouliaraki and Fairclough, 1999) and abductive methodologies (Wodak 2001). From the perspective of a critical discourse researcher, an analysis of social context precedes, and ultimately caps, a textual analysis that looks into the linguistic resources used. The major target of an integrative—social and linguistic—approach is to explore how *difference* is dialogized in social practice.

References

Allen, Paul. 2009. *Katyń: stalinowska masakra i triumf prawdy*. Warszawa: Świat Książki.

Bakhtin, Mikhail. 1981. *The Dialogical Imagination*. Austin: University of Texas Press.

Bilewicz, Michał. 2012. "Pawie i jaszczurki." *Polityka*: 7.

Bokszański, Zbigniew. 1996. "Tożsamość narodowa." In *Biografia a tożsamość narodowa*, ed. Marek Czyżewski, Andrzej Piotrowski, and Alicja Rokuszewska-Pawełek. Łódź: UŁ Press.

Bosiacki, Adam. 2012. *The Unfinished Business of Katyn*. (http://www.hoover.org/publications/hoover-digest/article/105461)

Celiński, Andrzej. 2012. "Stwórzmy wreszcie Muzeum Sukcesu!" *PASSA*, 23 August.

Chouliaraki, Lilie, and Norman Fairclough. *1999*. *Discourse in Late Modernity. Rethinking Critical Discourse Analysis*. Edinburgh: Edinburgh University Press.

Davis, Norman. 2004. *Powstanie '44*. Kraków: Znak.

Dubisz, Stanisław. 2011. *Kultura Językowych Zachowań. Od Dialogu do Polilogu*. Paper delivered at 8th Forum of Culture of the Word. Rzeszów, 20–22 October.

Dudzikowa, Maria and Maria Czerepaniak-Walczak, eds. 2008. *Wychowanie. Pojęcia, procesy, konteksty*. Vol. 5. Gdańsk: GWP.

Ensink, Titus and Christopher Sauer, eds. 2003. *The Art of Commemoration*. Amsterdam: John Benjamins.

Fairclough, Norman. 2003. *Analysing Discourse. Textual Analysis for Social Research*. London: Routledge.

Gilejko, Leszek. 2005. "Dylematy nowej tożsamości Polaków." In *Polacy o sobie*. ed. Piotr Kowalski. Łomża: Stopka.

Janion, Maria. 2009. "Klęska jest klęską." *Gazeta Wyborcza*: 29–30 August.

Kadell Franz. 2011. *Katyń*. Warszawa: PWN.

Kaźmierska, Kaja. 2002. "Narratives on World War II in Poland. When a life story is family story." *History of the Family* 7: 281–305.

Kochanowski, Jerzy. 2011. "Filtry przeszłości." *Polityka*: 16.

Kofta, Mirosław and Michał Bilewicz, eds. 2011. *Wobec obcych*. Warszawa: PWN.

Kowalski, Piotr, ed. 2005. *Polacy o sobie. Współczesna autorefleksja: jednostka, społeczeństwo, historia*. Łomża: Stopka.

Krzysztofek, Kazimierz. 2005. "(Ni)jaka tożsamość Polaków." In *Polacy o sobie*, ed. Piotr Kowalski. Łomża: Stopka

Kwiatkowski, Piotr, Lech Nijakowski, Barbara Szacka and Andrzej Szpociński. 2010. *Między codziennością a wielką historią. Druga wojna światowa w pamięci zbiorowej społeczeństwa polskiego*. Gdańsk: Scholar.

Łastawski, Kazimierz. 2004. *Polskość w Europie. Polska tożsamość narodowa w jednoczącej się Europie.* Warszawa: MON.

Machcewicz, Paweł. 2012. *Spory o historię 2000–2011.* Kraków: Znak.

Niewiara, Aleksandra. 2010. *Kształty polskiej tożsamości. Potoczny dyskurs narodowy w perspektywie etnolingwistycznej.* Katowice: UŚ.

Nijakowski, Lech. 2008. *Polska polityka pamięci. Esej socjologiczny.* Warszawa

Nijakowski, Lech N. 2010. Regionalne zróżnicowanie pamięci o II wojnie światowej. In *Między codziennością . . . .,* eds. Piotr Kwiatkowski et al. Gdańsk: Scholar.

Nowinowski, Sławomir, Jan Pomorski and Rafał Stobiecki, eds. 2008. *Pamięć i polityka historyczna. Doświadczenia Polski i jej sąsiadów.* Łódź: IPN

Olszewski. 2009. "Pornografia wojny." *Tygodnik Powszechny*: 13 September.

Pęczak, Mirosław. 2012. "Uciec w zbroi od buractwa." *Polityka*: 10.

Podgórska, Joanna. 2012. "Histeria." *Polityka*: 14.

Przecławska, Anna. 2008. "Bóg, honor i ojczyzna w recepcji współczesnej młodzieży." In *Wychowanie,* eds. Maria Dudzikowa and Maria Czerepaniak-Walczak. Gdańsk: GWP.

Samsonowicz, Henryk. 2008. "O niebezpieczeństwie manipulacji pamięcią." In *Wychowanie,* eds. Maria Dudzikowa and Maria Czerepaniak-Walczak. Gdańsk: GWP.

Sawicki Jacek, Zygmunt, ed. 2004. *Aresztowane powstanie.* Warszawa: IPN.

Skarżyńska, Krystyna. 2008. "Rodzaje patriotyzmu." In *Wychowanie,* eds. Maria Dudzikowa and Maria Czerepaniak-Walczak. Gdańsk: GWP.

Skarżyńska, Krystyna and Anna Golec de Zavala. 2006. "Poland and European integration: hopes, fears and national attitudes." In *Understanding Social Change: Political Psychology in Poland,* eds. Krystyna Skarżyńska and Anna Golec de Zavala. New York: Nova Science Publishers.

Szacka, Barbara. 2010. "II wojna światowa w pamięci rodzinnej." In *Między codziennością,* eds. Piotr Kwiatkowski et al. Gdańsk: Scholar.

Szpociński, Andrzej, ed. 2009. *Pamięć zbiorowa jako czynnik integracji i źródło konfliktów.* Warszawa: Scholar.

Wierzbicka, Anna. 1997. *Understanding Cultures through Their Key Words.* New York: OUP.

Wodak, Ruth 2001. "The Discourse-Historical Approach." In *Methods of Critical Discourse Analysis,* eds. Ruth Wodak and Martin Meyer. London: Sage.

Ziębińska-Witek, Anna. 2012. "Pop muzea." *Gazeta Wyborcza*: 11 April.

12

From the "Reunification of the Ukrainian Lands" to "Soviet Occupation": The Molotov-Ribbentrop Pact in the Ukrainian Political Memory

Tatiana Zhurzhenko

Introduction

As the seventieth anniversary of the Molotov-Ribbentrop Pact (MRP) in 2009 demonstrated, the meaning of this treaty goes far beyond diplomatic history or even history of World War II. In post–Cold War Europe, the pact between Nazi Germany and Stalin's Soviet Union does not only mark the outbreak of the Second World War, but symbolizes the subsequent division of the European continent that led to four decades of Communist rule in the countries behind the Iron Curtain. If 1989, the year of peaceful anti-Communist revolutions, is a positive symbol of the reunited Europe, 1939 has a good chance of becoming its negative counterpart. In some countries of Eastern Europe, first of all in Poland and in the Baltic states, the MRP has already become a national *lieu de mémoire*. These new EU members have been actively using European institutions for promoting and institutionalizing the narrative on the equal responsibility of Nazism and Communism. In 2009, as a result of their efforts, the European Parliament declared 23 August (the date of the signing of the Non-Aggression Treaty between the Nazi Germany and the Soviet Union in 1939) the European day of remembrance for the victims of all totalitarian and authoritarian regimes. However, as Stefan Troebst (2009) noted, 23 August can hardly be considered a European *lieu de mémoire* as it has different, often conflicting meanings in various parts of the European continent.

The role of the MRP in Ukrainian history as well as its place in collective memory is especially controversial. In brief, the territorial enlargement of the Ukrainian Soviet Socialist Republic at the costs of the ethnic Ukrainian territories in Eastern Poland was followed by the Stalinization of Western Ukraine and the eventual defeat of the Ukrainian nationalist movement. For contemporary Ukraine, the heritage of the MRP is related to such issues as the territorial integrity and legitimacy of its current borders, the de-Stalinization of collective memory, Ukraine's relations with Russia and Poland, and the European integration of Ukraine. Popular attitudes to the MRP differ within the country: while Western Ukrainians experienced its direct consequences in 1939, for the rest of Ukraine the war started only in 1941. The lack of consensus on the national memory of WWII (Hrynevych 2005; Jilge 2006) has also a geopolitical dimension, as Ukraine finds itself in the borderlands between the enlarged EU and post-Soviet Russia, with the latter actively using myths and symbols of the Great Patriotic War to secure its geopolitical influence in the "near abroad." Debates on how to remember WWII in Ukraine are connected to attempts of its pro-Western élites to redefine the country as a European nation and to escape the post-Soviet/Eurasian space (Zhurzhenko 2007).

In this chapter, I will discuss the ambivalent role of the Molotov-Ribbentrop Pact in Ukrainian collective memory and its implications for nation-building, regional politics, the relations with the neighbors, and the pro-European aspirations of the Ukrainian élites. Following the approach of Eva-Clarita Onken (2006: 25), who suggested a differentiation between three levels of memory politics (domestic memory politics, memory politics in bilateral relations, and memory politics in the European Union), I would like to add one more level of analysis: the regional/local one.

But before I start, let me briefly clarify some conceptual and methodological issues. Does the Molotov-Ribbentrop Pact indeed *exist* in the Ukrainian memory in the same way as the Nazi occupation or the Famine? Is it a *lieu de mémoire*, a narrative, a myth, or maybe simply a historical fact? Does the notion of collective memory, which has been rightly criticized in academic literature (e.g., Bell 2003) make sense in this case?

I am inclined to agree with political scientist Eric Langenbacher, who proposes to see *history*, *memory*, and *myth* not as competing but as dynamically related concepts: "History, with its 'thin' layer of interpretation, needs to be differentiated from memory and its 'thick', emotionalized, heavily mediated interpretations, and from myth, which has an extreme level of interpretation that sometimes borders on the fictional" (2010: 28). Collective memory may (or may not) correspond with historical facts, and it may (or may not) turn into a myth. Of course, people did not experience the Molotov-Ribbentrop Pact in the same way they experienced Nazi (or Soviet) occupation and in this sense cannot remember it. Some authors, however, introduced a useful distinction between "collected" and "collective" memories (Olick 1999) or in other words, between "mass individual memory" and "national memory" (Snyder 2002), the latter referring to generalized narratives produced by the élites. Similarly, Onken (2010: 280) suggests the notion of "political memory," which is a "form of structural power that works through radical selection and simplification, high symbolic intensity and emotional appeal." Pursuing political or "national" interests, it is the élite actors who "hammer out and validate the politically accepted memory regime, the public transcript of memory" (Langenbacher 2010: 31). At the same time, in a pluralist democracy "many different groups and individuals . . . continue to struggle for recognition, representation and participation in the construction of collective memories and political identities" (Onken 2010: 278).

Therefore, for my analysis of the MRP in Ukrainian memory I prefer the concept of "memory regime" (Langenbacher 2010: 30), which reflects both top-down and bottom-up dynamics and has two dimensions: synchronic as well as diachronic. The synchronic dimension contains dominant collective memories, political values, and symbols as well as supportive ethical and moral discourses. Applied to the MRP, the synchronic dimension of the new anti-Soviet memory regime includes: collective memories of Soviet invasion, Stalinization, political repressions, values and shared identities (anti-Communism, nationalism), and supportive moral discourses (Nazism and Communism as equally evil and equally responsible for WWII). The diachronic dimension relates the past to the present. It includes the master historical narrative explaining the causes of crucial memory-generating events (e.g., Stalin and Hitler were predestined to collaborate because the nature of both regimes was similar), and the master historical narrative about the history of the collective memory itself (totalitarian memory manipulation and historical falsification by the Soviet regime). This new memory regime opposes the old/modernized Soviet one, which is also based on collective memories (Nazi occupation, fighting in the Red Army), attached values, shared identities (Soviet Ukrainian/Russian patriotism), and moral discourses (Great Patriotic War, liberation of Europe from the Nazis). The master historical narrative in this case stresses Hitler's aggression against the Soviet Union and marginalizes the MRP as a pragmatic maneuver of the Soviet leadership, while the historical narrative of memory refers to the Nuremberg tribunal, whose decisions have to be protected from today's revisionism. As will be demonstrated in this chapter, memory regimes can change, collapse, and clash with each other.

The first section of the chapter addresses the role of the MRP in Ukrainian history, political memory, and post-Soviet nation-building. The second section moves to the European level of memory politics, briefly outlining the institutionalization of 23 August as a new (East-) European *lieu de mémoire* and the resulting tensions with Russia. The third section deals with Ukraine's half-hearted attempt to adopt the anti-Soviet memory regime, with some of its regional effects and with its implications for the Ukrainian-Russian and Ukrainian-Polish relations. Finally, the last section analyses the (mis)uses of the MRP as a historical analogy in today's Ukrainian discourses of Euro-skepticism.

Post-Communist Transition, Nation-Building, and Memory Regime Change

One of the motives behind Stalin's decision to make a pact with Hitler was the Ukrainian question. A considerable Ukrainian minority in interwar Poland had lost its fight for independence in 1919, but did not give up its national aspirations. While during the 1920s Moscow used pro-Soviet sympathies on the part of the Ukrainian minority to undermine the stability of the young Polish state, from the mid-1930s it was Stalin who perceived the growing Ukrainian nationalism in Poland as a threat to his control over Soviet Ukraine. Indeed, the Ukrainian nationalist underground in Poland saw the approaching war in Europe as an opportunity to reestablish the Ukrainian state in Eastern Galicia and, in case of Stalin's defeat, to reunite it with the other Ukrainian territories. The possibility of a Ukrainian state on the Soviet border that would be a satellite of Nazi Germany was a scenario Stalin wanted to prevent. The secret protocols to the Molotov-Ribbentrop Pact draw the demarcation line between the German and Soviet spheres of influence along the Narew, Vistula, and San rivers, giving Stalin control over more than a half of the Polish territory. However, when Hitler attacked Poland on 1 September 1939, Stalin did not rush to join him, afraid of getting involved in a war with France and Great Britain. Only on 17 September, Soviet troops entered the Polish territory, with the official justification "to take under their protection the life and property of the population of Western Ukraine and Western Belorussia." The Soviet occupation of Eastern Poland was presented by Stalin's propaganda as the liberation of the brotherly Ukrainians and Belarusians from the Polish yoke. On 28 September the German-Soviet Treaty of Friendship, Cooperation and Demarcation was signed. According to this treaty, Stalin's concession of the Lublin province and part of the Warsaw province was compensated by the transfer of Lithuania to the Soviet sphere of interests. The border created by this agreement roughly corresponded to the Curzon Line proposed by the British in 1919 as the eastern border of Poland. Stalin used the Curzon line as an argument during negotiations with the Allies at the Teheran and Yalta Conferences and succeeded in reestablishing this border after WWII. Poland received former German territories in the North and West as compensation.

In Soviet historiography, the invasion of eastern Poland in September 1939 was presented as the "re-unification of all Ukrainian lands in one Soviet Ukrainian state," a fulfillment of the centuries-old dream of the Ukrainian people. This event became part of the Soviet memory regime as the Golden September. In order to win the sympathies of the local Ukrainian population, Moscow initiated the Ukrainization of the education and local administration, and granted Ukrainian peasants land confiscated from its Polish owners (Hryciuk 2009). The situation of the Jewish population under Soviet rule was also considerably better than in Nazi-occupied Poland. It was the Polish military, state officials, landowners, and ideological opponents of the Soviets who were the primary target of arrests and deportations (Gross 1988). But soon repressions also followed against the Ukrainian nationalists, the Greek Catholic church and other disloyal strata. For ethnic Ukrainians, the political repressions, censorship, and forced collectivization were the dark side of the Golden September (Kulchytsky 2000). In October 1939, elections to the Belorussian and Ukrainian assemblies were held in the occupied territories to legitimize their incorporation into Soviet Ukraine and Soviet Belarussia.

For a short time, the nationalist dream of a Ukrainian Lviv became true, but the irony of history is that it was fulfilled by Stalin and in his own interests. The Ukrainian nationalist underground never accepted this reunification. After Hitler had attacked the Soviet Union on 22 June 1941, an independent Ukrainian state was declared in the Nazi-occupied Lviv. However, the Nazis were not interested the Ukrainian nationalists as allies, who were thus forced to fight at both fronts. Retreating Soviets executed thousands of their political prisoners in Western Ukraine, a fact used by the Nazis to provoke anti-Jewish pogroms. The participation of the local Ukrainian militia in these events is one of the hottest topics in contemporary Ukrainian debate on WWII (Himka 2011). As the Polish government in exile hoped for a restoration of the country's old borders, and the Ukrainian nationalist underground was not going to give up its plans of an independent state, a bloody Polish-Ukrainian ethnic conflict emerged on the territory of former Eastern Poland resulting in the expulsions and forced resettlements on both sides of the reestablished border. It took Moscow almost a decade after the end of WWII to suppress the anti-Soviet armed resistance in Western Ukraine.

Therefore, unlike in Poland and the Baltic states, where negative attitudes to the Soviet-German pact of 1939 dominate, in Ukraine the legacy of the MRP is ambivalent. As Wilfried Jilge (2006:55) has noted, "Ukrainian intellectuals and historians never questioned the legality of the 'reunification' of the Ukrainian territories in September 1939 despite their condemnation of the Ribbentrop-Molotov Pact."

Obviously, Ukraine in its current territorial shape (with the exception of the Crimea) emerged from WWII; its border with Poland (as well as the border with Romania) goes back to the MRP. But the price paid for the territorial integrity according to Stalin's scenario was high: giving up any hope of Ukrainian independence for decades, the Stalinization of Western Ukraine, millions of lives lost in the Ukrainian-Polish borderlands during military actions, repressions, the Holocaust, and the Polish-Ukrainian ethnic conflict. In the postwar decades, the narrative of the reunification and subsequent liberation in 1944 dominated the official discourse in Soviet Ukraine, underlining the role of the Red Army and the Communist Party in fulfilling the national aspirations of Ukrainians. The counter-memories of the local population in Western Ukraine were suppressed by the Soviet authorities; Soviet propaganda presented the Ukrainian nationalists as Nazi collaborators and enemies of the Ukrainian people.

With *perestroika* and *glasnost*, a flow of new publications and discussions on Soviet history shook the official myth of the Great Patriotic

War. The official denunciation of the secret protocols to the MRP by the Second Congress of the People's Deputies of USSR on 24 December 1989, was one of the highlights of the de-Stalinization process. The new public awareness that the Soviet Union acted in 1939 as an aggressor and, albeit for two years only, was an ally of Nazi Germany, contributed to the delegitimation of Soviet regime and collapse of the USSR. The demands to reveal the truth about the MRP had a tremendous mobilizing effect, especially in the Baltic republics. On 23 August 1989 (the fiftieth anniversary of the MRP), a human chain from Tallinn to Vilnius formed by two million people became a powerful manifestation of their desire for national independence. All these developments fostered the de-Stalinization of the collective memory in Ukraine.

Along with the Soviet narrative of the Great Patriotic War a new Ukrainian narrative of WWII emerged (Hrynevych 2005), with the beginning of war shifted from 22 June 1941 (Hitler's attack on Soviet Union), to September 1939 (the Soviet invasion of Eastern Poland). This new narrative had especially important consequences for Western Ukraine: instead of a reunification, it suggested the Soviet occupation of Western Ukraine, changing the meaning of 17 September from a positive to a negative symbol. What is more important, the new Ukrainian narrative of WWII as a war initiated by both Stalin and Hitler contributed to the legitimization of the memory of the nationalist underground and anti-Soviet resistance in Western Ukraine. The issue of the Ukrainian nationalists' collaboration with the Nazis, especially before and at the start of the war, was solved by referring to Stalin's ultimate act of collaboration in August 1939.

Instead of the reunification of 1939 and liberation of 1944 the Unification Act of 1919 (an agreement signed by the West Ukrainian People's Republic and the Ukrainian People's Republic in Kyiv) became the new symbol of Ukraine's territorial integrity and independence. In January 1990, hundred thousands of Ukrainians created a human chain from Kiev to Lviv, publically celebrating this day for the first time. In 1999, President Leonid Kuchma declared 22 January the Day of Unity and a state holiday. At the same time, Kuchma, known for his multivector politics, did not forget 17 September: a presidential decree from the same year ordered a large-scale celebration of the sixtieth anniversary of the reunification of the Ukrainian lands. This decision did not increase his popularity in Western Ukraine, and the local authorities in Lviv, to save the situation in the wake of the presidential elections, had to postpone the official celebrations in the city for a couple of days and shift the emphasis from the infamous reunification to the Day of Lviv (Stetsiuk 1999).

Thus, 17 September, the beginning of the Soviet invasion in Poland and a date closely connected to the Molotov-Ribbentrop Pact, remains ambivalent in Ukraine. Stanislav Kul'chytskyi (2000), the well-known Ukrainian historian and a leading expert in Stalinism and the Famine, does not agree with those who call for the removal this date from the national calendar:

> History rarely gives nations a second chance. Yet, the opportunity for the re-unification of the Ukrainian lands emerged twice in the 20th century; both times it was related to world wars. In 1919 the chance was missed. Without the events of 1939, the Yalta conference would not have pursued such large scale border changes in East-Central Europe to satisfy the interests of the two countries which suffered most in WWII, the Ukrainian SSR and Poland.

Similarly, Taras Vozniak, a prominent Lviv liberal intellectual and the editor of the pro-European *Ji* magazine, argues that apart from indisputably negative moral and human aspects of the Molotov-Ribbentrop Pact, its paradoxical political consequences cannot be ignored:

> Indeed, by the logic of circumstances and the evil will of Hitler and Stalin, Ukraine found itself under one boot for the first time, having achieved its unity in such a strange way. Soon Stalin incorporated the rest of the Ukrainian ethnic lands into the USSR, namely Bukovyna and Transcarpathia. In this way, he created the preconditions for the disintegration of the USSR and for an independent and united Ukrainian state. By including such big 'anti-Soviet' regions as the Baltics and Western Ukraine in the USSR, Stalin created the preconditions for resistance and the catalyst for the collapse of the empire. And eventually it happened (Vozniak 2002: 238).

Nazism and Stalinism as Equally Criminal: The Rise of the (East-)European Memory Regime

Since 1989, when Moscow officially recognized the fact of the secret protocols to the MRP, the issue has gained an international dimension. It first of all concerns the Russian-Polish and Russian-Baltic relations. While Poland was pressing for the disclosure of the full truth about the Katyn' massacre, Lithuania, Latvia, and Estonia sought Moscow's official acknowledgement of the forceful annexation of these countries in 1940. However, these disputes hardly went beyond bilateral relations of the concerned states with Russia; it was only since the mid-2000s that a new transnational discourse on the "equal criminality" of Nazism and Stalinism (Communism) has emerged. In this transnational discourse, the MRP is used as a powerful symbol for the global crimes committed by Communism, for the partition of the postwar Europe and for the equal responsibility of the two dictators for the outbreak of WWII. The new discourse also denies any principal differences between the two ideologies and implies that Hitler and Stalin were predestined to collaborate because the nature of their totalitarian regimes was very similar.

The transnationalization of this discourse and the rise of a new memory regime on the European level since the mid-2000s was related to the accession of the former Communist countries to the EU, on the one hand, and to Russia's self-assertive politics under President Putin on the other. The EU enlargement to the east strengthened the positions of Moscow's opponents, now EU members, and elevated the political debates about WWII to the European level. The starting point was the sixtieth anniversary of the end of WWII, celebrated on a large scale in Moscow in May 2005. By inviting the leaders of the European countries and the USA, Putin used this event as an opportunity to reassert Russia's geopolitical status after the collapse of the Soviet Union. As a gesture of considerable symbolic weight, US President George W. Bush on his way to Moscow made a stop in Riga to repudiate the Yalta treaty as "one of the greatest wrongs of history," trading the freedom of small nations for the goal of stability in Europe. In the new transnational round of memory wars, the new EU members used the European institutions to lobby for the political condemnation of Stalinism (Communism) as equally criminal to Nazism, while Russia instrumentalized the memory of the Holocaust in order to present Estonians, Latvians, and Lithuanians as willing Nazi collaborators and to compromise the new political élites of the Baltic States in the eyes of the West.

On 12 May 2005, the European Parliament (EP) passed a resolution on the end of the Second World War, noting that "for some nations the end of World War II meant renewed tyranny inflicted by the Stalinist Soviet Union" and reminding of "the magnitude of the suffering, injustice and long-term social, political and economic degradation endured by the captive nations located on the eastern side of what was to become the Iron Curtain" (European Parliament 2005). In June 2005, the center-right European People's Party (EPP), the largest political fraction in the European Parliament, officially condemned the MRP and the Soviet occupation of the Baltic States on request of Vytautas Landsbergis, a Lithuanian Member of the EP. In June 2005, the Parliamentary Assembly of the Council of Europe (PACE) adopted a resolution, including amendments suggested by the Baltic representatives, who demanded that Russia pay compensation for the citizens of the Baltic republics who had suffered deportation during the Soviet occupation (Asadova 2005). At the same time, The Union for a Europe of the Nations, a conservative political group in the EP with a good number of Baltic and Polish representatives, sponsored the production of the documentary *The Soviet Story* (2008), a film about the crimes of Soviet Communism and Soviet-German collaboration before 1941, underlining the close ideological, political, and organizational connections between the Nazi and the Soviet systems. On 18 March 2009, hearings on "European Conscience and Crimes of Totalitarian Communism: 20 Years after" took place in the European Parliament. Denouncing both totalitarian regimes, the resulting resolution suggested 23 August (the date of signature of the Molotov-Ribbentrop Pact) as a Europe-wide day of remembrance for the victims of all totalitarian and authoritarian regimes (European Parliament 2009). The thesis of "equal criminality" was also confirmed by the OSCE resolution Divided Europe Reunited, adopted in Vilnius in July 2009.

By promoting and institutionalizing the new memory regime on a European level, the Baltic states, Poland, and some other post-Communist countries sought to challenge the Western European consensus on WWII and to gain recognition for their narratives of collective victimhood, but also to acquire leverage over Russia and contain its geopolitical ambitions. The myth of the Great Patriotic War remains the core of Russia's memory politics, and the narrative of the liberation of Europe from Nazism is still used to legitimize the country's geopolitical status on the European continent. In Russia therefore, the Molotov-Ribbentrop Pact belongs to the most controversial aspects of World War II history. Little surprise that the Russian Duma denounced the 2009 OSCE resolution and accused the West of imposing a "false feeling of historical guilt" on Russia. Some Russian politicians suggested introducing criminal responsibility for denying the role of the Soviet Union in the defeat of Nazi Germany. In May 2009, in the wake of the Victory Day, the pro-presidential party United Russia drafted a law meant to protect the Soviet version of World War II from revisionist interpretations (Koposov 2010). The same year, President Medvedev established a special commission for fighting "falsifications" of history.

Counteracting the revisionism of World War II history was the main aim of Prime Minister Putin's official visit to Gdansk, where, on 1 September 2009, the European leaders met to commemorate the seventieth anniversary of the Nazi invasion of Poland and the beginning of World War II. In an article published by *Gazeta Wyborcza*, Putin admitted that the Molotov-Ribbentrop Pact was morally unacceptable but hardly avoidable under the circumstances and tried to relativize it by pointing to the Munich agreement one year before. He shifted the focus from the Molotov-Ribbentrop Pact to the creation of the anti-Hitler coalition, which he called "the turning point of the twentieth century, one of the most significant events of the last century" (Putin 2009).

Politics of Memory after the Orange Revolution: Memory Wars and Their Regional Effects

With the transnationalization and Europeanization of the debates on WWII, Ukraine found itself torn between the (East)European and the Russian regimes of memory. This became especially evident after the Orange Revolution. The memory politics of President Yushchenko, apart from their domestic political aims, were supposed to legitimize Ukraine's pro-European geopolitical choice. His most resonant initiatives, such as establishing the Museum of Soviet Occupation and the Institute of National Remembrance, the commemoration of the Great Famine in 1932–33 as a "genocide of the Ukrainian people," and the rehabilitation of the Ukrainian nationalist underground, were designed to de-Stalinize and de-colonize the Ukrainian collective memory. Yushchenko and his advisors were inspired by the more advanced policies of the new EU members (Poland and the Baltic states in particular). Among the multiple narratives of WWII Yushchenko preferred the one that presented the Ukrainian nation as a victim of two totalitarian regimes. Even if in the beginning of his presidency, Yushchenko paid tribute to the Great Patriotic War narrative, he invested it with new accents, calling for the reconciliation between the Soviet war veterans and the fighters of the anti-Soviet UPA. However, the idea of reconciliation did not work and was soon replaced by a politics of glorification of the UPA aimed at mobilizing the nationalist electorate concentrated in the western regions of the country. Presenting the UPA and its leaders Stepan Bandera and Roman Shukhevych as anti-Soviet symbols and, even more importantly, highlighting the Famine as a genocide of the Ukrainians organized by Stalin, Yushchenko presented his nation as the victim of the Communist regime imposed by Moscow. However, unlike

in the Baltic states, the MRP failed to become a symbol of national victimhood in Ukraine. This was not only because Yushchenko's political
opponents, the Party of Regions and the Communists, used the argument of Ukraine's current borders as a positive outcome of the Hitler-
Stalin Pact against the discourse of equal criminality, but also because
different parts of today's Ukraine experienced and remembered the
consequences of the Pact in different ways. Last but not least, having
Poland and Russia as its two main neighbors, Ukraine inevitably found
itself caught by their dispute on the MRP.

In the beginning of September 2009, when Poland discussed the
political message of Prime Minister Putin in Gdansk, Yushchenko
(2009) gave an interview to the Polish conservative newspaper *Rzeczpospolita* calling both Stalin and Hitler responsible for the beginning
of WWII. Yushchenko's political block Our Ukraine supported the
initiative of the European parliament and the OCSE to make 23 August
the all-European Day of the Victims of Totalitarianism and proposed
to ban all Communist symbols in Ukraine. Once again, pro-European
intellectuals made an effort to shift the accent from the positive Soviet
symbol of 17 September to the negative symbol of 23 August, and in
this way to change the meaning of the dominant narrative about WWII.
For example, Evhen Zakharov (2009a), the head of the Kharkiv Human
Rights Group, boldly stated in his article in *Ukrainska Pravda*, that to
celebrate the day of reunification is the same as if the Jews would celebrate the beginning of the Holocaust. Instead, he proposed to join the
newly established European memorial day on 23 August. For Kharkiv,
an academic and industrial center of Eastern Ukraine, 23 August 1943
is the date of the liberation from Nazi occupation and thus was chosen
as the Day of the City in the 1990s. In his article in the local newspaper
Glavnoe, Zakharov (2009b) proposed to turn 23 August from liberation
day into the day of mourning for all victims of war, Nazism and Stalinism, moving the Day of the City to another date. This would radically
change the meaning of the popular local holiday in Kharkiv, which is
still connected to the narrative of the Great Patriotic War.

The initiative of the EP and the OSCE aimed at turning the MRP into
a new European *lieu de mémoire* found much more support in Western Ukraine, but the proposed date of 23 August could not compete
with 17 September, which is deeply rooted in the local memory as the
symbol of a collective trauma. On 17 September 2009, the seventieth
anniversary of the Soviet occupation of Western Ukraine, various
commemorative events, from academic to purely political, took place

in the region, and this tradition has continued for the last three years. Flash mobs, historical enactments (costumed street performances), and provocative installations of political art have been organized by political activists from various Ukrainian nationalist organizations. For example, the borders of Ukraine were represented on a map drawn at a square in Ivano-Frankivsk and marked by barbed wire to symbolize the imposed character of the reunification (Bilyi 2011). In Lviv, young people dressed in Nazi and Soviet uniforms posed for photos and distributed "propaganda" leaflets. There were also more serious events: in September 2009, several academic institutions in Lviv, including the University, the Center for Urban History, the museum Lonsky Prison held a conference entitled "Golden September: liberation or occupation?".

The critical assessment of the Molotov-Ribbentrop pact, the interpretation of the Soviet invasion in eastern Galicia as aggression and occupation, and the condemnation of both Nazism and Stalinism have also become important elements for the Polish-Ukrainian reconciliation. The benefit of the formula "we all are victims" is its inclusive and nondiscriminatory character, allowing Ukrainians to downplay the conflicting ethnic narratives of collective suffering that had made Lviv a contested place for decades. A good example of such an approach to reconciliation is the exhibition "Lviv 1939–1941," opened on 2 July on the Market Square in Lviv. The display was jointly prepared by the Polish and Ukrainian Institutes of National Remembrance in cooperation with the Polish Embassy in Kiev and the Institute for Historical Research at Ivan Franko National University, Lviv.

In Kharkiv, in Eastern Ukraine, the seventieth anniversary of the Molotov-Ribbentrop Pact in September 2009 was also marked by a conference, but of a completely different political orientation. It was organized by the Party of Regions (which in 2009 had the majority in the city council and in the regional assembly) together with Russian partners, under the title "The Second World War: Lessons and Outcomes for Ukraine." The conference focused on the Molotov-Ribbentrop Pact and was one of numerous events in a large-scale Kremlin propaganda campaign aimed against the "falsifications of history"—a formula used to denounce attempts of some East-European countries to equate Nazism and Stalinism and officially condemn Stalin's deal with Hitler. It was also part of Moscow's information war against President Yushchenko, presented as a nationalist and consequently a Fascist who rehabilitates Nazi collaborators in Ukraine. In the course of the conference, political speeches denouncing the Orange Fascism in Ukraine dominated over academic presentations, and propaganda publications produced by the pro-Kremlin foundation Historical Memory (such as "The Molotov-Ribbentrop Pact in Questions and Answers" by Aleksandr Diukov [2009]) were distributed. Dmytro Tabachnyk, the ideological talking head of the Party of Regions (currently the controversial minister of education) was among the key speakers. Two weeks later, the Russian newspaper *Izvestia* published his article entitled "From Ribbentrop to Maydan" accusing Yushchenko of rehabilitating Nazism in Ukraine and defending Stalin's foreign policy. He went as far as to claim that the "Galicians" (Western Ukrainians) do not belong to the Ukrainian nation: "We have different enemies and different friends" (Tabachnyk 2009). Thus, the Molotov-Ribbentrop Pact has become a polarizing symbol in Ukraine, a country torn apart by memory wars between Russia and some new EU members promoting their version of WWII memory on the European level.

The Rise of Euro-Skepticism in Ukraine: The MRP as a Historical Analogy

Historian Jan-Werner Müller (2002: 27) once warned against the (mis) use of memory through historical analogies that "reduce complexity and short-circuit critical reflection." Indeed, politically charged analogies referring to the events of the past are often more than innocent comparisons between now and then. Those using them in political rhetoric seek to appropriate the moral capital accumulated in some popular sites of memory, symbols, or narratives and mobilize the related collective emotions and memories for their own purposes. It is probably the Holocaust that has been most often misused as a historical analogy. But in Eastern Europe, the Molotov-Ribbentrop Pact, highly charged with emotions and connotations of betrayal, conspiracy, and of ignoring the interests of the weak, has become another popular trope for political allusions. Indeed, if the MRP would not have taken place, it would have to be invented in today's Eastern Europe as a powerful symbol of geopolitical victimization.

The ghost of the MRP haunts the geopolitical imagination in Eastern Europe despite the fact that the EU and NATO enlargement provided the Baltic States, Poland, and other former Soviet satellites with strong guarantees of national security. However, from the mid-2000s, Russia's recovery from a decade of crisis, its growing geopolitical ambitions in Eastern Europe, and the perceived policy of double standards toward

Russia in Berlin and Paris—both allegedly interested in a special partnership with Moscow—have been nurturing the phobias of the former Soviet satellites. They fear a German-Russian rapprochement that threatens to change the balance of power in the EU. Energy politics is one field where Russia's interests (or more precisely the interests of the state-owned monopolist *Gasprom*) correspond with the interests of big German companies—consumers of Russian gas. Due to the Soviet-inherited infrastructure of gas pipelines, former Soviet satellites are dependent on the Russian monopoly. Besides, a considerable part of their state budget revenues consists of gas transit fees. As the Russian-Ukrainian gas wars from 2005 demonstrated, Moscow does not hesitate to use gas delivery as an instrument of political pressure. Therefore, some Eastern European politicians were worried when the project of the new North Steam pipeline was announced, which is supposed to run along the bed of the Baltic Sea delivering Russian gas directly to Germany and bypassing the former Soviet and satellite states. Many security experts and some Eastern European officials expressed concerns that the Russian-German venture will make these countries more vulnerable to pressure from Moscow: "For Eastern Europeans, the pipeline issue evokes deep memories of a darker era of occupation and collaboration, and has become a proxy debate over Russia's intentions towards the lands it ruled from the end of World War II to the fall of the Berlin Wall" (Kramer 2009). Radek Sikorski, the Polish foreign minister, compared the pipeline deal between Russia and Germany to the Molotov-Ribbentrop Pact, pointing particularly to the fact that the deal was made without consulting with the new EU members (Cf. Miodek 2009).

In Ukraine, the political bankruptcy of the Orange coalition, which led to Ukraine fatigue in the EU on the one hand, and the growing confrontation of Kyiv with the Kremlin on history and memory issues on the other hand, created fertile soil for conspiracy theories. Ukrainian commentators pointed to the numerous signals proving that Western Europe (more precisely Germany) sold Ukraine to Moscow. For example, in the summer of 2009, during her meeting with Putin in Sochi, Chancellor Angela Merkel essentially agreed with Putin's criticism of Yushchenko's politics and denounced his "nationalism" (Zilgalov 2009). On the website of the Lviv cultural journal *Ji*, the editor Taras Vozniak (2009) expressed his concern about the growing international isolation of Ukraine resulting from the failure of NATO and EU integration ambitions. He pointed to what he called the "crystallization of a Berlin-Paris-Moscow axis" joined by Warsaw. While the new Polish government pragmatically shifted political priorities from Kyiv to Moscow, and the memory wars have intensified in the Ukrainian-Polish borderlands, Germany, according to Vozniak, "tries to share its historical guilt for the Nazi crimes with Ukraine," to the satisfaction of Kremlin. Similar commentaries in the Ukrainian media, not only on nationalist websites but also in the liberal *Ukrainska Pravda*, evoked the case of Ivan Demianiuk, a Soviet POW accused of assisting in the mass murder of Jews in the Nazi extermination camp Sobibor. "In Munich a new 'Molotov-Ribbentrop Pact' was made, as responsibility for the German crimes were partly shifted to Demianiuk, in order to accuse Ukrainians of 'collaboration,'" wrote Lviv journalist Ivan Holod (2011). In fact, the journalist accused the German court of using evidence fabricated by the KGB. Interestingly, the MRP is a symbol used by the Ukrainian nationalists, national democrats, and liberals, but never by the Communists or the Party of Regions for whom it does not have any connotation of crime, betrayal, or conspiracy, but instead has a neutral or even a positive meaning. President Yanukovych, who has every reason to be irritated by Angela Merkel's position in the Tymoshenko case, would never refer to the MRP as a historical analogy.

As the examples above show, the use of the Molotov-Ribbentrop Pact as a historical analogy in contemporary Ukraine reflects the mutual frustration in EU-Ukrainian and German-Ukrainian relations, a growing feeling of political isolation, sensed especially by the Western part of the Ukrainian élites, and the new phenomenon of a Euro-skepticism resulting from the failure of the Orange Revolution and the EU's lack of enthusiasm concerning Ukraine's membership perspectives.

Conclusion

In Ukraine, as in other East European countries, the Molotov-Ribbentrop Pact has been at the center of public debates on the memory of World War II since 1989. In the last two decades, the Soviet myths of the Great Patriotic War and of the reunification of the Ukrainian lands in 1939 have been seriously challenged by processes of de-Stalinization of collective memory and partly replaced by narratives of the "Soviet-German war" and "Soviet occupation of Western Ukraine." These narratives correspond to the new transnational memory regime that has been promoted in the European Union by some post-Communist countries and is based on the thesis of Nazism and Stalinism as equally criminal and equally responsible for WWII. After the Orange Revolution, the attempt of the Ukrainian leadership to institutionalize this memory regime on the national level caused contradictory reactions in the Ukrainian regions and added to the political polarization in the country. It also had consequences for the relations with Ukraine's two most important neighbors, Poland and Russia. While in Western Ukraine liberal intellectuals used the narrative of "common suffering" of both Ukrainians and Poles under Stalin and Hitler to promote the reconciliation process, in the East the Party of Regions in collaboration with Moscow tried to denounce President Yushchenko as a Fascist for rehabilitating the anti-Soviet nationalist underground. From 2009, the growing frustration in EU-Ukrainian relations and Germany's pragmatic rapprochement with Russia led to the rise of Euro-skepticism among the pro-Western Ukrainian public. In this discourse the Molotov-Ribbentrop Pact has served as a useful historical analogy.

References

Asadova, Nargiz. 2005. "PACE Demanded Compensation for the Baltic Republics." *Kommersant – Russia's Daily Online*. 23 June. www.kommersant.com/ p586624/r_1/PACE_Demanded_Compensation_for_the_Baltic_Republics/ (Accessed 24 August 2012.)

Bell, Duncan S. A. 2003. "Mythscapes: memory, mythology, and national identity." *British Journal of Sociology*. 54 (1): 63–81.

Bilyi, Sehiy. 2011. "Ukraina za koliuchym drotom – pohliad UNP na 'Zolotyi veresen'." *Kolomyia Web Portal*. 19 September. http://kolomyya.org/se/sites/ pb/39434/ (Accessed 24 August 2012.)

Diukov, Aleksandr. 2009. *Molotov-Ribbentrop Pakt v voprosakh I otvetakh*. Moscow: Historical Memory Foundation.

European Parliament. 2005. "The Future of Europe Sixty Years after the Second World War." 12 May. www.europarl.europa.eu/sides/getDoc.do?pubRef=-// EP//TEXT+TA+P6-TA-2005-0180+0+DOC+XML+V0//EN (Accessed 24 August 2012.)

European Parliament. 2009. "On European Conscience and Totalitarianism." 2 April. http://www.europarl.europa.eu/sides/getDoc.do?pubRef=-//EP// TEXT+TA+P6-TA-2009-0213+0+DOC+XML+V0//EN (Accessed 24 August 2012.)

Gross, Jan T. [1988] 2002. *Revolution from Abroad: The Soviet Conquest of Poland's Western Ukraine and Western Belorussia*. Princeton: Princeton University Press.

Himka, John-Paul. 2011. "Debates in Ukraine over Nationalist Involvement in the Holocaust, 2004–2008." *Nationalities Papers*, 39 (3): 353–370.

Holod, Ihor. 2011. "U Nimechchyni zasudyly ukraintsia. Za nimets'ki zlochyny." *Ukrainska Pravda*. 19 May. www.istpravda.com.ua/columns/2011/05/19/39088/ (Accessed 24 August 2012.)

Hryciuk, Grzegorz. "Die Illusion der Freiheit. Belarussen und Ukrainer im September 1939." *Osteuropa*, 59 (7–8): 73–88.

Hrynevych, Vladyslav. 2005. "Raskolotaia pamiat'. Vtoraia mirovaia voina v istoricheskom soznanii ukrainskogo obshchestva." In *Pamiat' o voine 60 let spustia: Rossia, Germania, Evropa.* Moscow: NLO, 419–435.

Jilge, Wilfried. 2006. "The Politics of History and the Second World War in Post-Communist Ukraine (1986/1991–2004/2005)." *Jahrbücher für Geschichte Osteuropas.* 54 (1): 50–81.

Koposov, Nikolai. 2010. "Does Russia Need a Memory Law?" *OpenDemocracy,* 16 June. www.opendemocracy.net/od-russia/nikolai-koposov/does-russia-need-memory-law (Accessed 24 August 2012.)

Kramer, Andrew E. 2009. "Russia Gas Pipeline Heightens East Europe's Fears." *The New York Times.* 13 October.

Kulchyts'kyi, Stanislav. 2000. "I znovu pro 17 veresnia 1939 roku." *Den'.* 16 September.

Langenbacher, Eric. 2010. "Collective Memory as a Factor in Political Culture and International Relations." In *Power and the Past. Collective Memory and International Relations,* eds. Eric Langenbacher and Yossi Shain. Washington, DC: Georgetown University Press.

Miodek, Marcin. 2009. "'Das ist ein neuer Molotov-Ribbentrop Pakt!' Eine Historische Analogie in Polens Energiedebatte." *Osteuropa,* 59 (7–8): 295–305.

Müller, Jan Werner. 2002. "Introduction: the Power of Memory, the Memory of Power and the Power over Memory." In *Memory and Power in Post-War Europe. Studies in the Presence of the Past.* Ed. Jan-Werner Müller. Cambridge: Cambridge University Press.

Olik, Jeffrey. 1999. "Collective Memory: The Two Cultures." *Sociological Theory* 17 (3): 333–48.

Onken, Eva-Clarita. 2010. "Memory and Democratic Pluralism in the Baltic States – Rethinking the Relationship." *Journal of Baltic Studies,* 41 (3): 277–94.

Onken, Eva-Clarita. 2007. "The Baltic States and Moscow's 9 May Commemoration: Analysing Memory Politics in Europe." *Europe-Asia Studies,* 59 (1): 23–46.

Putin, Vladimir. 2009. "Karty historii – powod do wzajemnych pretensji czy podstawa pojednania i partnerstwa?" *Gazeta Wyborcza,* 31 August.

Snyder, Timothy. 2002. "Memory of Sovereignty and Sovereignty over Memory: Poland, Lithuania and Ukraine, 1939–1999." In *Memory and Power in Post-War Europe. Studies in the Presence of the Past.* Ed. Jan-Werner Müller, Cambridge: Cambridge University Press.

Stetsiuk, Valentyn. 1999. Sviatkuvannia dnia mista u L'vovi. *Brama,* 20 September.

Tabachnik, Dmitriy. 2009. "Ot Ribbentropa do Maydana." *Izvestiia,* 23 September.

Troebst, Stefan. 2009. "Der 23. August 1939: Ein europäischer *lieu de memoire?*" *Osteuropa,* 59 (7–8): 249–56.

Vozniak, Taras. 2002. "Skladnyi 'zolotyi veresen' trydtsiat' dev'iatoho." *Ji,* 26: 235–238.

Vozniak, Taras. 2009. "Zavershuiet'sia protses diplomatychnoi izoliatsii Ukrainy." *Ji – nasha posytsiia.* 17 August. www.ji-magazine.lviv.ua/position/2009/voznyak-aug09.htm (Accessed 24 August 2012.)

Yushchenko, Viktor (Interview). 2009. "Antypolskość nie jest cechą wrodzoną Ukraińców." *Rzeczpospolita.* 8 September.

Zakharov, Yevhen. 2009a. "Chy ie 17 veresnia sviatom v Ukraini?" *Ukrainska Pravda,* 17 September. www.pravda.com.ua/articles/2009/09/17/4190222/ (Accessed 24 August 2012.)

Zakharov, Yevhen. 2009b. "Sud vremeni." *Glavnoe,* 22 August.
Zhurzhenko, Tatiana. 2007. "The Geopolitics of Memory," in *Eurozine,* www.euro-zine.com/articles/2007-05-10-zhurzhenko-en.html (Accessed 24 August 2012.)
Zilgalov, Vasyl'. 2009. "Kreml' hotuie novyi pakt Molotova-Ribbentrops, nasam-pered proty Ukrainy." *Radio Svoboda.* 25 August. www.radiosvoboda.org/content/article/1807220.html (Accessed 24 August 2012.)

13

"Often Very Harmful Things Start Out with Things That Are Very Harmless": European Reflections on Guilt and Innocence Inspired by Art about the Holocaust in the 1990s

Diana I. Popescu

From Memorial Art to Installation Art Debates

Deliberations, argues political philosopher John Dryzek (2000: 5), are "critical moments that produce enduring changes in public opinion" as they help individuals create new norms that reshape the foundations of collective identity. Holocaust memorialization in Europe has been subjected to processes of negotiations many times. In Germany especially, the proposal for the Memorial to the Murdered Jews of Europe, publicized by the German journalist Leah Rosh during a colloquium on 24 August 1988, represented the incipient phase of a public discussion that developed into a twelve-year national debate and ended with the construction of American architect Peter Eisenman's field of pillars in 2005. Rosh's demand to erect "a site of remembrance, something that recalls this deed," "a clear sign . . . in the land of the perpetrators" (Rosh 1995: 3) launched a lengthy "German memorial process," dominated by multiple discussions about the relevance of commemoration in Germany, historical guilt and the "normalization" of history, the appropriateness of the architectural design, and the sitting of the memorial (Young 2000: 191). The search for common ground on which to build a new Germany and a renewed sense of nationhood inevitably led to a return to the two countries' shared past, with the Third Reich and the Holocaust the very cause of separation. As Jane Kramer noted, with the coming down of the Wall:

> After forty-four years of distraction, Germans began the excruciating process of connecting the kind of people they thought they were to the people they had been and the people they wanted to be. They discovered that it was hard to be ordinary folks – when you had a Holocaust in your history. (Kramer 1996: xvi)

Hearings, colloquia, unofficial meetings, and governmental sessions became sites of antagonism and "angry words," of "emotional displays and heated arguments, so hopelessly convoluted that one journalist suggested that a high wall be built around the site while everyone cools down" (Wiedmar 1999: 14). Was the construction of a Holocaust memorial a national duty, a redemptive act, a part of the mourning process, a cure for the national guilt? Did they want to "settle their crimes into 'history', to resolve a duty to remember and a longing to forget?" (Kramer 1996: 258). Martin Walser, on receiving the Peace Prize of the German Book Trade in October 1998, was among those opposing the construction of a Holocaust memorial. He reacted against what he termed the "milieu of intensive public memorialization," against "the exaggerated and coercive presence of memory in media and monuments," fearing that it might prevent individual confrontation with Holocaust guilt. In his view, every German individual should deal with the burden of the past through an act of "interiorization," by "letting the memory of Holocaust seep into the drain of privacy" (Walser cited by Assmann 2008: 129).

Walser argued for "the self-internalization of Holocaust remembrance and its expulsion from public memory" (quoted in Kamenetzky 1999: 258). Only in this manner could the unified German nation attain a sense of normality. In hindsight, one wonders whether the argument of interiorization proposed by Walser has not proved to be a more meaningful long-term approach, and whether collective memorialization is rather counter-productive for a younger generation that has reached maturity in the 1990s, the decade of the "hyperactive memory industry" (Cesarani 2005: 85). In this chapter, I would like to move away from public debates prompted by memorial art to what I view as an individual-oriented and private debate taking place in the public space of the art museum and proposed by art installation. In particular, I want to ask how third-generation Israeli artist Ram Katzir has opened up a space for dialogue and self-reflection about guilt and innocence, and the grey zones in between that characterize the connection to Nazism of several European countries, namely Germany, Holland, and Lithuania.

Debate-Centered Museums and Art Installations

Griselda Pollock and Joyce Zemans stress the symbiotic connection between art museums and society, reminding us that "art and thought are active and necessary processes, not isolated in the museum, but opened into the world. The museum/gallery is an opened space that can become their stage, where they are investigated and performed" (Pollock and Zemans 2007: xx). Since the 1960s, visual art has embraced theatricality and performance as part of a new artistic expression. According to some critics, it is installation art where this process is best realized (de Oliviera 2003: 32). It was installation art that came to be described as encouraging debate, a form of art which is not defined in terms of a traditional medium but rather in light of the message it conveys by whichever means. This new artistic expression is suggestive of "a shift from objective critique towards a new subjectivity which emphasizes uncertainty and brings both artist and viewer together in a discursive environment" (de Oliviera 2003: 32). If the art museum is likened to a stage, the question that arises is how the spectator participates in the artwork. In his newspaper article "No Stage, No Actors, but It Is Theatre and Art" (1999), art historian Robert Storr corroborates that installations have become "complete immersion environments." Storr insists that the theatrical aspect of a work of art that was once seen as a weakness, since it relied only on entertaining the audience, has recently been revalued. Hence, art that encourages audience interaction has gained a favorable position within the art world. There are several reasons to explain this trend. De Oliviera stresses the interconnectedness between the interactive character of the new forms of art expression and the construction of a museum's image, stating that:

> Interaction is not only an opportunity to ensure the audience's participation, but instead suggests a creative engagement with the content of the artwork which directly impacts on the evaluation of the museum itself. (2003: 46)

Hence, the work of art turns into a "space of exchange" and interactivity, as artworks and exhibitions act as catalysts that generate "communicative processes" and make possible "a state of encounter" (Bourriaud 1998).

Art exhibitions, due to their theatrical and performative aspect, become open arenas where meanings are negotiated between artists, viewers, and the institutions that house them. This interplay is made particularly apparent in an art installation project entitled *Your Coloring Book* by Ram Katzir, artist and grandchild of Holocaust survivors. Its very title conveys the idea that ownership of the artwork does not pertain exclusively to its author. The coloring book can belong to anyone willing to engage in the process of coloring and filling its black and white drawings with content. Indeed, assuming responsibility for the created image is a crucial element of this artwork.

The Wandering Coloring Book Project (1996–1998)

Your Coloring Book does not betray the artist's enduring mission to "subvert expectations, surprising and disorienting the spectator." His images "often have a dualistic nature: inside is outside, the tragic is comical, and what seems far away is actually very near. The result is a world in which the foreign and the familiar coexist in unexpected ways" (Heingartner 2012).

Katzir was a graduate of the Rietveld Academy of Art in Amsterdam, when Casco Project Space invited him to present his work with them in Utrecht in 1995. He discovered that during 1942–1945 their building had housed the printers of the Dutch Nazi newspaper, located near the Dutch Nazi party's former offices. To his surprise, the space, now converted into an art gallery, did not betray any signs of this dark past. As an artist taking inspiration in places, Katzir felt compelled to create a work of art that could uncover the hidden history underlying this seemingly innocent space. A children's coloring book became the central piece of an installation that turned into a wandering project. The installation travelled for two years, 1996 to 1998, to "places where people would rather not see the book," namely to cities with specific historical connections to the Holocaust: Utrecht, Enschede, Vilnius, Kraków, Berlin, and Jerusalem (Katzir 1997). The project concluded in Amsterdam's Stedelijk Museum, with an exhibition documenting responses from participants of all previous exhibitions.

Entering an exhibition space filled with old school benches arranged in symmetrical lines, on which children's coloring books were neatly placed, visitors were invited to color within the lines of seemingly innocent images. Although there were no guidelines with regard to how one should approach the coloring book, most visitors took a seat. The book revealed thirteen simple drawings, some of them idyllic, depicting scenes including a group of pupils saluting their teacher with hands raised upward; a crowd of boys and girls queuing in front of what look like train carriages; youngsters singing, their hands protruding as if reaching outside the frame of the drawing toward the visitor; a solitary bench in a park; a young girl offering what could be flowers and facing a man whose identity is hidden; airplanes in flying formation; a fatherly figure reading to children from what appears to be a book of fairytales.

On the last page one discovered that Katzir's drawings had replicated historical photographs depicting Nazi propaganda against, and persecution of, the Jews. The visitors started coloring the sketchy images, which seemed harmless at first. As they turned the pages, doubt about the pictures' provenance would be raised. At closer inspection, one drawing revealed a small Star of David attached to the coat of a child waiting in line in front of a train carriage, the airplanes were arranged in the shape of a swastika, and the children's salute looked very similar to the Nazi salute. However, only on the last page of the book could the drawings be positively identified as reproductions of historical photographs. What initially seemed to create innocent settings, in due course revealed a different story. The man on the cover of the coloring book could be identified in one historical photograph as Adolf Hitler; the father reading bedtime stories turned into Joseph Goebbels, the Third Reich's propaganda minister, reading to his daughters; the cheerful crowd was welcoming Hitler to the *Bückerberg Erntedankfest* (Harvest Festival) rally in Germany; the pupils were greeting their teacher with the Nazi salute; and the children were queuing for a train that would deport them from Łódź Ghetto to a concentration camp. Katzir had worked with images collected in an especially designed book entitled *Deutschland Erwacht: Werden, Kampf und Sieg der NSDAP*, which consisted of photographic Nazi propaganda against Jews that had been printed on cigarette cards by the *Cigaretten Bilderdienst* between 1933–1940. Katzir had also included drawings based on photographs depicting scenes in Nazi concentration camps, and of the deportation and persecution of Jews held at Yad Vashem Archives. The resemblance between the originals and their reproduction in Katzir's drawings was not very close. The artist deliberately withheld vital visual information, luring the visitors into working on a scene whose meaning they could not fully understand. The photographs were selected for their iconic value but also because "they had the same kind of Walt Disney allure. They looked very sweet and attractive, but actually what was behind them was different" (Interview with Katzir 2009). Visitors who did not check the evidence on the last page of the book might have felt duped into doing something they would never knowingly have done. Yet, those few but noticeable references to the Holocaust make us doubt whether the visitors could in fact miss the real meaning of the images. Art historian Gary Schwartz (1998: 36–37) argues on this account that:

> By the time visitors have sat down and begun to color, it is clear that each one has traversed an inner barrier between not knowing and knowing, between innocence and guilty knowledge. It is hard to get that far in the project without sensing that there is a shameful secret attached to it.

Having gained full awareness of the idea informing the exhibition, visitors variously stayed and took responsibility for the images they had given color to, rebelled and challenged the very concept of the project, or responded by writing their views on the book itself, or on the visitor books placed at the entrance of the exhibition halls. Many became very involved with the process, leaving behind thousands of colored books now stored in the artist's personal archive in Amsterdam.

Consequently, some three thousand colored books now reflect individual Europeans' responses to history. They remained anonymous, unless they felt the need to sign their contributions. Such anonymity, one might conclude, enabled visitors to more freely interrogate the content of public memorialization discourses or school history textbooks. Arguably, the process also offered opportunities to variously confess a real or inherited sense of guilt, or to articulate detachment from events known and accessed only by means of representations. A selection of colored images by visitors in Enschede, Berlin, and Vilnius, accessible on the artist's webpage, show participants engaged in a process of reflection on the Holocaust and their countries' dominant approaches to the past. In what follows, I briefly describe how Katzir adapted the installation space to fit what he saw as the historical profiles of Germany, the Netherlands, and Lithuania. This is followed by a discussion of how several anonymous visitors in these countries engaged with the coloring books, suggesting that these individuals were given the opportunity to express private negotiations of public memory discourses and, occasionally, to openly endorse their countries' narratives of postwar collective identities. In addition to my own readings of the colored images, I examine the interpretations given by the local media and place them within a broader context of the respective countries' memory narratives.

Several limitations of this analysis need to be acknowledged. Firstly, there is no available information about visitors' demographic profiles. One might assume, however, that a large number of the responses reflect the attitudes of the middle class, since visitors to art galleries tend to belong predominantly to this category. Another constraint comes from the lack of full access to the three thousand visitor comments gathered by the artist. The particular visitors' responses quoted in this chapter draw on a selection made by the artist, documentary filmmakers, and newspaper journalists. Hence, questions arise about the criteria applied when choosing these specific comments over others. While the selected responses were clearly deemed interesting and relevant by Katzir himself or the journalists, one cannot know how representative of the views of the local population they are. Because of the anonymous character of the project and the lack of relevant statistics, it is impossible to gauge to what extent these responses, both textual and visual, represent majority opinions.

My choice of visitors' responses, then, takes into account the extent to which they enter into a dialogue with existing memory narratives. This leads me to ask how these comments resonate with, or challenge, dominant views, and whether they enter a process of negotiation with established discourses about WWII in their respective national contexts. My interpretations of the colored images and of the statements made by visitors should be regarded as a springboard for discussion and further reflection. Furthermore, they can be viewed as snapshots illustrating certain discourses or self-understandings already contained in scholarly literature about the development of European national memories of World War II.

Berlin, January–March 1998

The exhibition hall in Berlin was reminiscent of Bavarian beer halls, former meeting places for members of the national-socialist party. Visitors entered a space where one could see an old school desk from the 1930s, when education served to indoctrinate students with the National Socialist worldview. The lamps in the ceiling concealed a video projector, from which an animation film of drawings turning into photographs was projected as a haunting loop, onto the walls of the exhibition space. The element of surprise was no longer important, as these images are well-known to the German public and part of the nation's conscience, argued Katzir. It is clear from this set-up that the artist attempted to reinforce on his visitors a sense of guilt, by recreating in minute detail a space reminiscent of the Nazi period. The invitation to the exhibition took the form of a beer-mat, with pencils placed in beer mugs. Katzir's endeavor to enforce onto the German visitors a confrontation with the past, and to place them in locations formerly occupied by Nazi customers (i.e., in Bavarian beer halls), succeeded in the sense that participants indeed engaged deeply with the images. Katzir further notes that, unlike other places in Europe, the dialogue created by the exhibition was the most interesting (2009). Katharina Kaiser, director of the Haus Am Kleistpark, which hosted the project, saw it as a "contribution to the current discussion about the Holocaust memorial in Berlin" (quoted in Stepken 1998). Inspired by the exhibition, a conference at the Wannsee Building soon followed, focusing on the "loss of images," "the culture of memory," and the validity and limits of representation (Kaiser quoted in Stepken 1998). In the blank spaces inside the drawings, visitors were offered chances to variously inscribe their own connection to the events, their immediate reactions to the particular images, and also their sense of confusion or disapproval of the artist's intentions.

The documentary film carrying the same title as the exhibition records one visitor's unease at the thought of interacting with Katzir's reproductions of historical evidence. Initially the visitor rejects the invitation to color, on the grounds that the images are "too silly," only to confirm later on, that most of the photographs are all too familiar to him, and more importantly "these are photos from *our* history, and *I* can't color it" (Anonymous visitor Berlin, 1998, my emphasis). Even though he does not further explain his refusal to get involved, it is obvious that the images do not leave him indifferent. This leaves room for interpretation of course. However, given the dominant presence of the Holocaust in German public discourse in the late 1980s and throughout the 1990s, triggered by the *Historians' Debate* (*Historikerstreit*) of 1986–1987 and the Holocaust memorial debate (1988–2005), one can safely conclude that this visitor shows acute awareness of the issues addressed by the artist (Geyer and Hasen 1994). It seems to be his historical sensitivity that stops him from coloring, since changing the meaning of the images can be a form of denial, which would of course go against the now established narrative of acceptance and acknowledgment of historical guilt that gained centrality in Germany after the fall of the Berlin Wall. While this visitor recognizes these images as part of his national history, it seems—one might plausibly conclude—that, for him, engaging in the playful activity of coloring would be tantamount to reducing the gravity of the crimes committed by Nazi Germany, and to sanction activities that might lead to Holocaust trivialization. After all, the notion of trivialization already appeared in the *Historikerstreit*, which raised questions about the perils of normalizing German history, by comparing the Nazi genocide with the Soviet Gulag. It was argued that by normalizing German history, one runs the risk of trivializing the tragedy of European Jewry (Habermas 1988).

"I had some trouble sitting down here," confesses another visitor. We see him coloring with great care the shoe of a child lined up in front of a deportation train, and admitting that the coloring "gives you time to concentrate on this special subject, and it's a good way to remember the history." Unlike the previous visitor, this participant feels that he needs to change the reality of the photograph by giving "the picture a positive sense," of what could have been if Nazism had never existed in the first place. This visitor seemingly feels empowered by the act of coloring to create a different fate for the Jewish children, and through this escape into wishful thinking, he appears to find a personal way of remembering and interacting with a history that cannot be altered. Reflecting on the coloring book, a female visitor shares what she sees as its central message:

> I think the lesson is that often very harmful things start out with things that are very harmless. And, before you know it, you get more and more involved, and by that time you are emotionally so committed that you don't want to admit that it has become harmful. (Visitor, 1998 Berlin)

She articulates awareness of how propaganda entraps its subjects and takes root due to people's ignorance, complacency, and lack of initiative.

Many visitors accepted Katzir's invitation. Undaunted, argues journalist Angelika Stepken (1998), members of younger generations "colored hair blond, and mouths red. Some added interpretative signs, projected skulls onto faces, tied a swastika necktie round the innocent deer's neck." Others inscribed the word *Deutschland* on the drawing of a deer, to symbolize how the country was misguided into committing atrocious acts by an evil shepherd, or drew Hitler moustaches onto the faces of children gathered for a picnic, to express the omnipresence of Nazi ideology and the dissolution of individual identities under a regime that led to previously unimaginable acts and entirely changed our understanding of humanity.

At the same time, members of the older generation showed difficulty in dealing with some images, and they tended "to deny the image and seek the word, jotting down memories, poems" (Stepken 1998). One visitor wrote on the image of children being deported to concentration camps: "*Sag mir wo die Kinder sind*?," reminiscent of the folk song "Where have all the flowers gone?," written by American Pete Seeger in 1955 and later recorded and performed by Marlene Dietrich in German with the title "*Sag mir wo die Blumen sind*?." The song is well-known for its nostalgic tones and widely regarded as a meditation on death. Whereas this visitor expressed a seemingly deeply felt sense of loss and mourning, other visitors conveyed a sense of anger and revolt. On the drawing based on the original photograph of a school girl handing flowers to Hitler during a street parade, one visitor attached a swastika band on Hitler's arm, exchanged the flowers for dynamite and a knife, and entitled the scene a "missed opportunity." Indeed, many of the colored images are indicative of their authors' willingness to engage with the past. This is perhaps not surprising, since Germany's unification and assumption of a leading role in the European Union were accompanied by a continued commitment to come to terms with history, via debate, and as shown here, also through the medium of art. Hermann Pfütze (1998) observes: "You can color Hitler's boots neatly or scrawl all over them, you can stab Goebbels' face with your crayon and obliterate Nazi symbols. Everything is allowed, there are no recriminations." What the visitor is left with, this journalist suggests, is "the experience of having had to deal with these images."

Enschede, March 1997

Situated on the eastern border with Germany, Enschede is the largest town in the province of Overijssel and the center of the Dutch cotton industry. In line with the Nazi policy to single out the Jewish population, yellow star badges were distributed and enforced throughout the Netherlands in April 1942. These cotton badges were produced by De Nijverheid, a textile company that had been owned by Jews before the German occupation. Decades later, Katzir hoped to confront the Dutch people with their own past as collaborators with Nazism. He argued that whilst Israelis had formed a favorable image of the Dutch as those who had helped the Jews, he doubted that this reflected the reality (Katzir 2009). Of the approximately 140,000 Dutch Jews living in the prewar Netherlands, 107,000 were deported to the East and at least 102,000 were murdered in the Nazi camps. Around 73 percent of the Dutch-Jewish population perished, an unusually high percentage compared to other occupied countries in Western Europe, such as Belgium (40 percent) and France (25 percent) (Griffioen and Zeller 2011). In Holland, there is comprehensive historiography of the Dutch Jewry, looking at various aspects of Jewish life and persecution by Nazis (among the earliest studies see Presser 1969). The story of Anne Frank and the opening of Anne Frank House—a must-see for tourists in Amsterdam—have shaped Dutch public discourse about Holocaust memorialization. Five years prior to the exhibition, a new and contentious area of research focused on the role of the Dutch Civil Service and especially of the police in facilitating the arrests and deportations of Jews (Houwink ten Cate 1990). With this historical debate taking place mainly in academia, one wonders to what extent the Dutch public acknowledges their nation's portion of historical guilt. Unlike Berlin with its Topography of Terror site, a permanent signifier of historical guilt is missing; Katzir, as a Dutch citizen, argues that:

> In Holland people swept [collaboration with Nazism] to the other side of the fence, and kept on saying the Germans were horrible. But, if it was not for the Dutch collaboration, they would not have been so successful. I decided to do a project which dealt with this horrible feeling I had, because everything looked so pretty, but behind it there was a much darker story. (Katzir 2009)

The exhibition in the basement of the Gemeentelijk Kunstcentrum M17 was called "*Kinderspel*" (*Child's Play*), and consisted of a hall with 150 tables. In order to emphasize the shift from victim to perpetrator, hunter, and the hunted, Katzir installed seventeen surveillance cameras overlooking the visitors, while upstairs a TV monitor showed the visitors engaged in coloring. "The visitors will feel watched. Here the exhibition is about obeying and conforming. About looking on and doing nothing," explained Katzir.

A selection of colored images reveals two opposing ways of dealing with this subject. One confirms Katzir's impression that people in the Netherlands have engaged with the Holocaust in a superficial manner, while repressing Dutch involvement with Nazism. The other attests to individuals' personal acts of commemorating the victims. Among the most suggestive images is an entirely blackened page, on the bottom of which a visitor wrote: "A black page in our history." Another drawing shows black bands covering the eyes of children as they now blindly give their teacher the Nazi salute. Yet another portrays Hitler as a wolf, while an innocent fawn falls into his hands just as in the folktale Little Red Riding Hood.

Other colored images contain striking elements of ambiguity and allow for various interpretations. A drawing of a group of planes flying in swastika formation was altered in such a way that the initial meaning was completely erased. Instead of planes, this visitor drew butterflies and colored them in orange, purple and green. Another drawing of a group of girls within a window frame became a murder scene, with girls now depicted as collaborators cheering a man who shoots a Jew wearing the yellow badge. The captions say: "It was only a Jew," and "Hitler is the best." Both examples arguably reveal a playful manner of (dis)engaging with the topic. One may further wonder whether this playfulness denotes undue light-heartedness on the part of the visitors and even an inclination toward anti-Semitism. From the documentary film recording public reactions in Enschede, one discovers that the visitor who had drawn the butterflies was a young lady who explained: "I'm trying to make it a little more positive although it really is not." So, one wonders, are we to read this as another personal attempt to find alternatives to a distraught history, as this visitor wished that war planes could turn into harmless butterflies?

"It is a psychological test," since coloring allows one to explore one's own personality, argued another visitor. This is also the case for an older participant who recognized the book as being about the war, but who had trouble admitting that the picture he was coloring—of a group of schoolchildren to whose hands he attached German flags—arguably said as much about his own past history as a member of the Nationale Jeugdstorm (NJS), the Dutch Hitler Youth, as it did about the Germans. In fact, the NJS faithfully copied the Hitler Jugend and expanded after the German occupation of Holland, counting up to sixteen thousand members by 1942. It is perhaps not surprising that for this ex-member of the NJS, being reminded of his own past involvement as a child was challenging. It is also notable that articles in the Dutch press applauded the educational aspect of the exhibition, but preferred to speak about how it was received in Jerusalem rather than reflecting on what it said about Dutch visitors (Stigter 1997; Bouman 1997). Constructions of victim-identity in the aftermath of WWII characterized many European countries' postwar narratives. Identification with the victims has its own benefits as it keeps feelings of guilt and moral responsibility at bay, and allows the perpetuation of a comfortable state of denial. For art historian Ernst van Alphen, Dutch teaching about the war and the Holocaust seemed almost hypocritical, as stories about death and unimaginable destruction were framed by proud heroism, and Holland situated itself among those numerous "we" who had "won" the war. "The telling and retelling of the events were not so much part of a mourning ritual or of an education in moral sensibility; it was in fact a ritual reconfiguration of a nation's proud self-image as heroic victor," a narrative that did not appeal to van Alphen. "War narratives," he confesses "were dull to me, almost dulled me, as a young child because they were told in such a way that I was not allowed to have my own response to them" (van Alphen 1997: 2). Katzir's project, an example of teaching through art that places the audience responses at its very core, resonates with the issues highlighted by van Alphen. It endows the Dutch visitors with a personal voice that, following Van Alphen's argument, has been weakened by the country's official narratives.

Vilnius, April–May 1997

The thriving culture of Vilna's Jewish community was doubly erased by World War II and the Soviet regime. The Holocaust wiped out some 90 percent of the 240,000-strong prewar Jewish population, and Soviet dominance made religious or ethnic revival difficult if not impossible (Sydney and Alice Goldstein 1997:107). The early 1990s were characterized by the Lithuanian movement's (*Sąjūdis*) struggle for independence, which led to processes of social and political realignment and Lithuanian national redefinition as a democratic republic freed from the Russian influence. In the process, Lithuanian prewar attitudes toward the Jews started to be interrogated, and a particular subject of historical debate was the role of the Lithuanian Activist Front (LAF), the main anti-Soviet resistance movement, and of its controversial offshoot, the Lithuanian Provisional Government, in the murder of the Jews of Kaunas (25–29 June 1941). Massacres were committed again on 29 October 1941 when nearly ten thousand Lithuanian Jews were slaughtered at Fort IX in Kaunas by the Nazis and their local collaborators. "Never had so many been killed on Lithuanian soil in so short a time. It is small wonder, then, that the painful record of 1941 continues to confront, embarrass and annoy Lithuanian society," argues historian Saulius Sužiedėlis (2001). One such confrontation occurred in September 2000 when the Lithuanian parliament passed a resolution defining the above-mentioned Provisional Government as a restorer of sovereignty, arousing protests and public debate about the country's history of anti-Semitism and involvement in crimes against the Jews (Sužiedėlis 2001; Eidintas, 2001). Only after Lithuania's EU-accession in October 2002, and after it became a full member of the International Task Force in the same year, did the Holocaust come to feature on political leaders' agenda. Yet, the political (self-)portrayal of "Lithuania's sincere and continuous efforts towards perpetuating the memory of the Holocaust victims" (Lithuanian Foreign Minister Audronius Ažubalis 2012) is challenged by skeptical critics, including Efraim Zuroff, director of the Simon Wiesenthal Center in Israel, who argues that commemorative activities have largely a ceremonial function, which meets EU memorialization objectives but hides increasingly anti-Semitic attitudes. He points to counter-evidence, including "the government's abysmal failure to punish a single Lithuanian Holocaust perpetrator despite an abundance of potential suspects, and the continuing efforts of government leaders and officials to promote the canard of historical equivalency between Communist and Nazi crimes" (Zuroff 2012).

Katzir's own views of Lithuanian attitudes toward the Holocaust are closer to the lines of argumentation sketched by Zurroff. The exhibition space Katzir created in the basement of the Contemporary Art Centre of Vilnius was painted baby blue and golden brown, a reference to the predominant colors of a church in Vilnius built on the grounds of a former Jewish synagogue, whose history had thus been completely erased and replaced with Christian symbolism. The exhibition named *Nuspalvink Pats* (Coloring Yourself) consisted of a hall with mirrors hung on both walls, so that visitors could see themselves in endless repetition. The small selection of colored images from the exhibition's art catalogue suggests that the intended historical (self-) reflection indeed did happen. These images showed a deep engagement on the part of the audience with the victims of the Holocaust and, arguably, a clear identification with the plight of the victimized Jews.

To the image depicting the deportation of Jewish children one visitor added the warning: "Children Stop! Don't enter this train! It will bring you to gas chambers, to death!" Other participants changed the naïve connotation of the drawings into grotesque ones, and attempted to remember those perished in the camps, by writing Jewish names and dates on the drawing representing suitcases belonging to Auschwitz victims. One response provided by an anonymous visitor is particularly noteworthy. The color red predominates a drawing based on a photograph showing human bodies used for anatomical experiments in Danzig in 1944. On this image the visitor wrote: "Meat processing factory, but was animal meat processed here?" A beautiful landscape peers through the open window, to which the visitor added: "It is so beautiful outdoors but what is it like in here?" On the drawings of containers he or she writes: "People are identified with animals, whole leg, whole arm, lungs, heart, liver. Horror" (Visitors, 1997 Vilnius).

There is, however, a clear discrepancy between these individual visitors' engagement and how the Lithuanian press covered the event. Journalist Ruta Miksioniene, for instance, protested against Katzir's intention to reflect on Lithuanians' anti-Semitism during the war. She disliked the installation of mirrors in the exhibition space, which allegedly "forced everyone to look at themselves and feel the guilt of the murder of 94% of Lithuania's Jews." She stated:

> In fact the situation undergoes a paradoxical change; that glimpse in the mirror makes you feel a victim. It evokes memories of postwar deportations, confiscation of farmers' properties, murders of our brothers in the forests and damp cellars of KGB. The best part of Lithuanian society as well as other nationalities in Lithuania were killed, deported or forced to emigrate. (Miksioniene 1997)

This resonates with a dominant Lithuanian victim narrative, equating Jewish persecution with Lithuanian suffering; both are here presented as part of what this journalist calls "an internal private experience," and the emphasis is clearly placed on of the traumas of Communism, since "for us, the war only finished five years ago and those who were born free in Lithuania are still toddlers." A sense of indignation at Katzir becomes apparent in Miksioniene's further comment: "Even a remarkable education and his nation's tragedy have not helped [Katzir] create a work equal to S. Spielberg's *Schindler's List*, which is able to reach peoples' hearts and minds everywhere." Another criticism leveled against Katzir's points at his alleged ignorance of Lithuania's recent history of victimization by the Soviet regime, and of the country's desire to construct a positive national identity, as his placing of pencils in the colors of the national flag is described as "not a declaration of [patriotism] but a very vivid protest." The journalist in question reproaches Katzir, reminding him that "during the Soviet regime school children would have spent more than a month or two in the KGB's interrogation rooms for making a similar gesture" (Miksioniene 1997). A similar argument is made by another journalist who writes: "the public was made indignant not by the artist's concept, but by the way it was expressed, which was understood as a lack of respect for the suffering of an oppressed and exterminated nation" (Zoviene 1997). Such emphases on Lithuanian martyrology in journalistic accounts corroborate Sužiedėlis's argument

(2001) that these views, adopted at national level, risk creating "a rigid pattern of collective memories."

These accounts in the Lithuanian media arguably also add weight to Zurroff's (2012) criticism that the Lithuanian government has generally "de-emphasize[d] the history of local participation in Holocaust crimes, and focus[ed] attention on the suffering of the victims of Communism in Eastern Europe." Conversely, it may be objected that Katzir perhaps went too far by pouring salt on a wound caused by Soviet rule that had not yet healed, or by prematurely asking a victimized public to understand someone else's victimization, subtly pointing the finger at Lithuanian anti-Semitism. It may well be that his exhibition came too early at the time when Lithuania was still a vulnerable society, having just emerged from Soviet domination. Nonetheless, the colored images discussed above show individual Lithuanians' sensitivity to others' suffering and they reveal understanding and compassion toward the Jewish plight. In the anonymity of the process of coloring some visitors found a personal way of dealing with history unfettered by narratives imposed from above.

Conclusion

Katzir's project proved powerful in transcending the boundaries of the gallery space, and in intruding into visitors' lives, who were no longer passive witnesses to the effect of art, but directly responsible for giving meaning to the kinds of historical images that had previously only entered their consciousness by means of formal education, or via popular culture and the media. The control over pictures that had previously belonged to the realm of the documentary was passed on to the participants in the installation. The visitors of these exhibitions were entrusted with a moral responsibility of working on the significance of particular images and were thereby given the opportunity to comment on their connections to the historical event.

The colored images show a range of reactions to, and understandings of, the postwar identity narratives of their respective countries that warrant careful consideration. Some attest to individual views that resonate with dominant postwar narratives or their later transformation, including the struggle to come to terms with the past, *Vergangenheitsbewältigung*, in Germany; or an ambivalent public discourse in Holland, which, on one hand, shows commitment to Holocaust memorialization, and on the other hand, an uneasiness when it comes to acknowledging Dutch collaboration with the Nazis. Individual visitor responses in

Lithuania, meanwhile, showed great empathy with the victims of the Holocaust, while the journalistic responses discussed above reflected the dominant national self-image of Lithuania as a victim of both the Nazi and the Soviet regimes. In the privacy and anonymity of their coloring, some individual visitors went beyond the confining memory discourses of their countries, and showed an ability to reflect upon a dark chapter of history that has profoundly challenged our understanding of humanity. Some such individual responses thus revealed more nuanced and complex interpretations that transcended the overarching national narratives of WWII and of the Holocaust commonly adopted in their wider national contexts.

Finally, within the dialogical space created between the artist's interpretations of the historical images, on one hand, and the visitors' personal interpretations of the artist's drawings and their own perception of the historical photographs, on the other, one is able to discern a genuine endeavor to think history afresh and to create links with a past that is ever more distant.

References

Art Catalog

Katzir, Ram. 1998. *Your Coloring Book, a Wandering Installation*. Amsterdam: Stedelijk Museum.

Schwartz, Gary. 1998. "Teach It to the Children." In *Your Coloring Book*. Amsterdam: Stedelijk Museum.

Documentary Film

Brunnen, Eleanor. 1998. *Your Colouring Book, a documentary film*. Amsterdam: Phantavision.

Interview

Interview with Ram Katzir, Amsterdam 2009.

Academic Literature

Assmann, Aleida. 2003. "Two Forms of Resentment: Jean Améry, Martin Walser and German Memorial Culture." *New German Critique* 90: 123–33.

Cesarani, David. 2005. "Holocaust Controversies in the 1990s: The Revenge of History or the History of Revenge?" In *After Eichmann Collective Memory and the Holocaust since 1961*, ed. David Cesarani. London: Routledge.

De Oliviera, Nicolas and Michael Petry. 2003. *Installation Art in the New Millennium: The Empire of the Senses*. London: Thames & Hudson.

Dryzek, John. 2000. *Deliberative Democracy and Beyond*. New York: Oxford University Press.

Eidintas, Alfonsas. 2001. *Lietuvos žydų žudynių byla: dokumentų ir straipsnių rinkinys*. Vilnius: Vaga.

Geyer, Michael and Miriam Hasen. 1994. "German-Jewish memory and national consciousness." In *Holocaust Remembrance: The Shapes of Memory*, ed. Geoffrey H. Hartman. Oxford: Blackwell.

Goldstein, Sidney and Alice. 1993. *Lithuanian Jewry, 1993: A Demographic and Socio-Cultural Profile*. Jerusalem: Avraham Harman Institute of Contemporary Jewry, Hebrew University of Jerusalem.

Griffioen, Pim and Ron Zeller. 2011. *Jodenvervolging in Nederland, Frankrijk en België, 1940–1945: overeenkomsten, verschillen, oorzaken*. Amsterdam: Uitgeverij Boom.

Habermas, Jürgen. 1988. "Special Issue on Historikerstreit." In *New German Critique* 44 Spring/Summer.

Houwink ten Cate, J. 1990. "De justitie en de Joodsche Raad." In *Geschiedenis en Cultuur: achttien opstellen*, ed. Jonker, E and Van Rossem, M. The Hague. 149–168.

Kamenetzky, David. 1999. "The Debate on National Identity and the Martin Walser Speech: How Does Germany Reckon with its Past?" *SAIS Review* 19 (2): 257–266.

Kramer, Jane. 1996. *The Politics of Memory: Looking for Germany in the new Germany*. New York: Random House.

Pollock, Griselda and Joyce Zemans. 2007. *Museums after Modernism: Strategies of Engagement*. Malden, MA: Blackwell.

Presser, Jacob. 1969. *The Destruction of the Dutch Jews*. Trans. Arnold Pomerans. New York: Dutton.

Sužiedėlis, Saulius. 2001. "The Burden of 1941." In *Lithuanian Quarterly Journal of Arts and Sciences* 47 (4): http://www.lituanus.org/2001/01_4_04.htm. Accessed on 7 July 2012.

Van Alphen, Ernst. 1997. *Caught by History: Holocaust Effects in Contemporary Art, Literature, and Theory*. Stanford, Calif.: Stanford University Press.

Wiedmer, Caroline. 1999. *The Claims of Memory: Representations of the Holocaust in Contemporary Germany and France*. Ithaca: Cornell University Press.

Young, James. 2000. *At Memory's Edge: After-Images of the Holocaust in Contemporary Art and Architecture*. New Haven: Yale University Press.

Webpages

Bourriaud, Nicolas. 1998. *Relational Aesthetics*, http://www.creativityandcognition.com/blogs/legart/wp-content/uploads/2006/07/Borriaud.pdf (Accessed 7 July 2012.)

http://www.holocausttaskforce.org/membercountries/member-lithuania.html (Accessed 7 July 2012.)

Heingartner, Douglas, Statement retrieved http://www.ramkatzir.com/#/about/bio/ (Accessed 7 July 2012.)

http://www.ramkatzir.com/#/worklist/your-coloring-book/ (Accessed 7 July 2012.)

Zurroff, Efraim. 2012. "Lithuania 2012: Holocaust Distortion as Background for Increased Anti- Semitism. A Simon Wiesenthal Center Report." http://www.wiesenthal.com/atf/cf/%7B54d385e6-f1b9-4e9f-8e94-890c3e6dd277%7D/%20LITHUANIA%202012-%20HOLOCAUST%20DISTORTION%20AS%20BACKGROUND%20FOR%20INCREASED%20FOR%20ANTI-SEMITISM-FINAL-%204-19-2012%20.PDF (Accessed 7 July 2012.)

Newspaper Articles

Bouman, Solomon. 21 February 1997. "Exhibition in Jerusalem arouses strong emotions." *NRC Handelsblad*.

Miksioniene, Ruta. 15 April 1997. "The installation has failed to resist the pressure of horrible reality." *Muza Malunas*.

Pfütze, Hermann. April 1998. "Ram Katzir – 6th stop: Malzeit." *Kunstforum*.

Stepken, Angelika. March 1998. "Malzeit The Israeli artist Ram Katzir in Berlin." In *Neue Bildende Kunst*.

Stigter, Bianca. 21 February 1997. "I want to go to places where people do not want to see the book." *NRC Handelsblad*.

Storr, Robert. 28 November 1999. "No Stage, No Actors, But It's Theater (and Art)." *New York Times*.

Zoviene, Danute. 11–17 April 1997. "There is always a choice." *Lietuvos Zinios*.

14

Epilogue

Christian Karner and Bram Mertens

"Do you want total austerity?" asks a graffiti artist in central Vienna, as depicted in the image appearing here in the epilogue. An intertextual allusion to Goebbels's infamous "total war speech" in Berlin in February 1943, this encapsulates the crux of our volume, or at least in part: the Second World War in its many facets and dimensions, as viewed and remembered from heterogeneous political positions throughout the second half of the twentieth century and perhaps even more so at the beginning of the twenty-first century, has provided people across Europe with an interpretative prism for contemporary ills, anxieties, and tensions. As our contributors have shown, such discursive connections between the present and a very particular historical context have been made, and are continue to be made, not only across the continent, but also across ideological divides, at different levels of political hierarchies, in order to make sense of a multitude of current issues, fears, and (perceived) injustices. Crucially, as we have seen throughout, any such invocations can only be understood in the various contexts—often predominantly national, but also regional and at times European—of the different political and discursive frames, through which memories of World War II have been articulated, transmitted, or contested since the postwar era.

The preceding chapters have spanned large geographical distances and have covered diverse data, involving various social actors. Due to the quality and coherence of our contributors' analyses, they can and should be left to speak for themselves. Moreover, the conceptual backdrop outlined in the introduction needs no repetition at this stage. Yet, and by way not so much of a conclusion but as a pointer toward further questions raised by this book, two issues warrant flagging up on these final pages. Their foci pertain to questions of ethics and historicity respectively.

What Jaspal and Yampolsky (2011) have revealed in Israel, the continuing centrality of the Second World War and particularly of the Holocaust as anchors for interpretations of present circumstances utilized across the national political spectrum, has here been shown to also feature prominently in Europe's diverse contexts. These contexts were of course the setting to the Shoah and to many other defining facets of World War Two. Their memory and utilization in the here and now also poses difficult questions to the backdrop of the current crisis: are Europeans capable of being molded into what Avishai Margalit (2002: 7–8; 69–70) famously describes as a "community of memory" based on "thick," meaningful, and ethical relations of mutual solidarity and grounded in a "shared past," as commonly encountered amongst more narrowly defined groups including "families, clans, tribes, religious communities and nations"?

Partly diverging from contemporary detractors of the idea or desirability of a shared historical consciousness on a European scale (see Berger 2010: 135), the analyses presented here have revealed spaces and instances of remembering involving *both* profound tensions *and* partial agreement in *both* national *and* transnational settings. In other words, close attention to local, regional, national, and transnational contexts confirms the contestability of any narrative of the past, articulated on any political or geographical scale, while also allowing for the possibility of a shared consciousness across contexts, premised on discussion and engagement with *the other* rather than on unifying consensus (see also Pakier and Stråth 2010: 13). Yet, as suggested by several of our contributions querying some deeply problematic historical analogies currently in circulation, there are undeniably both factual and ethical outer limits to any historical consciousness, however debated and internally diverse such a consciousness may be. In other words, there is also a fundamental ethical dimension to the central question facing memory scholars—not only "when [and] where [but also] *how, and for whom* ... the remembered past matter[s] for individuals making sense of and acting in the present" (Griffin and Bollen 2009: 610, *italics added*).

This ethical dimension acquires particular pertinence when we find ourselves confronted by some of the analogical misuses of the history of World War II examined in some of our chapters. Also highly relevant here is Maximilian Gottschlich's (2012: 38–39) discussion of a new anti-Semitism: its defining topoi include deeply troubling discursive equations of contemporary Israel with Nazi Germany, which aim to delegitimize and demonize Israel and to variously reject, project, and invert historical guilt. A major call for further research and for close attention emanating from the present volume concerns the political intentions and effects of such and similar analogies. What is more, these analogies and our responses to them matter on any given scale of remembering, local, regional, national, and indeed European.

Partly to avoid complicity in reifying, at times positively primordialist definitions of nations as "natural communities of memory" (Margalit 2002: 26), some of our discussions have invoked Bell's (2003) notion of the national mythscape. Grounded in constructivist ontology, this concept defines nations as inherently negotiated projects, and competing memories as intrinsic parts of their contested ideological terrains. However, and this is where we encounter wider issues of historicity, we need to entertain the possibility that a growing skepticism and more widespread contestation of "governing myths" may be amongst the peculiarities and defining features of our current post- or "liquid" modern era (Bauman 2000).

This emerges from Andreas Huyssen's seminal account of a present "crisis of history" and the concomitant weakening of the "stable links" formerly provided by historical pasts that once legitimized political structures:

> Historical memory today is not what it used to be. It used to mark the relation of a community or nation to its past, but the boundary between past and present used to be stronger and more stable. . . . The past has become part of the present in ways simply unimaginable in earlier centuries . . . temporal boundaries have weakened just as the experiential dimension of space has shrunk as a result of modern means of transportation and communication. . . . For about two centuries, history in the West was quite successful in its project to anchor the ever more transitory present of modernity and the nation in a multifaceted but strong narrative of historical time. . . . This model no longer works. (Huyssen 2003: 1–2)

This resonates with several earlier chapters in ways that need no further explanation. What matters here is that this argument also historicizes national mythscapes. Their defining disagreements over the past arguably become hallmarks of postmodernity. Furthermore, this raises difficult questions about possible connections between the proliferation of competing memories, on the one hand, and a growing skepticism of politics and concomitant diminishing of political legitimacy, on the other, which in turn echo parts of this book. Paraphrasing an argument Karl Wilds touches on in his chapter, we may close with the following hypothesis awaiting further research: do memories and historical allusions gain in appeal and salience to the same extent as the political blueprints on offer lose in plausibility? Or, put differently, do we increasingly turn to the past, often or usually to a thoroughly decontextualized past, when the present holds few promises and no certainties?

Along with some of the examples discussed by our contributors, the above-quoted question by a Viennese graffiti artist—"*Do you want total austerity?*"—can plausibly be read in these terms. More than an isolated invocation of Europe's darkest historical chapter, the

272

question inadvertently condenses parts of the continent's contemporary *Zeitgeist*. Confronted by complex issues and far-reaching crises, Europeans appear to turn, and not for the first time, to World War II as a template for comparison, interpretation or even prediction. As we have also seen, there are ethical and historiographical reasons to be wary of, and often positively opposed to, many such invocations. Yet, the underlying circumstances and anxieties giving rise to comparisons and analogies of this kind must of course be taken very seriously indeed. While different historical crises cannot be conflated, or only at considerable intellectual and ethical peril, they all demand cogent and humane responses. Present crises are awaiting theirs.

References

Bauman, Zygmunt. 2000. *Liquid Modernity*. Cambridge: Polity.

Bell, Duncan. 2003. "Mythscape: memory, mythology, and national identity." *British Journal of Sociology* 54 (1): 63–81.

Berger, Peter. 2010. "Remembering the Second World War in Western Europe, 1945–2005." In *A European Memory?* eds. Małgorzata Pakier and Bo Stråth. New York: Berghahn.

Griffin, Larry and Kenneth Bollen. 2009. "What do these memories do? Civil rights remembrance and racial attitudes." *American Sociological Review* 74 (4): 594–614.

Gottschlich, Maximilian. 2012. *Die große Abneigung*. Wien: Czernin.

Huyssen, Andreas. 2003. *Present Pasts: Urban Palimpsests and the Politics of Memory*. Stanford: Stanford University Press.

Jaspal, Rusi and Maya Yampolsky. 2011. "Social representations of the Holocaust and Jewish Israeli identity construction: insights from identity process theory." *Social Identities* 17 (2): 201–224.

Margalit, Avishai. 2002. *The Ethics of Memory*. Cambridge, Massachusetts: Harvard University Press.

Pakier, Małgorzata and Bo Stråth. 2010. "Introduction: A European Memory?" In *A European Memory?* eds. Małgorzata Pakier and Bo Stråth. New York: Berghahn.

List of Contributors

Giorgos Bithymitris is a research fellow in the Department of Political Science and History at Panteion University of Social and Political Sciences, Greece. His research focuses on union movements and political ideologies. He is currently conducting research on the ideological and organizational preconditions of labor incidents in the context of the Greek economic crisis. He has published articles about mass media ideology, trade union strategies, and employee relations.

Joseph Burridge is a senior lecturer in sociology at the University of Portsmouth. His primary research interest lies in the sociology of food. As well as teaching about that, he also teaches social research methods across the curriculum. The research upon which his chapter is based was conducted as part of an ESRC-funded PhD studentship (R4220134082) and an ESRC Postdoctoral Research Fellowship (PTA-026-27-0591). He is grateful to the University of Portsmouth's Centre for European and International Studies Research (CEISR) for funding his attendance at the conference from which this volume is derived.

Anna Duszak is full professor of linguistics, and head of the Division of Discourse Studies at the Institute of Applied Linguistics, University of Warsaw. Her research interests cover discourse analysis, pragmatics, anthropological linguistics, and critical discourse studies. Her publications include a monograph, *Tekst, dyskurs, komunikacja międzykulturowa* (1998, PWN), and some ninety papers in scholarly collections and journals. She edited *Culture and Styles of Academic Discourse* (1997, Mouton de Gruyter) and *Us and Others. Social Identities across Languages, Discourses and Cultures* (2002, John Benjamins). She co-edited several volumes in English and Polish, most recently: *Language, Culture and the Dynamics of Age* (Mouton de Gruyter, 2011).

Rosario Forlenza is a postdoctoral visiting scholar at the Center for European and Mediterranean Studies, New York University. He is a historian whose main fields of expertise are political anthropology, symbolic and cultural politics, cinema and propaganda, and memories studies. He is author of *Le elezioni amministrative della Prima repubblica. Politica e propaganda locale nell'Italia del secondo dopoguerra, 1946–1956* (Rome: Donzelli, 2008) and *La Repubblica del Presidente. Gli anni di Carlo Azeglio Ciampi, 1999–2006* (Diabasis: Reggio Emilia, 2011). His most recent articles have appeared in *Modern Italy, Journal of Modern Italian Studies, History&Memory, Contemporary European History.*

Henning Grunwald is DAAD lecturer in Modern European History at the University of Cambridge and fellow of Pembroke College. After undergraduate and graduate study at Cambridge he moved to Berlin as postdoctoral fellow at the Institute for Theatre Studies of Freie Universität before serving as assistant to the president of Humboldt-Universität. From 2006 he held an assistant professorship at Vanderbilt University, where he also served as associate director of the Max-Kade-Center for European and German Studies. Grunwald has published on the concept of crisis, the performativity of justice, and the legal and political culture of Weimar Germany. His most recent publication is *Courtroom to Revolutionary Stage: Performance and Ideology in Weimar Political Trials* (Oxford University Press 2012).

Christian Karner is associate professor of sociology in the School of Sociology and Social Policy at the University of Nottingham. He has researched and published widely within urban sociology (i.e., with David Parker in a long-term project on inner-city Birmingham) and on the negotiations of ethnic, religious, national, and local identities across various empirical contexts, particularly in Austria, and to the wider backdrop of contemporary globalization. His books include *Negotiating National Identities* (2011, Ashgate), *Ethnicity and Everyday Life* (2007, Routledge) and *Writing History, Constructing Religion* (co-edited with James Crossley, 2005, Ashgate).

Zinovia Lialiouti is a postdoctoral researcher at the Aristotle University of Thessaloniki, Greece. The subject of her research, which is conducted in collaboration with the UCD Clinton Institute for

American Studies, is the ideology of Americanism and the image of Greece during the post-war period. She holds a PhD from the Department of Politics and History, Panteion University, Athens. The title of her thesis is *Greek anti-Americanism, 1947–1989*. She has published papers on the phenomenon of anti-Americanism, American studies, cold war culture, as well as the study of political discourse and Greek political culture.

Bram Mertens is a lecturer in German and Dutch in the Department of German Studies at the University of Nottingham, United Kingdom. He is the author of *Dark Images, Secret Hints: Walter Benjamin, Gershom Scholem and Franz Joseph Molitor* (London: Peter Lang, 2007), as well as of several articles on the history of German ideas and twentieth-century Belgian history. He is particularly interested in the history and ideology of the Flemish Movement from the Interbellum to the present day, as well as the construction of memories and narratives of the Second World War in Belgium.

Jovana Mihajlović Trbovc is a junior research fellow at the Peace Institute Ljubljana and a PhD candidate in Balkan Studies at the University of Ljubljana, with a thesis examining "Public Narratives of the Past in the Framework of Transitional Justice Processes: The Case of Bosnia and Herzegovina." She holds an MA in nationalism studies from the Central European University, Budapest, and BA degrees in international relations from the University of Belgrade and the London School of Economics. She researches transitional justice, post conflict memory-making, and issues of national identity.

Tamara Pavasovic Trost holds a PhD in sociology from Harvard University. Her academic interests include ethnic identity, nationalism, collective memory, and political socialization, with a focus on the Balkans. Her previous research has examined ethnonationalist socialization through history curriculum, determinants of ethnic distance among youth, football hooliganism and nationalism, and the relationship between class and everyday identity. Her doctoral dissertation, *Dealing with the Past: History and Identity in Serbia and Croatia*, examines the construction and the expressions of everyday identity among youth in Serbia and Croatia. She currently teaches at the University of Graz, Austria.

Diana Popescu has recently completed her PhD thesis exploring public responses to visual art about the Holocaust among Jewish-American and Israeli postwar generations and the changing public discourses of Holocaust memorialization in the late 1990s and early 2000s. An alumnus of University of Southampton, Parkes Institute, she is of Romanian origin. Several of her contributions can be found in the *Jewish Renaissance Magazine* and *Images: A journal of Jewish art and visual culture*, and new articles will appear in *Jewish History and Culture and Holocaust Studies* journal.

Tanja Schult is assistant professor at the Hugo Valentin Center at Uppsala's University, Sweden. Having studied history of art, Scandinavian studies and theatre- and media studies in Erlangen, Lund, and Berlin, she completed her PhD in 2007 at Humboldt University, Berlin. She was the curator of the Stockholm exhibition Raoul Wallenberg Images (2008) and is the author of *A Hero's Many Faces: Raoul Wallenberg in Contemporary Monuments* (Palgrave Macmillan 2009/2012). From 2009 to 2012 Schult was a researcher and lecturer at Stockholm University; her research project, financed by Riksbankens Jubileumsfond, focused on the influence of the Holocaust on Swedish art.

Paul Smith is associate professor and senior lecturer in the Department of French and Francophone Studies at the University of Nottingham. His work focuses mainly on French constitutional history and political institutions in the nineteenth and twentieth centuries. His published monographs include *Feminism and the Third Republic: Women's Political and Civil Rights in France 1918–1945* (OUP 1996), *A History of the French Senate 1870–2004* (Edwin Mellen, 2 vols 2005 and 2006), and *The Senate of the Fifth French Republic* (Palgrave Macmillan 2009).

Bjørn Thomassen is associate professor in the Department of Society and Globalisation, Roskilde University, Denmark. His current teaching and research engages anthropological theory, urban anthropology, social theory, memory and identity, Italian politics, and contemporary Italian history. He has done research on nationalism and the anthropology of borders and boundaries, with fieldwork carried out in the border area between Italy and Slovenia and the Istrian peninsula (the focus of his PhD thesis). He is particularly interested in how anthropological ideas and approaches can inform political and social theory and the study of contemporary politics.

Karl Wilds teaches nineteenth- and twentieth-century German history and politics in the department of German studies at the University of Nottingham. His research interests include German cultural memories of the twentieth century, and he is currently working on a project examining the post-unification phenomenon of Ostalgie in the former East Germany.

Tatiana Zhurzhenko is currently a postdoctoral research fellow at the Aleksanteri Institute, University of Helsinki, where she works on memory of WWII in Russia. She studied political economy and social philosophy at V.N. Karazin Kharkiv National University (Ukraine), where she later worked as an assistant, then associate professor (1993–2010). From 2007 to 2011 she was an Elise Richter research fellow at the Department of Political Science, University of Vienna, where she worked on her project "Politics of Memory and National Identities in Post-Soviet Borderlands: Ukraine/Russia and Ukraine/ Poland." Her most recent book is *Borderlands into Bordered Lands: Geopolitics of Identity in Post-Soviet Ukraine* (Stuttgart 2010).

Index